T0070241

Quality of Life, Balance of Power and Nuclear Weapons

Quality of Life, Balance of Power and Nuclear Weapons

A Statistical Yearbook for Statesmen and Citizens 2014

Alexander V. Avakov

Volume 7

Algora Publishing
New York

© 2014 by Algora Publishing.
All Rights Reserved
www.algora.com

No portion of this book (beyond what is permitted by Sections 107 or 108 of the United States Copyright Act of 1976) may be reproduced by any process, stored in a retrieval system, or transmitted in any form, or by any means, without the express written permission of the publisher.

Library of Congress Cataloging-in-Publication Data —

Avakov, Aleksandr V. (Aleksandr Vladimirovich), 1954-

Quality of life, balance of power and nuclear weapons: a statistical yearbook for statesmen and citizens / Alexander V. Avakov.

p. cm.

Includes bibliographical references and index.

ISBN 978-1-62894-012-1 (soft: alk. paper) — ISBN 978-1-62894-013-8 (hard cover: alk. paper) — ISBN 978-1-62894-014-5 (ebook: alk. paper) 1. Economic indicators. 2. Social indicators. 3. Quality of life—Statistics. 4. Armed Forces—Appropriations and expenditures—Statistics.. 5. Nuclear weapons—Statistics. 6. Health status indicators. I. Title.

HC59.3.A83 2008
306.09'0511021—dc22

2008003446

Printed in the United States

Table of Contents

Introduction

This statistical annual presents fundamental data in three sections: (1) Quality of Life, (2) Balance of Powers, (3) Developed Market Economies since 1960.

The advantage of this yearbook is that it contains data generally not available elsewhere. Sections 1 and 2 give statistics for 235 countries. By comparison, the World Bank and Encyclopedia Britannica provide statistical data for a maximum of about 160 countries. The actual number of countries in World Bank statistical tables is even smaller. The CIA World Factbook gives data for about 230 countries, but that data is limited by scope and is imprecise. Other statistical publications are in even less satisfactory. I managed to increase the number of countries tallied by writing proprietary software utilizing statistical regressions, selecting data which, first of all, is important and, second, is relatively reliable, offering high correlation coefficients for these regressions.

Section 1 concentrates on data that reflect the quality of life. First, I focused on major economic and demographic indicators. In addition to data about the quality of life as measured strictly in economic terms, I sought to produce a methodologically rigorous estimate of a human rights index. The latter measures civil and political rights as well as socio-economic rights. I also computed an integrated economico-political quality-of-life index.

In Section 2, the book deals with major indicators of balance of power. In addition to data about each country's economic power, military personnel and military expenditures, it includes data about nuclear delivery systems and provides the number of nuclear warheads of all nuclear powers. This is based on information from reputable sources. Among others, it includes estimates of the Israeli nuclear arsenal which usually do not appear in the press. I also give a rough account of countries possessing, pursuing or capable of acquiring other weapons of mass destruction. Chances are that if American public were more familiar with this statistics, some Middle East foreign policy failures might have been avoided.

It should also be underscored that many official estimates, for example, of Russian military expenditures distributed by U.S. and British intelligence communities are methodologically flawed. Such estimates claim to give a picture of the military expenditures of the countries of the world at market exchange rates; at the same time, they apparently cite the figures of the Russian military expense figures at purchasing power parities, thus inflating these numbers in comparison to other countries. Such deceptive practices of the Anglo-American intelligence services should be counterbalanced by presenting two different tables, showing military expenditure estimates both at market exchange rates and at purchasing power parities. Members of the U.S. Congress and others who care about the foundations of power politics in the nuclear age will find facts that speak for themselves in this section.

In Section 3, I give data on the hot topic of health care. It seems that public health expenditures as a share of total health expenditures has a stronger correlation with the comparative level (and the rates of improvement) of main health care indicators than the absolute level (measured as percent of GDP) of total health expenditures. It is also worth noting that, as the data demonstrates, the U.S. has the least public health expenditures of developed market economies and is increasingly lagging behind other countries of this group by main health care indicators. The proposed introduction of national health insurance in the U.S. would probably mean some sort of tax increase. I therefore also try to shed light on modern ideological debates about the share of taxation in GDP and its influence on rates of growth. Surprisingly enough, the empirical data for the developed market economies does not seem to support the popular idea that low taxes are strongly correlated with higher rates of growth; depending on how the data is analyzed, the appropriate correlations are either low or even the reverse of what is commonly believed.

Sources

The sources are shown in the form: XX(Source), or XX(Source)W, or XX(Source A/SourceB), where XX is a year, W after (Source) means that data is weighted against the World Bank data for the U.S., and (Source) (or Source A or Source B) is one of the following:

WB	The World Bank (1)
E	Encyclopedia Britannica
CIA	Central Intelligence Agency
CALC(CIA)	Calculated using data of the Central Intelligence Agency
UN	United Nations Development Programme
GPI	Global Peace Index
USAID	U.S. Agency For International Development
FH	Freedom House
IISS	International Institute for Strategic Studies
JDW	Jane's Defense Weekly
SIPRI	Stockholm International Peace Research Institute
BULL	Bulletin of the Atomic Scientists
UCS	Union of Concerned Scientists
WIKI	Wikipedia
Reg	Regression
Est	Estimate
PRIN1(EQL)	Principal Component 1 of Economic Quality-of-Life Indicators

PRIN1(PQL)	Principal Component 1 of Political Quality-of-Life Indicators
PRIN1(EPQL)	Principal Component 1 of Economico-Political Quality-of-Life Indicators
POP*GPC	Obtained by multiplication of Population by GDP per Capita at Market Exchange Rates
POP*GPCPPP	Obtained by multiplication of Population by GDP per Capita at Purchasing Power Parities
GDP*MILGDP+MILAID	Obtained by multiplication of GDP at Market Exchange Rates by Percent of Military Expenditures as Share of GDP plus Foreign Military Aid
GDPPPP*MILGDP+MILAID	Obtained by multiplication of GDP at Purchasing Power Parities by Percent of Military Expenditures as Share of GDP plus Foreign Military Aid

Regions

AFR	Africa
CPA	Centrally Planned Asia
DME	Developed Market Economies
EEU	Eastern Europe
LAM	Latin America
MEA	Middle East
SAS	South Asia
SEA	South-East Asia and Pacific
USR	Former U.S.S.R.

Abbreviations

OBS	Number of Countries Observed
GPC	Gross National Income at Market Exchange Rates Per Capita
INFMRT	Infant Mortality
LIFEXP	Life Expectancy
GPCPPP	Gross Domestic Product at Purchasing Power Parities Per Capita
EQLX	Economic Quality-of-Life Index
SCINTX	Societal Integration Index
CPRX	Civil and Political Rights Index
HDX	Human Development Index
GINI	Gini Coefficient of Income Inequality
PQLX	Political Quality-of-Life Index
EPQLX	Economico-Political Quality-of-Life Index
POP	Population
GDPPPP	Gross Domestic Product at Purchasing Power Parities
GDP	Gross National Income at Market Exchange Rates
ARMY	Armed Forces Personnel
MILGDP	Military Expenditures as Share of GDP

MILAID	Foreign Military Aid
MILXPP	Military Expenditures at Purchasing Power Parities Plus Foreign Military Aid
MILEXP	Military Expenditures at Market Exchange Rates Plus Foreign Military Aid
GPCXX	Gross National Income Per Capita at Market Exchange Rates, Year XX
GRPCMER	Growth Rates of GNI Per Capita at Market Exchange Rates
GPCPPPXX	Gross Domestic Product Per Capita at Purchasing Power Parities, Year XX
GRPCPPP	Growth Rates of GDP Per Capita at Purchasing Power Parities
INFMRTXX	Infant Mortality, Year XX
DRIM	Decrease Rates of Infant Mortality
LIFEXPXX	Life Expectancy, Year XX
GRLE	Growth Rates of Life Expectancy
HLTGDP	Total Health Expenditures as Percent of GDP
PUBHLT	Public Health Expenditures as Percent of Total Health Expenditures
TAXGDPXX	Taxes as Share of GDP, Year XX

Quality of Life

Table 1.1 Gross National Income at Market Exchange Rates, Per Capita, 2011				
Rank	Region	Country	GPC	Source
1	DME	Monaco	157,252	10(WB)
2	DME	Liechtenstein	145,035	09(WB)
3	DME	Bermuda	132,567	09(E)
4	DME	Norway	88,870	11(WB)
5	MEA	Qatar	80,440	11(WB)
6	DME	Luxembourg	77,390	11(WB)
7	DME	Switzerland	76,350	11(WB)
8	DME	Isle of Man	66,923	11(E)
9	DME	Jersey	66,104	09(E)
10	DME	Denmark	60,160	11(WB)
11	LAM	Cayman Islands	56,118	09(E)
12	DME	Falkland Islands	54,910	07(CIA)
13	DME	Sweden	53,170	11(WB)
14	DME	San Marino	50,344	11(CIA)
15	DME	Australia	49,790	11(WB)
16	DME	Netherlands	49,660	11(WB)
17	DME	United States	48,620	11(WB)
18	DME	Faroe Islands	48,485	09(E)
19	DME	Austria	48,170	11(WB)
20	DME	Finland	47,760	11(WB)
21	DME	Guernsey	47,674	11(E)
22	MEA	Kuwait	46,877	11(CIA)
23	SEA	Macao	46,669	10(WB)
24	LAM	Virgin Islands, Brit.	46,312	08(CIA)
25	DME	Belgium	45,930	11(WB)
26	DME	Canada	45,550	11(WB)
27	DME	Japan	44,900	11(WB)
28	DME	Germany	44,230	11(WB)
29	LAM	Virgin Islands, U.S.	43,397	10(E)
30	SEA	Singapore	42,930	11(WB)
31	DME	France	42,420	11(WB)
32	DME	Andorra	42,386	08(WB)
33	DME	Gibraltar	41,604	06(CIA)
34	MEA	United Arab Emirates	40,760	11(WB)
35	SEA	New Caledonia	39,281	09(E)
36	DME	Ireland	39,150	11(WB)
37	DME	New Zealand	38,303	11(CIA)
38	DME	Greenland	38,095	11(CIA)
39	DME	United Kingdom	37,780	11(WB)
40	SEA	Brunei	36,967	11(CIA)
41	LAM	Curacao	36,505	08(CIA)
42	SEA	Hong Kong	36,010	11(WB)
43	DME	Italy	35,320	11(WB)
44	DME	Iceland	34,820	11(WB)
45	DME	Spain	30,930	11(WB)

Table 1.1 Gross National Income at Market Exchange Rates, Per Capita, 2011				
Rank	Region	Country	GPC	Source
46	DME	Israel	28,930	11(WB)
47	LAM	Martinique	27,936	07(E)
48	LAM	Guadeloupe	26,710	09(E)
49	SEA	Guam	25,866	09(E)
50	SEA	French Polynesia	25,541	10(E)
51	LAM	Aruba	24,493	09(E)
52	DME	Greece	24,490	11(WB)
53	AFR	Reunion	24,064	10(E)
54	MEA	Oman	23,772	11(CIA)
55	EEU	Slovenia	23,600	11(WB)
56	MEA	Cyprus	22,987	11(CIA)
57	LAM	Bahamas	22,500	11(CIA)
58	LAM	Saint Martin	21,851	99(E)
59	SEA	Taiwan	21,759	11(CIA)
60	LAM	Sint Maarten	21,445	09(E)
61	DME	Portugal	21,370	11(WB)
62	SEA	Korea, South	20,870	11(WB)
63	MEA	Bahrain	19,925	11(CIA)
64	LAM	Guiana, French	19,529	10(E)
65	DME	Malta	19,115	10(WB)
66	EEU	Czech Republic	18,700	11(WB)
67	MEA	Saudi Arabia	17,820	11(WB)
68	LAM	Puerto Rico	17,001	10(WB)
69	EEU	Slovakia	16,190	11(WB)
70	LAM	Barbados	15,884	11(CIA)
71	AFR	Equatorial Guinea	15,670	11(WB)
72	USR	Estonia	15,260	11(WB)
73	LAM	Trinidad & Tobago	15,040	11(E)
74	DME	St. Pierre & Miquelon	14,716	(REG)
75	SEA	Northern Mariana Is.	14,715	09(E)
76	EEU	Croatia	13,540	11(WB)
77	USR	Latvia	13,320	11(WB)
78	USR	Lithuania	12,980	11(WB)
79	EEU	Hungary	12,730	11(WB)
80	LAM	St. Kitts & Nevis	12,610	11(WB)
81	EEU	Poland	12,380	11(WB)
82	MEA	Libya	12,379	10(CIA)
83	LAM	Anguilla	12,296	09(CIA)
84	LAM	Chile	12,280	11(WB)
85	LAM	Antigua & Barbuda	11,940	11(WB)
86	LAM	Uruguay	11,860	11(WB)
87	LAM	Venezuela	11,820	11(WB)
88	AFR	Seychelles	11,270	11(WB)
89	LAM	Turks & Caicos Is.	10,829	(REG)
90	LAM	Brazil	10,720	11(WB)

Table 1.1 Gross National Income at Market Exchange Rates, Per Capita, 2011				
Rank	Region	Country	GPC	Source
91	USR	Russia	10,650	11(WB)
92	MEA	Turkey	10,410	11(WB)
93	SEA	Cook Islands	9,905	05(CIA)
94	LAM	Argentina	9,740	11(E)
95	LAM	Mexico	9,420	11(WB)
96	MEA	Lebanon	9,140	11(WB)
97	SEA	Malaysia	8,770	11(WB)
98	USR	Kazakhstan	8,260	11(WB)
99	EEU	Romania	8,140	11(WB)
100	SEA	Samoa, American	8,085	07(E)
101	AFR	Gabon	8,080	11(WB)
102	AFR	Mauritius	8,040	11(WB)
103	LAM	Suriname	7,840	11(WB)
104	AFR	Mayotte	7,645	09(CIA)
105	LAM	Costa Rica	7,640	11(WB)
106.5	AFR	Botswana	7,470	11(WB)
106.5	LAM	Panama	7,470	11(WB)
108	SEA	Niue	7,351	03(CIA)
109	LAM	Grenada	7,350	11(WB)
110	EEU	Montenegro	7,140	11(WB)
111	LAM	Dominica	7,030	11(WB)
112	AFR	South Africa	6,960	11(WB)
113	LAM	St. Lucia	6,820	11(WB)
114	EEU	Bulgaria	6,640	11(WB)
115	SEA	Palau	6,510	11(WB)
116	MEA	Iran	6,381	11(CIA)
117.5	LAM	Colombia	6,070	11(WB)
117.5	LAM	St. Vincent	6,070	11(WB)
119	USR	Belarus	5,830	11(WB)
120	SAS	Maldives	5,720	11(WB)
121	EEU	Serbia	5,690	11(WB)
122	SEA	Nauru	5,631	09(E)
123	USR	Azerbaijan	5,290	11(WB)
124	LAM	Cuba	5,251	10(CIA)
125	LAM	Dominican Republic	5,240	11(WB)
126	LAM	Peru	5,150	11(WB)
127	LAM	Jamaica	4,980	11(E)
128	SEA	Tuvalu	4,950	11(WB)
129	CPA	China	4,940	11(WB)
130	EEU	Macedonia	4,810	11(WB)
131	USR	Turkmenistan	4,800	11(WB)
132	EEU	Bosnia	4,780	11(WB)
133	AFR	Namibia	4,700	11(WB)
134	MEA	Algeria	4,470	11(WB)
135	SEA	Thailand	4,440	11(WB)
136	MEA	Jordan	4,380	11(WB)

TABLE 1.1 GROSS NATIONAL INCOME AT MARKET EXCHANGE RATES, PER CAPITA, 2011

Rank	Region	Country	GPC	Source
137	LAM	Ecuador	4,200	11(WB)
138	MEA	Tunisia	4,020	11(WB)
139	EEU	Albania	3,980	11(WB)
140	SEA	Marshall Islands	3,910	11(WB)
141	AFR	Angola	3,830	11(WB)
142	SEA	Tonga	3,820	11(WB)
143	SEA	Fiji	3,720	11(WB)
144	LAM	Belize	3,710	11(WB)
145	AFR	St. Helena	3,594	(REG)
146	AFR	Cape Verde	3,540	11(WB)
147	EEU	Kosovo	3,510	11(WB)
148	LAM	El Salvador	3,480	11(WB)
149	AFR	Swaziland	3,470	11(WB)
150	USR	Armenia	3,360	11(WB)
151	SEA	Samoa	3,160	11(WB)
152	USR	Ukraine	3,130	11(WB)
153	MEA	Syria	3,116	11(CIA)
154	LAM	Paraguay	3,020	11(WB)
155	MEA	Morocco	2,970	11(WB)
156	SEA	Indonesia	2,940	11(WB)
157	LAM	Guyana	2,930	11(CIA)
158	LAM	Guatemala	2,870	11(WB)
159.5	USR	Georgia	2,860	11(WB)
159.5	SEA	Micronesia	2,860	11(WB)
161	SEA	East Timor	2,803	10(WB)
162	LAM	Montserrat	2,768	(REG)
163	SEA	Vanuatu	2,730	11(WB)
164	SEA	Wallis & Futuna	2,675	(REG)
165	MEA	Iraq	2,640	11(WB)
166	MEA	Egypt	2,600	11(WB)
167	SAS	Sri Lanka	2,580	11(WB)
168	CPA	Mongolia	2,310	11(WB)
169	AFR	Congo, Republic	2,250	11(WB)
170	SEA	Philippines	2,210	11(WB)
171	SAS	Bhutan	2,130	11(WB)
172	SEA	Kiribati	2,030	11(WB)
173	LAM	Bolivia	2,020	11(WB)
174.5	LAM	Honduras	1,980	11(WB)
174.5	USR	Moldova	1,980	11(WB)
176	MEA	West Bank	1,856	08(CIA)
177	AFR	Djibouti	1,548	11(CIA)
178.5	LAM	Nicaragua	1,510	11(WB)
178.5	USR	Uzbekistan	1,510	11(WB)
180	SEA	Papua New Guinea	1,480	11(WB)
181	SAS	India	1,420	11(WB)
182	AFR	Ghana	1,410	11(WB)
183	AFR	Western Sahara	1,393	(REG)

Table 1.1 Gross National Income at Market Exchange Rates, Per Capita, 2011				
Rank	Region	Country	GPC	Source
184	AFR	Sao Tome & Principe	1,350	11(WB)
185	AFR	Sudan	1,310	11(WB)
186	AFR	Nigeria	1,280	11(WB)
187	CPA	Vietnam	1,270	11(WB)
188	MEA	Gaza Strip	1,238	08(CIA)
189.5	AFR	Cameroon	1,210	11(WB)
189.5	AFR	Lesotho	1,210	11(WB)
191	AFR	Zambia	1,160	11(WB)
192	CPA	Laos	1,130	11(WB)
193	SAS	Pakistan	1,120	11(WB)
194	SEA	Solomon Islands	1,110	11(WB)
195	AFR	Ivory Coast	1,090	11(WB)
196.5	AFR	Senegal	1,070	11(WB)
196.5	MEA	Yemen	1,070	11(WB)
198	AFR	Mauritania	1,030	11(WB)
199	CPA	Korea, North	997	09(E)
200	SEA	Tokelau	970	(REG)
201	USR	Kyrgyzstan	900	11(WB)
202	USR	Tajikistan	870	11(WB)
203.5	CPA	Cambodia	820	11(WB)
203.5	AFR	Kenya	820	11(WB)
205.5	SAS	Bangladesh	780	11(WB)
205.5	AFR	Benin	780	11(WB)
207	AFR	Comoros	770	11(WB)
208	AFR	Chad	720	11(WB)
209	LAM	Haiti	700	11(WB)
210	AFR	Zimbabwe	660	11(WB)
211	AFR	Mali	610	11(WB)
212	AFR	Guinea-Bissau	600	11(WB)
213	AFR	Burkina Faso	580	11(WB)
214.5	AFR	Rwanda	570	11(WB)
214.5	AFR	Togo	570	11(WB)
216.5	SAS	Nepal	540	11(WB)
216.5	AFR	Tanzania	540	11(WB)
218	AFR	Uganda	510	11(WB)
219	AFR	Gambia	500	11(WB)
220	AFR	Central African Rep.	480	11(WB)
221	SAS	Afghanistan	470	11(WB)
222.5	AFR	Mozambique	460	11(WB)
222.5	AFR	Sierra Leone	460	11(WB)
225	AFR	Eritrea	430	11(WB)
225	AFR	Guinea	430	11(WB)
225	AFR	Madagascar	430	11(WB)
227	CPA	Burma	402	09(E)
228	AFR	Ethiopia	370	11(WB)

Table 1.1 Gross National Income at Market Exchange Rates, Per Capita, 2011				
Rank	Region	Country	GPC	Source
229.5	AFR	Malawi	360	11(WB)
229.5	AFR	Niger	360	11(WB)
231	AFR	Liberia	330	11(WB)
232	AFR	Burundi	250	11(WB)
233	AFR	Somalia	245	10(CIA)
234	AFR	Congo, Dem. Republic	190	11(WB)
235	AFR	South Sudan	93	07(E)

Table 1.2 Infant Mortality Rate Per 1,000 Live Births, 2011				
Rank	Region	Country	INFMRT	Source
1	DME	San Marino	1.60	11(WB)
2	DME	Iceland	1.70	11(WB)
3	DME	Liechtenstein	1.80	11(WB)
4	SEA	Singapore	2.00	11(WB)
5	EEU	Slovenia	2.10	11(WB)
6	DME	Sweden	2.20	11(WB)
7.5	DME	Finland	2.30	11(WB)
7.5	DME	Luxembourg	2.30	11(WB)
9	DME	Japan	2.40	11(WB)
10	DME	Bermuda	2.47	11(CIA)
11.5	MEA	Cyprus	2.60	11(WB)
11.5	DME	Norway	2.60	11(WB)
13	DME	Portugal	2.70	11(WB)
14.5	DME	Andorra	2.80	11(WB)
14.5	USR	Estonia	2.80	11(WB)
16	SEA	Hong Kong	2.90	11(CIA)
17	DME	Denmark	3.10	11(WB)
18	SEA	Macao	3.18	11(CIA)
20.5	EEU	Czech Republic	3.20	11(WB)
20.5	DME	Ireland	3.20	11(WB)
20.5	DME	Italy	3.20	11(WB)
20.5	DME	Monaco	3.20	11(WB)
23	DME	Germany	3.30	11(WB)
24.5	DME	France	3.40	11(WB)
24.5	DME	Netherlands	3.40	11(WB)
26	LAM	Anguilla	3.47	11(CIA)
28.5	DME	Austria	3.50	11(WB)
28.5	DME	Belgium	3.50	11(WB)
28.5	DME	Israel	3.50	11(WB)
28.5	DME	Spain	3.50	11(WB)
31	DME	Guernsey	3.55	11(CIA)
32	DME	Greece	3.70	11(WB)
33	DME	Falkland Islands	3.73	(REG)
34	USR	Belarus	3.90	11(WB)
35	DME	Jersey	3.98	11(CIA)
36	DME	Switzerland	4.00	11(WB)
37.5	DME	Australia	4.10	11(WB)
37.5	SEA	Korea, South	4.10	11(WB)
39	DME	Isle of Man	4.32	11(CIA)
40.5	EEU	Croatia	4.40	11(WB)
40.5	DME	United Kingdom	4.40	11(WB)
42	LAM	Cuba	4.50	11(WB)
43	SEA	Wallis & Futuna	4.67	11(CIA)
44.5	USR	Lithuania	4.70	11(WB)
44.5	DME	New Zealand	4.70	11(WB)
46.5	DME	Canada	4.90	11(WB)
46.5	EEU	Poland	4.90	11(WB)

TABLE 1.2 INFANT MORTALITY RATE PER 1,000 LIVE BIRTHS, 2011

Rank	Region	Country	INFMRT	Source
48	DME	Malta	5.10	11(WB)
49	SEA	Taiwan	5.18	11(CIA)
50	EEU	Hungary	5.40	11(WB)
52	SEA	Brunei	5.60	11(WB)
52	SEA	Malaysia	5.60	11(WB)
52	MEA	United Arab Emirates	5.60	11(WB)
54	SEA	New Caledonia	5.71	11(CIA)
55	SEA	Northern Mariana Is.	5.79	11(CIA)
56.5	SEA	Guam	5.83	11(CIA)
56.5	AFR	Reunion	5.83	07(E)
58	DME	Faroe Islands	6.06	11(CIA)
59.5	EEU	Serbia	6.10	11(WB)
59.5	LAM	St. Kitts & Nevis	6.10	11(WB)
62.5	LAM	Antigua & Barbuda	6.40	11(WB)
62.5	LAM	Martinique	6.40	09(E)
62.5	MEA	Qatar	6.40	11(WB)
62.5	DME	United States	6.40	11(WB)
65	LAM	Saint Martin	6.49	(REG)
66.5	EEU	Montenegro	6.50	11(WB)
66.5	EEU	Slovakia	6.50	11(WB)
68	LAM	Sint Maarten	6.56	(REG)
69	LAM	Cayman Islands	6.63	11(CIA)
70	DME	Gibraltar	6.69	11(CIA)
71	EEU	Bosnia	6.70	11(WB)
72	USR	Latvia	7.10	11(WB)
73	LAM	Virgin Islands, U.S.	7.24	11(CIA)
74	SEA	French Polynesia	7.27	11(CIA)
75	MEA	Oman	7.30	11(WB)
76	DME	St. Pierre & Miquelon	7.47	11(CIA)
77	LAM	Chile	7.70	11(WB)
78	MEA	Saudi Arabia	7.90	11(WB)
79	EEU	Kosovo	7.98	10(E)
80	MEA	Lebanon	8.00	11(WB)
81	LAM	Puerto Rico	8.07	11(CIA)
82	LAM	Guadeloupe	8.09	05(E)
83.5	MEA	Bahrain	8.60	11(WB)
83.5	LAM	Costa Rica	8.60	11(WB)
85	SEA	Nauru	8.66	11(CIA)
87	EEU	Macedonia	8.70	11(WB)
87	USR	Ukraine	8.70	11(WB)
87	LAM	Uruguay	8.70	11(WB)
89	LAM	Curacao	8.86	10(E)
90	SAS	Maldives	9.20	11(WB)
91	MEA	Kuwait	9.30	11(WB)

Table 1.2 Infant Mortality Rate Per 1,000 Live Births, 2011				
Rank	Region	Country	INFMRT	Source
92	SEA	Samoa, American	9.66	11(CIA)
93	USR	Russia	9.80	11(WB)
94	DME	Greenland	10.05	11(CIA)
95	LAM	Guiana, French	10.24	09(E)
96	LAM	Grenada	10.30	11(WB)
97	SAS	Sri Lanka	10.50	11(WB)
98.5	EEU	Bulgaria	10.60	11(WB)
98.5	SEA	Thailand	10.60	11(WB)
100	LAM	Dominica	10.70	11(WB)
101	EEU	Romania	10.80	11(WB)
102	SEA	Vanuatu	11.40	11(WB)
103	MEA	Turkey	11.50	11(WB)
104	AFR	Seychelles	11.90	11(WB)
105	LAM	Turks & Caicos Is.	11.97	11(CIA)
106.5	LAM	Argentina	12.60	11(WB)
106.5	CPA	China	12.60	11(WB)
109	EEU	Albania	12.80	11(WB)
109	MEA	Libya	12.80	11(WB)
109	AFR	Mauritius	12.80	11(WB)
111	LAM	Venezuela	12.90	11(WB)
112	LAM	Aruba	12.92	11(CIA)
113	LAM	El Salvador	13.10	11(WB)
114.5	MEA	Syria	13.20	11(WB)
114.5	SEA	Tonga	13.20	11(WB)
116	LAM	Mexico	13.40	11(WB)
117	LAM	Virgin Islands, Brit.	13.63	11(CIA)
118.5	USR	Moldova	13.80	11(WB)
118.5	LAM	St. Lucia	13.80	11(WB)
120.5	LAM	Brazil	13.90	11(WB)
120.5	MEA	Tunisia	13.90	11(WB)
123	LAM	Bahamas	14.10	11(WB)
123	SEA	Fiji	14.10	11(WB)
123	LAM	Peru	14.10	11(WB)
125	SEA	Palau	14.30	11(WB)
126	LAM	Belize	14.50	11(WB)
127	MEA	West Bank	14.92	11(CIA)
128	SEA	Niue	15.09	94(CIA)
129	LAM	Montserrat	15.23	11(CIA)
130	LAM	Colombia	15.40	11(WB)
131	USR	Armenia	15.60	11(WB)
132	LAM	Jamaica	15.70	11(WB)
133	SEA	Cook Islands	15.81	11(CIA)
134	SEA	Samoa	16.00	11(WB)
135	AFR	St. Helena	16.38	11(CIA)
136	LAM	Panama	16.70	11(WB)
137	MEA	Gaza Strip	17.12	11(CIA)
138	CPA	Vietnam	17.30	11(WB)
139	LAM	Barbados	17.70	11(WB)

Table 1.2 Infant Mortality Rate Per 1,000 Live Births, 2011				
Rank	Region	Country	INFMRT	Source
140.5	MEA	Egypt	18.00	11(WB)
140.5	MEA	Jordan	18.00	11(WB)
142.5	AFR	Cape Verde	18.20	11(WB)
142.5	LAM	Honduras	18.20	11(WB)
144	USR	Georgia	18.30	11(WB)
145	SEA	Solomon Islands	18.40	11(WB)
146	LAM	Paraguay	19.10	11(WB)
147	LAM	St. Vincent	19.50	11(WB)
148	LAM	Ecuador	19.60	11(WB)
149	SEA	Philippines	20.20	11(WB)
150	AFR	Botswana	20.30	11(WB)
151	LAM	Dominican Republic	20.90	11(WB)
152	MEA	Iran	21.10	11(WB)
153	LAM	Nicaragua	21.60	11(WB)
154	SEA	Marshall Islands	22.10	11(WB)
155	LAM	Guatemala	24.20	11(WB)
156	LAM	Trinidad & Tobago	24.50	11(WB)
157	SEA	Indonesia	24.80	11(WB)
158	USR	Kazakhstan	25.00	11(WB)
159	SEA	Tuvalu	25.10	11(WB)
160	CPA	Mongolia	25.50	11(WB)
161	MEA	Algeria	25.60	11(WB)
162	LAM	Suriname	26.00	11(WB)
163	CPA	Korea, North	26.30	11(WB)
164	USR	Kyrgyzstan	27.00	11(WB)
165	MEA	Morocco	28.20	11(WB)
166	LAM	Guyana	29.40	11(WB)
167	AFR	Namibia	29.60	11(WB)
168	MEA	Iraq	30.90	11(WB)
169	SEA	Micronesia	33.50	11(WB)
170	CPA	Laos	33.80	11(WB)
171	SEA	Tokelau	34.25	01(CIA)
172	AFR	South Africa	34.60	11(WB)
173	CPA	Cambodia	36.20	11(WB)
174	SAS	Bangladesh	36.70	11(WB)
175	SEA	Kiribati	37.70	11(WB)
176	AFR	Rwanda	38.10	11(WB)
177	USR	Azerbaijan	38.50	11(WB)
178	SAS	Nepal	39.00	11(WB)
179	LAM	Bolivia	39.30	11(WB)
180	USR	Uzbekistan	41.50	11(WB)
181	SAS	Bhutan	42.00	11(WB)
182.5	AFR	Madagascar	42.80	11(WB)
182.5	AFR	Zimbabwe	42.80	11(WB)
184	USR	Turkmenistan	44.60	11(WB)

Table 1.2 Infant Mortality Rate Per 1,000 Live Births, 2011				
Rank	Region	Country	INFMRT	Source
185	SEA	Papua New Guinea	44.80	11(WB)
186	AFR	Tanzania	45.40	11(WB)
187	SEA	East Timor	45.80	11(WB)
188	AFR	Eritrea	46.30	11(WB)
189	AFR	Senegal	46.70	11(WB)
190	SAS	India	47.20	11(WB)
191	CPA	Burma	47.90	11(WB)
192	AFR	Kenya	48.30	11(WB)
193	AFR	Gabon	49.30	11(WB)
194	AFR	Ethiopia	51.50	11(WB)
195	AFR	Ghana	51.80	11(WB)
196	AFR	Zambia	52.70	11(WB)
197	USR	Tajikistan	52.80	11(WB)
198.5	LAM	Haiti	52.90	11(WB)
198.5	AFR	Malawi	52.90	11(WB)
200	AFR	Mayotte	53.91	10(CIA)
201	AFR	Sudan	56.60	11(WB)
202	MEA	Yemen	57.00	11(WB)
203	AFR	Gambia	57.60	11(WB)
204	AFR	Uganda	57.90	11(WB)
205.5	AFR	Liberia	58.20	11(WB)
205.5	AFR	Sao Tome & Principe	58.20	11(WB)
207	AFR	Comoros	58.80	11(WB)
208	SAS	Pakistan	59.20	11(WB)
209	AFR	Western Sahara	60.44	11(CIA)
210	AFR	Lesotho	62.60	11(WB)
211	AFR	Congo, Republic	63.80	11(WB)
212	AFR	Niger	66.40	11(WB)
213	AFR	Benin	67.90	11(WB)
214	AFR	Swaziland	69.00	11(WB)
215	AFR	Mozambique	71.60	11(WB)
216	AFR	Djibouti	71.80	11(WB)
217	SAS	Afghanistan	72.70	11(WB)
218	AFR	Togo	72.90	11(WB)
219	AFR	Mauritania	75.60	11(WB)
220	AFR	South Sudan	76.00	11(WB)
221	AFR	Nigeria	78.00	11(WB)
222	AFR	Guinea	78.90	11(WB)
223	AFR	Cameroon	79.20	11(WB)
224	AFR	Equatorial Guinea	79.60	11(WB)
225	AFR	Ivory Coast	81.20	11(WB)
226	AFR	Burkina Faso	81.60	11(WB)
227	AFR	Burundi	86.30	11(WB)
228	AFR	Angola	96.40	11(WB)
229	AFR	Chad	97.10	11(WB)
230	AFR	Guinea-Bissau	98.00	11(WB)

TABLE 1.2 INFANT MORTALITY RATE PER 1,000 LIVE BIRTHS, 2011				
Rank	Region	Country	INFMRT	Source
231	AFR	Mali	98.20	11(WB)
232	AFR	Central African Rep.	108.20	11(WB)
233	AFR	Somalia	108.30	11(WB)
234	AFR	Congo, Dem. Republic	110.60	11(WB)
235	AFR	Sierra Leone	119.20	11(WB)

Table 1.3 Life Expectancy at Birth - Average Between Male and Female, 2011				
Rank	Region	Country	LIFEXP	Source
1	DME	Monaco	89.730	11(CIA)
2	SEA	Hong Kong	83.422	11(WB)
3	DME	San Marino	83.323	11(WB)
4	DME	Switzerland	82.695	11(WB)
5	DME	Japan	82.591	11(WB)
6	DME	Andorra	82.430	11(CIA)
7	DME	Iceland	82.359	11(WB)
8	DME	Spain	82.327	11(WB)
9	DME	Guernsey	82.160	11(CIA)
10	DME	Italy	82.088	11(WB)
11	DME	Malta	82.005	11(WB)
12	DME	Faroe Islands	81.929	11(WB)
13	SEA	Singapore	81.893	11(WB)
14	DME	Australia	81.846	11(WB)
15	DME	Sweden	81.802	11(WB)
16	DME	Israel	81.756	11(WB)
17	DME	France	81.668	11(WB)
18	DME	Jersey	81.380	11(CIA)
19	DME	Norway	81.295	11(WB)
20	DME	Netherlands	81.205	11(WB)
21	DME	Austria	81.032	11(WB)
22	SEA	Macao	81.019	11(WB)
23	DME	Luxembourg	80.988	11(WB)
24	DME	Canada	80.929	11(WB)
25	DME	New Zealand	80.905	11(WB)
26	LAM	Anguilla	80.870	11(CIA)
27	SEA	Korea, South	80.866	11(WB)
28	DME	Falkland Islands	80.762	(REG)
29	DME	United Kingdom	80.754	11(WB)
30	DME	Greece	80.744	11(WB)
31	DME	Germany	80.741	11(WB)
32	DME	Portugal	80.722	11(WB)
33	LAM	Cayman Islands	80.680	11(CIA)
34	DME	Isle of Man	80.640	11(CIA)
35	DME	Ireland	80.495	11(WB)
36	DME	Belgium	80.485	11(WB)
37	DME	Finland	80.471	11(WB)
38	DME	Liechtenstein	80.310	11(CIA)
39	EEU	Slovenia	79.971	11(WB)
40	DME	St. Pierre & Miquelon	79.870	11(CIA)
41	DME	Denmark	79.800	11(WB)
42	LAM	Guadeloupe	79.750	11(E)
43	LAM	Martinique	79.650	11(E)
44	MEA	Cyprus	79.563	11(WB)
45	LAM	Costa Rica	79.315	11(WB)

Table 1.3 Life Expectancy at Birth - Average Between Male and Female, 2011				
Rank	Region	Country	LIFEXP	Source
46	LAM	Virgin Islands, U.S.	79.306	11(WB)
47	DME	Bermuda	79.289	11(WB)
48	LAM	Cuba	79.126	11(WB)
49	LAM	Turks & Caicos Is.	79.110	11(CIA)
50	LAM	Puerto Rico	79.028	11(WB)
51	LAM	Chile	79.017	11(WB)
52	SEA	Wallis & Futuna	78.980	11(CIA)
53	AFR	St. Helena	78.760	11(CIA)
54	DME	Gibraltar	78.680	11(CIA)
55	DME	United States	78.641	11(WB)
56	SEA	Taiwan	78.320	11(CIA)
57	MEA	Qatar	78.249	11(WB)
58	AFR	Reunion	78.096	06(E)
59	SEA	Brunei	78.065	11(WB)
60	LAM	Saint Martin	77.924	(REG)
61	EEU	Czech Republic	77.873	11(WB)
62	AFR	Mayotte	77.670	10(WB)
63	LAM	Virgin Islands, Brit.	77.630	11(CIA)
64	SEA	Northern Mariana Is.	77.080	11(CIA)
65	EEU	Albania	77.042	11(WB)
66	LAM	Mexico	76.890	11(WB)
67	SAS	Maldives	76.883	11(WB)
68	EEU	Croatia	76.876	11(WB)
69	EEU	Poland	76.746	11(WB)
70	MEA	United Arab Emirates	76.743	11(WB)
71	LAM	Barbados	76.739	11(WB)
72	LAM	Curacao	76.693	09(WB)
73	SEA	New Caledonia	76.611	11(WB)
74	LAM	Guiana, French	76.450	11(E)
75	LAM	Uruguay	76.412	11(WB)
76	SEA	Guam	76.169	11(WB)
77	LAM	Panama	76.148	11(WB)
78	USR	Estonia	76.127	11(WB)
79	LAM	Sint Maarten	76.121	09(WB)
80	LAM	Belize	76.053	11(WB)
81	LAM	Dominica	75.980	11(CIA)
82	EEU	Slovakia	75.959	11(WB)
83	MEA	Syria	75.844	11(WB)
84	LAM	Grenada	75.827	11(WB)
85	LAM	Argentina	75.798	11(WB)
86	LAM	Ecuador	75.630	11(WB)
87	EEU	Bosnia	75.553	11(WB)
88	LAM	Antigua & Barbuda	75.480	11(CIA)
89	LAM	Bahamas	75.452	11(WB)
90	SEA	French Polynesia	75.256	11(WB)
91	MEA	Bahrain	75.156	11(WB)

Table 1.3 Life Expectancy at Birth - Average Between Male and Female, 2011				
Rank	Region	Country	LIFEXP	Source
92	LAM	Aruba	75.113	11(WB)
93	CPA	Vietnam	75.051	11(WB)
94	MEA	West Bank	75.010	11(CIA)
95	MEA	Libya	74.950	11(WB)
96	SAS	Sri Lanka	74.902	11(WB)
97	EEU	Hungary	74.859	11(WB)
98	EEU	Macedonia	74.788	11(WB)
99	MEA	Tunisia	74.754	11(WB)
100	MEA	Kuwait	74.728	11(WB)
101	SEA	Cook Islands	74.700	11(CIA)
102	LAM	St. Lucia	74.611	11(WB)
103	LAM	St. Kitts & Nevis	74.600	11(CIA)
104	EEU	Serbia	74.585	11(WB)
105	EEU	Romania	74.512	11(WB)
106	EEU	Montenegro	74.504	11(WB)
107	LAM	Venezuela	74.312	11(WB)
108	SEA	Malaysia	74.261	11(WB)
109	SEA	Samoa, American	74.210	11(CIA)
110	EEU	Bulgaria	74.163	11(WB)
111	SEA	Thailand	74.091	11(WB)
112	MEA	Saudi Arabia	74.058	11(WB)
113	LAM	Nicaragua	73.996	11(WB)
114	LAM	Peru	73.976	11(WB)
115	MEA	Turkey	73.944	11(WB)
116	MEA	Gaza Strip	73.920	11(CIA)
117	AFR	Cape Verde	73.917	11(WB)
118	USR	Armenia	73.916	11(WB)
119	LAM	Colombia	73.642	11(WB)
120	USR	Latvia	73.576	11(WB)
121	USR	Lithuania	73.563	11(WB)
122	CPA	China	73.486	11(WB)
123	AFR	Seychelles	73.456	11(WB)
124	LAM	Dominican Republic	73.438	11(WB)
125	LAM	Brazil	73.435	11(WB)
126	MEA	Jordan	73.429	11(WB)
127	USR	Georgia	73.420	10(WB)
128	MEA	Oman	73.342	11(WB)
129	AFR	Mauritius	73.267	11(WB)
130	MEA	Egypt	73.202	11(WB)
131	LAM	Montserrat	73.160	11(CIA)
132	LAM	Honduras	73.113	11(WB)
133	MEA	Algeria	73.080	11(WB)
134	LAM	Jamaica	73.076	11(WB)
135	MEA	Iran	72.999	11(WB)
136	MEA	Lebanon	72.587	11(WB)
137	SEA	Samoa	72.543	11(WB)
138	LAM	Paraguay	72.485	11(WB)

Table 1.3 Life Expectancy at Birth - Average Between Male and Female, 2011

Rank	Region	Country	LIFEXP	Source
139	LAM	St. Vincent	72.295	11(WB)
140	SEA	Tonga	72.286	11(WB)
141	MEA	Morocco	72.132	11(WB)
142	LAM	El Salvador	71.945	11(WB)
143	SEA	Palau	71.780	11(CIA)
144	SEA	Marshall Islands	71.760	11(CIA)
145	SEA	Vanuatu	71.098	11(WB)
146	LAM	Guatemala	71.072	11(WB)
147	DME	Greenland	70.960	11(CIA)
148	USR	Ukraine	70.809	11(WB)
149	USR	Azerbaijan	70.653	11(WB)
150	USR	Belarus	70.651	11(WB)
151	LAM	Suriname	70.581	11(WB)
152	EEU	Kosovo	70.149	11(WB)
153	LAM	Trinidad & Tobago	69.963	11(WB)
154	LAM	Guyana	69.863	11(WB)
155	USR	Kyrgyzstan	69.602	11(WB)
156	SEA	Fiji	69.349	11(WB)
157	SEA	Indonesia	69.319	11(WB)
158	USR	Moldova	69.212	11(WB)
159	SEA	Tokelau	69.145	05(CIA)
160	USR	Russia	69.005	11(WB)
161	MEA	Iraq	68.985	11(WB)
162	SEA	Micronesia	68.948	11(WB)
163	SAS	Bangladesh	68.937	11(WB)
164	USR	Kazakhstan	68.893	11(WB)
165	SEA	Philippines	68.757	11(WB)
166	SAS	Nepal	68.726	11(WB)
167	CPA	Korea, North	68.676	11(WB)
168	CPA	Mongolia	68.488	11(WB)
169	USR	Uzbekistan	68.265	11(WB)
170	SEA	Solomon Islands	67.863	11(WB)
171	USR	Tajikistan	67.536	11(WB)
172	CPA	Laos	67.432	11(WB)
173	SAS	Bhutan	67.285	11(WB)
174	AFR	Madagascar	66.696	11(WB)
175	LAM	Bolivia	66.577	11(WB)
176	SEA	Niue	65.557	94(CIA)
177	SAS	India	65.478	11(WB)
178	MEA	Yemen	65.452	11(WB)
179	SAS	Pakistan	65.449	11(WB)
180	SEA	Nauru	65.350	11(CIA)
181	CPA	Burma	65.150	11(WB)
182	USR	Turkmenistan	64.998	11(WB)
183	SEA	Tuvalu	64.750	11(CIA)
184	AFR	Sao Tome & Principe	64.592	11(WB)
185	SEA	Kiribati	64.390	11(CIA)

Table 1.3 Life Expectancy at Birth - Average Between Male and Female, 2011				
Rank	Region	Country	LIFEXP	Source
186	AFR	Ghana	64.224	11(WB)
187	CPA	Cambodia	62.977	11(WB)
188	SEA	Papua New Guinea	62.801	11(WB)
189	AFR	Gabon	62.691	11(WB)
190	SEA	East Timor	62.461	11(WB)
191	AFR	Namibia	62.332	11(WB)
192	AFR	South Sudan	62.066	08(WB)
193	LAM	Haiti	62.062	11(WB)
194	AFR	Sudan	61.448	11(WB)
195	AFR	Eritrea	61.417	11(WB)
196	AFR	Western Sahara	61.130	11(CIA)
197	AFR	Comoros	61.042	11(WB)
198	AFR	Senegal	59.272	11(WB)
199	AFR	Ethiopia	59.243	11(WB)
200	AFR	Mauritania	58.547	11(WB)
201	AFR	Gambia	58.485	11(WB)
202	AFR	Tanzania	58.151	11(WB)
203	AFR	Djibouti	57.909	11(WB)
204	AFR	Congo, Republic	57.356	11(WB)
205	AFR	Kenya	57.081	11(WB)
206	AFR	Togo	57.027	11(WB)
207	AFR	Liberia	56.743	11(WB)
208	AFR	Benin	56.014	11(WB)
209	AFR	Ivory Coast	55.421	11(WB)
210	AFR	Rwanda	55.395	11(WB)
211	AFR	Burkina Faso	55.358	11(WB)
212	AFR	Niger	54.691	11(WB)
213	AFR	Malawi	54.136	11(WB)
214	AFR	Guinea	54.092	11(WB)
215	AFR	Uganda	54.074	11(WB)
216	AFR	Botswana	53.018	11(WB)
217	AFR	South Africa	52.615	11(WB)
218	AFR	Nigeria	51.863	11(WB)
219	AFR	Cameroon	51.576	11(WB)
220	AFR	Mali	51.372	11(WB)
221	AFR	Zimbabwe	51.236	11(WB)
222	AFR	Somalia	51.195	11(WB)
223	AFR	Equatorial Guinea	51.137	11(WB)
224	AFR	Angola	51.059	11(WB)
225	AFR	Burundi	50.337	11(WB)
226	AFR	Mozambique	50.151	11(WB)
227	AFR	Chad	49.523	11(WB)
228	AFR	Zambia	48.969	11(WB)
229	SAS	Afghanistan	48.681	11(WB)
230	AFR	Swaziland	48.659	11(WB)
231	AFR	Congo, Dem. Republic	48.369	11(WB)

Table 1.3 Life Expectancy at Birth - Average Between Male and Female, 2011				
Rank	Region	Country	LIFEXP	Source
232	AFR	Central African Rep.	48.346	11(WB)
233	AFR	Guinea-Bissau	48.113	11(WB)
234	AFR	Lesotho	47.984	11(WB)
235	AFR	Sierra Leone	47.776	11(WB)

Table 1.4 Gross Domestic Product at Purchasing Power Parities Per Capita, 2011				
Rank	Region	Country	GPCPPP	Source
1	DME	Liechtenstein	148,823	09(CIA)
2	DME	Monaco	131,420	(REG)
3	DME	Bermuda	114,254	(REG)
4	DME	Luxembourg	88,797	11(WB)
5	MEA	Qatar	88,314	11(WB)
6	SEA	Macao	77,079	11(WB)
7	DME	Jersey	64,502	05(CIA)
8	SEA	Singapore	60,688	11(WB)
9	DME	Norway	60,392	11(WB)
10	LAM	Cayman Islands	56,322	09(CIA)
11	DME	Falkland Islands	54,994	07(CIA)
12	SEA	Brunei	51,760	11(WB)
13	DME	Switzerland	51,227	11(WB)
14	SEA	Hong Kong	50,513	11(WB)
15	DME	Guernsey	50,470	05(CIA)
16	DME	United States	48,112	11(WB)
17	MEA	United Arab Emirates	47,893	11(WB)
18	DME	Gibraltar	46,848	08(CIA)
19	LAM	Virgin Islands, Brit.	45,972	04(CIA)
20	LAM	Virgin Islands, U.S.	45,742	(REG)
21	DME	Netherlands	42,779	11(WB)
22	DME	Austria	42,172	11(WB)
23	SEA	New Caledonia	42,154	(REG)
24	DME	Australia	41,974	11(WB)
25	DME	Sweden	41,484	11(WB)
26	DME	Denmark	40,933	11(WB)
27	DME	Ireland	40,868	11(WB)
28	MEA	Kuwait	40,700	11(CIA)
29	DME	Canada	40,420	11(WB)
30	DME	Isle of Man	39,607	05(CIA)
31	DME	Germany	39,456	11(WB)
32	DME	Belgium	38,723	11(WB)
33	SEA	Taiwan	37,900	11(CIA)
34	DME	Greenland	37,619	11(CIA)
35	DME	Finland	37,455	11(WB)
36	DME	Andorra	37,200	11(CIA)
37	DME	Iceland	36,483	11(WB)
38	AFR	Equatorial Guinea	36,202	11(WB)
39	DME	United Kingdom	35,598	11(WB)
40	DME	San Marino	35,500	11(CIA)
41	DME	France	35,247	11(WB)
42	DME	Japan	33,668	11(WB)
43	DME	Italy	32,672	11(WB)
44	MEA	Cyprus	32,254	11(WB)
45	DME	Spain	32,087	11(WB)

Table 1.4 Gross Domestic Product at Purchasing Power Parities Per Capita, 2011

Rank	Region	Country	GPCPPP	Source
46	LAM	Bahamas	31,978	11(WB)
47	LAM	Martinique	31,879	(REG)
48	DME	Faroe Islands	31,382	08(CIA)
49	DME	New Zealand	31,082	11(WB)
50	LAM	Guadeloupe	30,727	(REG)
51	SEA	Korea, South	29,834	11(WB)
52	DME	Israel	28,809	11(WB)
53	MEA	Oman	28,684	11(WB)
54	AFR	Reunion	28,209	(REG)
55	DME	Malta	27,504	11(WB)
56	MEA	Bahrain	27,300	11(CIA)
57	EEU	Slovenia	26,943	11(WB)
58	EEU	Czech Republic	26,332	11(WB)
59	LAM	Saint Martin	26,064	(REG)
60	DME	Greece	25,858	11(WB)
61	AFR	Seychelles	25,788	11(WB)
62	DME	Portugal	25,564	11(WB)
63	LAM	Trinidad & Tobago	25,074	11(WB)
64	LAM	Aruba	24,582	09(CIA)
65	MEA	Saudi Arabia	24,268	11(WB)
66	EEU	Slovakia	24,095	11(WB)
67	LAM	Guiana, French	23,771	(REG)
68	LAM	Barbados	23,600	11(CIA)
69	USR	Estonia	21,997	11(WB)
70	USR	Russia	21,921	11(WB)
71	EEU	Hungary	21,661	11(WB)
72	SEA	French Polynesia	21,493	04(CIA)
73	USR	Lithuania	21,480	11(WB)
74	EEU	Poland	21,085	11(WB)
75	LAM	Curacao	20,669	08(CIA)
76	DME	St. Pierre & Miquelon	19,541	03(CIA)
77	EEU	Croatia	19,487	11(WB)
78	USR	Latvia	18,951	11(WB)
79	LAM	Antigua & Barbuda	18,492	11(WB)
80	LAM	Puerto Rico	18,011	10(CIA)
81	LAM	Chile	17,270	11(WB)
82	LAM	Argentina	17,250	11(E)
83	LAM	St. Kitts & Nevis	17,226	11(WB)
84	SEA	Northern Mariana Is.	17,143	00(CIA)
85	MEA	Turkey	17,110	11(WB)
86	SEA	Guam	16,974	05(CIA)
87	LAM	Mexico	16,588	11(WB)
88	SEA	Malaysia	16,051	11(WB)
89	EEU	Romania	15,983	11(WB)
90	AFR	Gabon	15,852	11(WB)
91	LAM	Sint Maarten	15,845	08(CIA)

Table 1.4 Gross Domestic Product at Purchasing Power Parities Per Capita, 2011

Rank	Region	Country	GPCPPP	Source
92	LAM	Panama	15,589	11(WB)
93	EEU	Bulgaria	15,083	11(WB)
94	LAM	Uruguay	15,078	11(WB)
95	LAM	Turks & Caicos Is.	15,027	02(CIA)
96	USR	Belarus	14,938	11(WB)
97	AFR	Botswana	14,746	11(WB)
98	MEA	Lebanon	14,609	11(WB)
99	MEA	Libya	14,554	10(CIA)
100	AFR	Mauritius	14,420	11(WB)
101	SEA	Palau	13,758	11(WB)
102	EEU	Montenegro	13,432	11(WB)
103	LAM	Dominica	13,288	11(WB)
104	AFR	Mayotte	13,168	09(CIA)
105	USR	Kazakhstan	13,099	11(WB)
106	LAM	Venezuela	12,749	11(WB)
107	LAM	Anguilla	12,341	09(CIA)
108	MEA	Iran	12,200	11(CIA)
109	LAM	Costa Rica	12,157	11(WB)
110	EEU	Serbia	11,887	11(WB)
111	LAM	Brazil	11,640	11(WB)
112	LAM	St. Lucia	11,597	11(WB)
113	EEU	Macedonia	11,561	11(WB)
114	AFR	South Africa	10,960	11(WB)
115	LAM	Grenada	10,837	11(WB)
116	LAM	St. Vincent	10,715	11(WB)
117	SEA	Cook Islands	10,298	05(CIA)
118	LAM	Peru	10,234	11(WB)
119	LAM	Cuba	10,219	10(CIA)
120	USR	Azerbaijan	10,062	11(WB)
121	LAM	Colombia	10,033	11(WB)
122	LAM	Dominican Republic	9,796	11(WB)
123	USR	Turkmenistan	9,420	11(WB)
124	MEA	Tunisia	9,317	11(WB)
125	EEU	Bosnia	9,076	11(WB)
126	SAS	Maldives	8,871	11(WB)
127	EEU	Albania	8,866	11(WB)
128	LAM	Ecuador	8,669	11(WB)
129	MEA	Algeria	8,655	11(WB)
130	SEA	Thailand	8,646	11(WB)
131	CPA	China	8,400	11(WB)
132	LAM	Suriname	8,355	11(WB)
133	SEA	Samoa, American	8,304	07(CIA)
134	LAM	Jamaica	7,770	11(E)
135	SEA	Tuvalu	7,716	(REG)
136	LAM	Guyana	7,500	11(CIA)
137	SEA	Niue	7,300	03(CIA)
138	USR	Ukraine	7,208	11(WB)

TABLE 1.4 GROSS DOMESTIC PRODUCT AT PURCHASING POWER PARITIES PER CAPITA, 2011

Rank	Region	Country	GPCPPP	Source
139	LAM	El Salvador	6,831	11(WB)
140	AFR	Namibia	6,801	11(WB)
141	LAM	Belize	6,672	11(WB)
142	EEU	Kosovo	6,500	11(CIA)
143	MEA	Egypt	6,281	11(WB)
144	AFR	Swaziland	6,053	11(WB)
145	MEA	Jordan	5,966	11(WB)
146	AFR	Angola	5,920	11(WB)
147	SAS	Bhutan	5,846	11(WB)
148	AFR	St. Helena	5,844	11(CIA)
149	USR	Armenia	5,789	11(WB)
150	SEA	Nauru	5,658	05(CIA)
151	SAS	Sri Lanka	5,582	11(WB)
152	LAM	Paraguay	5,501	11(WB)
153	USR	Georgia	5,465	11(WB)
154	MEA	Syria	5,182	11(CIA)
155	LAM	Bolivia	5,099	11(WB)
156	MEA	Morocco	4,952	11(WB)
157	LAM	Guatemala	4,928	11(WB)
158	SEA	Tonga	4,886	11(WB)
159	SEA	Fiji	4,757	11(WB)
160	CPA	Mongolia	4,742	11(WB)
161	LAM	Montserrat	4,673	08(CIA)
162	SEA	Indonesia	4,636	11(WB)
163	SEA	Wallis & Futuna	4,538	04(CIA)
164	SEA	Samoa	4,475	11(WB)
165	SEA	Vanuatu	4,379	11(WB)
166	AFR	Congo, Republic	4,360	11(WB)
167	SEA	Philippines	4,119	11(WB)
168	AFR	Cape Verde	4,095	11(WB)
169	LAM	Honduras	4,047	11(WB)
170	MEA	Iraq	3,864	11(WB)
171	LAM	Nicaragua	3,812	11(WB)
172	SAS	India	3,650	11(WB)
173	MEA	West Bank	3,629	09(CIA)
174.5	SEA	Micronesia	3,412	11(WB)
174.5	CPA	Vietnam	3,412	11(WB)
176	USR	Moldova	3,369	11(WB)
177	USR	Uzbekistan	3,287	11(WB)
178	SEA	Solomon Islands	2,923	11(WB)
179	CPA	Laos	2,790	11(WB)
180	SAS	Pakistan	2,745	11(WB)
181	SEA	Papua New Guinea	2,676	11(WB)
182	AFR	Djibouti	2,600	11(CIA)
183	AFR	Western Sahara	2,595	07(CIA)
184	SEA	Marshall Islands	2,572	08(CIA)
185	AFR	Nigeria	2,533	11(WB)

TABLE 1.4 GROSS DOMESTIC PRODUCT AT PURCHASING POWER PARITIES PER CAPITA, 2011				
Rank	Region	Country	GPCPPP	Source
186	AFR	Mauritania	2,532	11(WB)
187	MEA	Gaza Strip	2,419	09(CIA)
188	USR	Kyrgyzstan	2,402	11(WB)
189	AFR	Cameroon	2,359	11(WB)
190	CPA	Cambodia	2,358	11(WB)
191	SEA	Kiribati	2,337	11(WB)
192	MEA	Yemen	2,333	11(WB)
193	AFR	Sudan	2,325	11(WB)
194	USR	Tajikistan	2,324	11(WB)
195	AFR	Sao Tome & Principe	2,077	11(WB)
196	AFR	Senegal	1,967	11(WB)
197	SEA	Tokelau	1,903	93(CIA)
198	AFR	Ghana	1,871	11(WB)
199	AFR	Gambia	1,809	11(WB)
200	CPA	Korea, North	1,800	11(CIA)
201	AFR	Ivory Coast	1,789	11(WB)
202	SAS	Bangladesh	1,777	11(WB)
203	AFR	Kenya	1,710	11(WB)
204	AFR	Lesotho	1,691	11(WB)
205	AFR	Zambia	1,621	11(WB)
206	AFR	Benin	1,619	11(WB)
207	SEA	East Timor	1,578	11(WB)
208	AFR	Tanzania	1,512	11(WB)
209	AFR	Chad	1,498	11(WB)
210	AFR	Uganda	1,345	11(WB)
211	AFR	Burkina Faso	1,302	11(WB)
212	CPA	Burma	1,300	11(CIA)
213	AFR	Rwanda	1,282	11(WB)
214	AFR	Guinea-Bissau	1,270	11(WB)
215	SAS	Nepal	1,252	11(WB)
216	LAM	Haiti	1,171	11(WB)
217	SAS	Afghanistan	1,139	11(WB)
218	AFR	Sierra Leone	1,131	11(WB)
219	AFR	Guinea	1,124	11(WB)
220	AFR	Comoros	1,110	11(WB)
221	AFR	Ethiopia	1,109	11(WB)
222	AFR	Mali	1,091	11(WB)
223	AFR	Togo	1,049	11(WB)
224	AFR	Mozambique	975	11(WB)
225	AFR	Madagascar	966	11(WB)
226	AFR	Malawi	893	11(WB)
227	AFR	Central African Rep.	810	11(WB)
228	AFR	Niger	727	11(WB)
229	AFR	Somalia	619	10(CIA)
230	AFR	Burundi	604	11(WB)
231.5	AFR	Eritrea	585	11(WB)
231.5	AFR	Liberia	585	11(WB)

Table 1.4 Gross Domestic Product at Purchasing Power Parities Per Capita, 2011				
Rank	Region	Country	GPCPPP	Source
233	AFR	Zimbabwe	500	11(CIA)
234	AFR	Congo, Dem. Republic	373	11(WB)
235	AFR	South Sudan	297	(REG)

TABLE 1.5 ECONOMIC QUALITY-OF-LIFE INDEX PRINCIPAL COMPONENT 1 OF THE ECONOMIC QUALITY-OF-LIFE INDICATORS, 2011

Rank	Region	Country	EQLX	Source
1	DME	Monaco	2.504	PRIN1(EQL)
2	DME	Liechtenstein	1.890	PRIN1(EQL)
3	DME	Bermuda	1.700	PRIN1(EQL)
4	DME	Luxembourg	1.655	PRIN1(EQL)
5	DME	San Marino	1.613	PRIN1(EQL)
6	DME	Norway	1.587	PRIN1(EQL)
7	SEA	Singapore	1.559	PRIN1(EQL)
8	DME	Switzerland	1.501	PRIN1(EQL)
9	SEA	Hong Kong	1.491	PRIN1(EQL)
10	DME	Sweden	1.491	PRIN1(EQL)
11	DME	Iceland	1.485	PRIN1(EQL)
12	SEA	Macao	1.465	PRIN1(EQL)
13	DME	Jersey	1.453	PRIN1(EQL)
14	DME	Japan	1.443	PRIN1(EQL)
15	DME	Guernsey	1.417	PRIN1(EQL)
16	DME	Andorra	1.407	PRIN1(EQL)
17	DME	Finland	1.375	PRIN1(EQL)
18	DME	Falkland Islands	1.374	PRIN1(EQL)
19	DME	Netherlands	1.351	PRIN1(EQL)
20	DME	Australia	1.336	PRIN1(EQL)
21	DME	Denmark	1.329	PRIN1(EQL)
22	DME	Austria	1.327	PRIN1(EQL)
23	DME	France	1.309	PRIN1(EQL)
24	DME	Isle of Man	1.300	PRIN1(EQL)
25	DME	Italy	1.300	PRIN1(EQL)
26	DME	Germany	1.299	PRIN1(EQL)
27	MEA	Qatar	1.292	PRIN1(EQL)
28	DME	Ireland	1.281	PRIN1(EQL)
29	DME	Belgium	1.275	PRIN1(EQL)
30	DME	Spain	1.265	PRIN1(EQL)
31	LAM	Cayman Islands	1.241	PRIN1(EQL)
32	DME	Canada	1.224	PRIN1(EQL)
33	DME	Israel	1.202	PRIN1(EQL)
34	EEU	Slovenia	1.188	PRIN1(EQL)
35	DME	Faroe Islands	1.184	PRIN1(EQL)
36	DME	United Kingdom	1.184	PRIN1(EQL)
37	DME	New Zealand	1.150	PRIN1(EQL)
38	MEA	Cyprus	1.150	PRIN1(EQL)
39	DME	Portugal	1.136	PRIN1(EQL)
40	DME	United States	1.102	PRIN1(EQL)
41	DME	Greece	1.087	PRIN1(EQL)
42	SEA	Brunei	1.078	PRIN1(EQL)
43	LAM	Virgin Islands, U.S.	1.071	PRIN1(EQL)
44	SEA	Korea, South	1.070	PRIN1(EQL)
45	DME	Gibraltar	1.061	PRIN1(EQL)
46	DME	Malta	1.046	PRIN1(EQL)

Table 1.5 Economic Quality-of-Life Index Principal Component 1 of the Economic Quality-of-Life Indicators, 2011				
Rank	Region	Country	EQLX	Source
47	MEA	United Arab Emirates	1.028	PRIN1(EQL)
48	SEA	New Caledonia	0.986	PRIN1(EQL)
49	LAM	Martinique	0.969	PRIN1(EQL)
50	SEA	Taiwan	0.955	PRIN1(EQL)
51	EEU	Czech Republic	0.953	PRIN1(EQL)
52	LAM	Guadeloupe	0.903	PRIN1(EQL)
53	AFR	Reunion	0.875	PRIN1(EQL)
54	LAM	Virgin Islands, Brit.	0.863	PRIN1(EQL)
55	USR	Estonia	0.848	PRIN1(EQL)
56	LAM	Anguilla	0.843	PRIN1(EQL)
57	MEA	Kuwait	0.826	PRIN1(EQL)
58	LAM	Saint Martin	0.810	PRIN1(EQL)
59	DME	St. Pierre & Miquelon	0.736	PRIN1(EQL)
60	LAM	Curacao	0.729	PRIN1(EQL)
61	EEU	Croatia	0.723	PRIN1(EQL)
62	SEA	Guam	0.711	PRIN1(EQL)
63	EEU	Poland	0.693	PRIN1(EQL)
64	LAM	Puerto Rico	0.688	PRIN1(EQL)
65	SEA	French Polynesia	0.672	PRIN1(EQL)
66	EEU	Slovakia	0.669	PRIN1(EQL)
67	MEA	Oman	0.654	PRIN1(EQL)
68	SEA	Northern Mariana Is.	0.654	PRIN1(EQL)
69	DME	Greenland	0.642	PRIN1(EQL)
70	LAM	Sint Maarten	0.636	PRIN1(EQL)
71	LAM	Chile	0.635	PRIN1(EQL)
72	MEA	Bahrain	0.634	PRIN1(EQL)
73	EEU	Hungary	0.613	PRIN1(EQL)
74	LAM	Guiana, French	0.607	PRIN1(EQL)
75	USR	Lithuania	0.606	PRIN1(EQL)
76	LAM	Bahamas	0.579	PRIN1(EQL)
77	MEA	Saudi Arabia	0.576	PRIN1(EQL)
78	LAM	Antigua & Barbuda	0.551	PRIN1(EQL)
79	LAM	Aruba	0.550	PRIN1(EQL)
80	LAM	St. Kitts & Nevis	0.528	PRIN1(EQL)
81	LAM	Cuba	0.519	PRIN1(EQL)
82	USR	Latvia	0.487	PRIN1(EQL)
83	LAM	Turks & Caicos Is.	0.485	PRIN1(EQL)
84	LAM	Costa Rica	0.471	PRIN1(EQL)
85	LAM	Uruguay	0.469	PRIN1(EQL)
86	SEA	Malaysia	0.462	PRIN1(EQL)
87	LAM	Barbados	0.451	PRIN1(EQL)
88	AFR	Seychelles	0.394	PRIN1(EQL)
89	LAM	Mexico	0.364	PRIN1(EQL)
90	EEU	Montenegro	0.363	PRIN1(EQL)
91	USR	Belarus	0.356	PRIN1(EQL)

TABLE 1.5 ECONOMIC QUALITY-OF-LIFE INDEX PRINCIPAL COMPONENT 1 OF THE ECONOMIC QUALITY-OF-LIFE INDICATORS, 2011				
Rank	Region	Country	EQLX	Source
92	LAM	Argentina	0.352	PRIN1(EQL)
93	MEA	Libya	0.326	PRIN1(EQL)
94	MEA	Turkey	0.321	PRIN1(EQL)
95	EEU	Serbia	0.318	PRIN1(EQL)
96	MEA	Lebanon	0.312	PRIN1(EQL)
97	EEU	Romania	0.300	PRIN1(EQL)
98	LAM	Dominica	0.290	PRIN1(EQL)
99	USR	Russia	0.271	PRIN1(EQL)
100	LAM	Venezuela	0.268	PRIN1(EQL)
101	LAM	Grenada	0.261	PRIN1(EQL)
102	EEU	Bulgaria	0.247	PRIN1(EQL)
103	EEU	Bosnia	0.245	PRIN1(EQL)
104	SAS	Maldives	0.244	PRIN1(EQL)
105	LAM	Panama	0.233	PRIN1(EQL)
106	SEA	Wallis & Futuna	0.227	PRIN1(EQL)
107	EEU	Macedonia	0.207	PRIN1(EQL)
108	AFR	Mauritius	0.196	PRIN1(EQL)
109	LAM	Brazil	0.187	PRIN1(EQL)
110	SEA	Samoa, American	0.184	PRIN1(EQL)
111	LAM	Trinidad & Tobago	0.163	PRIN1(EQL)
112	SEA	Cook Islands	0.160	PRIN1(EQL)
113	LAM	St. Lucia	0.150	PRIN1(EQL)
114	EEU	Albania	0.109	PRIN1(EQL)
115	SEA	Palau	0.080	PRIN1(EQL)
116	SEA	Thailand	0.064	PRIN1(EQL)
117	LAM	Peru	0.052	PRIN1(EQL)
118	LAM	Colombia	0.044	PRIN1(EQL)
119	MEA	Tunisia	0.020	PRIN1(EQL)
120	AFR	St. Helena	0.019	PRIN1(EQL)
121	CPA	China	0.016	PRIN1(EQL)
122	MEA	Iran	-0.004	PRIN1(EQL)
123	AFR	Mayotte	-0.020	PRIN1(EQL)
124	LAM	Belize	-0.026	PRIN1(EQL)
125	LAM	Ecuador	-0.039	PRIN1(EQL)
126	LAM	St. Vincent	-0.041	PRIN1(EQL)
127	LAM	Jamaica	-0.063	PRIN1(EQL)
128	LAM	Dominican Republic	-0.065	PRIN1(EQL)
129	EEU	Kosovo	-0.081	PRIN1(EQL)
130	USR	Ukraine	-0.082	PRIN1(EQL)
131	SAS	Sri Lanka	-0.086	PRIN1(EQL)
132	MEA	Syria	-0.091	PRIN1(EQL)
133	USR	Kazakhstan	-0.101	PRIN1(EQL)
134	LAM	El Salvador	-0.141	PRIN1(EQL)
135	MEA	Jordan	-0.160	PRIN1(EQL)
136	USR	Armenia	-0.161	PRIN1(EQL)
137	LAM	Suriname	-0.165	PRIN1(EQL)
138	SEA	Nauru	-0.167	PRIN1(EQL)

Table 1.5 Economic Quality-of-Life Index Principal Component 1 of the Economic Quality-of-Life Indicators, 2011

Rank	Region	Country	EQLX	Source
139	MEA	Algeria	-0.177	PRIN1(EQL)
140	SEA	Tonga	-0.184	PRIN1(EQL)
141	SEA	Niue	-0.198	PRIN1(EQL)
142	MEA	Egypt	-0.245	PRIN1(EQL)
143	USR	Georgia	-0.254	PRIN1(EQL)
144	LAM	Montserrat	-0.255	PRIN1(EQL)
145	AFR	Cape Verde	-0.259	PRIN1(EQL)
146	SEA	Vanuatu	-0.262	PRIN1(EQL)
147	SEA	Samoa	-0.272	PRIN1(EQL)
148	LAM	Paraguay	-0.282	PRIN1(EQL)
149	USR	Azerbaijan	-0.286	PRIN1(EQL)
150	SEA	Fiji	-0.291	PRIN1(EQL)
151	MEA	West Bank	-0.309	PRIN1(EQL)
152	AFR	Botswana	-0.360	PRIN1(EQL)
153	AFR	Gabon	-0.371	PRIN1(EQL)
154	LAM	Honduras	-0.385	PRIN1(EQL)
155	SEA	Tuvalu	-0.394	PRIN1(EQL)
156	LAM	Guyana	-0.402	PRIN1(EQL)
157	AFR	Equatorial Guinea	-0.409	PRIN1(EQL)
158	MEA	Morocco	-0.410	PRIN1(EQL)
159	LAM	Guatemala	-0.410	PRIN1(EQL)
160	CPA	Vietnam	-0.419	PRIN1(EQL)
161	SEA	Marshall Islands	-0.448	PRIN1(EQL)
162	LAM	Nicaragua	-0.455	PRIN1(EQL)
163	USR	Moldova	-0.466	PRIN1(EQL)
164	SEA	Indonesia	-0.472	PRIN1(EQL)
165	USR	Turkmenistan	-0.490	PRIN1(EQL)
166	SEA	Philippines	-0.509	PRIN1(EQL)
167	AFR	Namibia	-0.518	PRIN1(EQL)
168	MEA	Gaza Strip	-0.527	PRIN1(EQL)
169	CPA	Mongolia	-0.536	PRIN1(EQL)
170	AFR	South Africa	-0.565	PRIN1(EQL)
171	MEA	Iraq	-0.588	PRIN1(EQL)
172	SEA	Micronesia	-0.620	PRIN1(EQL)
173	SAS	Bhutan	-0.656	PRIN1(EQL)
174	LAM	Bolivia	-0.694	PRIN1(EQL)
175	SEA	Solomon Islands	-0.695	PRIN1(EQL)
176	USR	Uzbekistan	-0.803	PRIN1(EQL)
177	USR	Kyrgyzstan	-0.817	PRIN1(EQL)
178	CPA	Laos	-0.857	PRIN1(EQL)
179	CPA	Korea, North	-0.875	PRIN1(EQL)
180	SEA	Kiribati	-0.889	PRIN1(EQL)
181	SAS	India	-0.889	PRIN1(EQL)
182	SEA	Tokelau	-0.920	PRIN1(EQL)
183	SEA	Papua New Guinea	-0.990	PRIN1(EQL)
184	SAS	Bangladesh	-0.992	PRIN1(EQL)
185	SEA	East Timor	-1.001	PRIN1(EQL)

Table 1.5 Economic Quality-of-Life Index Principal Component 1 of the Economic Quality-of-Life Indicators, 2011				
Rank	Region	Country	EQLX	Source
186	AFR	Congo, Republic	-1.009	PRIN1(EQL)
187	AFR	Swaziland	-1.025	PRIN1(EQL)
188	USR	Tajikistan	-1.042	PRIN1(EQL)
189	SAS	Pakistan	-1.042	PRIN1(EQL)
190	AFR	Angola	-1.058	PRIN1(EQL)
191	CPA	Cambodia	-1.061	PRIN1(EQL)
192	MEA	Yemen	-1.073	PRIN1(EQL)
193	AFR	Ghana	-1.075	PRIN1(EQL)
194	AFR	Sao Tome & Principe	-1.081	PRIN1(EQL)
195	AFR	Western Sahara	-1.112	PRIN1(EQL)
196	AFR	Sudan	-1.122	PRIN1(EQL)
197	SAS	Nepal	-1.145	PRIN1(EQL)
198	AFR	Senegal	-1.186	PRIN1(EQL)
199	AFR	Djibouti	-1.195	PRIN1(EQL)
200	AFR	Mauritania	-1.269	PRIN1(EQL)
201	AFR	Kenya	-1.306	PRIN1(EQL)
202	AFR	Madagascar	-1.307	PRIN1(EQL)
203	CPA	Burma	-1.321	PRIN1(EQL)
204	LAM	Haiti	-1.337	PRIN1(EQL)
205	AFR	Nigeria	-1.351	PRIN1(EQL)
206	AFR	Tanzania	-1.368	PRIN1(EQL)
207	AFR	Comoros	-1.378	PRIN1(EQL)
208	AFR	Cameroon	-1.383	PRIN1(EQL)
209	AFR	Gambia	-1.395	PRIN1(EQL)
210	AFR	Rwanda	-1.397	PRIN1(EQL)
211	AFR	Ivory Coast	-1.401	PRIN1(EQL)
212	AFR	Zambia	-1.407	PRIN1(EQL)
213	AFR	Benin	-1.425	PRIN1(EQL)
214	AFR	Lesotho	-1.446	PRIN1(EQL)
215	AFR	Ethiopia	-1.504	PRIN1(EQL)
216	AFR	Uganda	-1.528	PRIN1(EQL)
217	AFR	Eritrea	-1.540	PRIN1(EQL)
218	AFR	Togo	-1.565	PRIN1(EQL)
219	AFR	Burkina Faso	-1.574	PRIN1(EQL)
220	AFR	Chad	-1.641	PRIN1(EQL)
221	AFR	Malawi	-1.647	PRIN1(EQL)
222	AFR	Zimbabwe	-1.655	PRIN1(EQL)
223	AFR	Guinea	-1.666	PRIN1(EQL)
224	AFR	Mali	-1.708	PRIN1(EQL)
225	SAS	Afghanistan	-1.711	PRIN1(EQL)
226	AFR	Mozambique	-1.721	PRIN1(EQL)
227	AFR	Liberia	-1.726	PRIN1(EQL)
228	AFR	Guinea-Bissau	-1.727	PRIN1(EQL)
229	AFR	Niger	-1.733	PRIN1(EQL)
230	AFR	Sierra Leone	-1.847	PRIN1(EQL)
231	AFR	Central African Rep.	-1.876	PRIN1(EQL)

Rank	Region	Country	EQLX	Source
232	AFR	Burundi	-1.962	PRIN1(EQL)
233	AFR	Somalia	-2.002	PRIN1(EQL)
234	AFR	South Sudan	-2.041	PRIN1(EQL)
235	AFR	Congo, Dem. Republic	-2.193	PRIN1(EQL)

Table 1.6 Societal Integration Index, Intensity of Open Political Process, 2011				
Rank	Region	Country	SCINTX	Source
1	LAM	Brazil	0.900	11(CALC(CIA))
2	DME	Belgium	0.881	11(CALC(CIA))
3	SEA	Vanuatu	0.874	11(CALC(CIA))
4	SEA	Hong Kong	0.867	11(CALC(CIA))
5	DME	Israel	0.852	11(CALC(CIA))
6	DME	Netherlands	0.851	11(CALC(CIA))
7	MEA	Morocco	0.849	11(CALC(CIA))
8	SEA	New Caledonia	0.842	11(CALC(CIA))
9	LAM	Haiti	0.841	11(CALC(CIA))
10	EEU	Kosovo	0.839	11(CALC(CIA))
11	SEA	Indonesia	0.838	11(CALC(CIA))
12	AFR	Liberia	0.829	11(CALC(CIA))
13	DME	Finland	0.828	11(CALC(CIA))
14	USR	Lithuania	0.828	11(CALC(CIA))
15	LAM	Chile	0.827	11(CALC(CIA))
16	DME	Denmark	0.822	11(CALC(CIA))
17	DME	Switzerland	0.820	11(CALC(CIA))
18	EEU	Bosnia	0.816	11(CALC(CIA))
19	DME	Faroe Islands	0.808	11(CALC(CIA))
20	AFR	Congo, Dem. Republic	0.805	11(CALC(CIA))
21	MEA	Algeria	0.804	11(CALC(CIA))
22	LAM	Colombia	0.802	11(CALC(CIA))
23	SEA	Papua New Guinea	0.801	11(CALC(CIA))
24	AFR	Mali	0.798	11(CALC(CIA))
25	USR	Kyrgyzstan	0.796	11(CALC(CIA))
26	AFR	Mauritania	0.796	11(CALC(CIA))
27	AFR	Reunion	0.789	11(CALC(WIKI))
28	EEU	Slovenia	0.788	11(CALC(CIA))
29	SAS	India	0.788	11(CALC(CIA))
30	SEA	Solomon Islands	0.787	11(CALC(CIA))
31	MEA	Iraq	0.781	11(CALC(CIA))
32	DME	Sweden	0.780	11(CALC(CIA))
33	USR	Latvia	0.779	11(CALC(CIA))
34	EEU	Czech Republic	0.778	11(CALC(CIA))
35	MEA	Tunisia	0.776	11(CALC(CIA))
36	SEA	East Timor	0.771	11(CALC(CIA))
37	AFR	Niger	0.771	11(CALC(CIA))
38	DME	Austria	0.766	11(CALC(CIA))
39	SAS	Nepal	0.764	11(CALC(CIA))
40	DME	Iceland	0.761	11(CALC(CIA))
41	SAS	Pakistan	0.759	11(CALC(CIA))
42	LAM	Costa Rica	0.758	11(CALC(CIA))
43	LAM	Guatemala	0.754	11(CALC(CIA))
44	DME	Norway	0.754	11(CALC(CIA))

Table 1.6 Societal Integration Index, Intensity of Open Political Process, 2011				
Rank	Region	Country	SCINTX	Source
45	EEU	Slovakia	0.750	11(CALC(CIA))
46	EEU	Serbia	0.749	11(CALC(CIA))
47	DME	San Marino	0.748	11(CALC(CIA))
48	LAM	Curacao	0.748	11(CALC(CIA))
49	DME	Germany	0.748	11(CALC(CIA))
50	LAM	Peru	0.748	11(CALC(CIA))
51	SAS	Afghanistan	0.740	11(CALC(CIA))
52	USR	Estonia	0.740	11(CALC(CIA))
53	LAM	Guiana, French	0.739	11(CALC(WIKI))
54	LAM	Panama	0.726	11(CALC(CIA))
55	DME	Luxembourg	0.724	11(CALC(CIA))
56	EEU	Romania	0.720	11(CALC(CIA))
57	USR	Uzbekistan	0.717	11(CALC(CIA))
58	SAS	Maldives	0.716	11(CALC(CIA))
59	LAM	Martinique	0.712	11(CALC(WIKI))
60	DME	Ireland	0.712	11(CALC(CIA))
61	LAM	Ecuador	0.711	11(CALC(CIA))
62	LAM	Paraguay	0.707	11(CALC(CIA))
63	USR	Armenia	0.703	11(CALC(CIA))
64	MEA	Egypt	0.702	11(CALC(CIA))
65	EEU	Bulgaria	0.698	11(CALC(CIA))
66	USR	Ukraine	0.697	11(CALC(CIA))
67	EEU	Poland	0.693	11(CALC(CIA))
68	AFR	Kenya	0.693	11(CALC(CIA))
69	USR	Moldova	0.691	11(CALC(CIA))
70	LAM	Suriname	0.688	11(CALC(CIA))
71	DME	Greenland	0.685	11(CALC(CIA))
72	AFR	Lesotho	0.681	11(CALC(CIA))
73	MEA	Kuwait	0.680	11(CALC(CIA))
74	LAM	Argentina	0.678	11(CALC(CIA))
75	DME	Italy	0.675	11(CALC(CIA))
76	MEA	Cyprus	0.674	11(CALC(CIA))
77	LAM	Mexico	0.670	11(CALC(CIA))
78	AFR	Zambia	0.661	11(CALC(CIA))
79	SEA	Kiribati	0.661	11(CALC(CIA))
80	DME	Australia	0.661	11(CALC(CIA))
81	LAM	El Salvador	0.660	11(CALC(CIA))
82	AFR	Mayotte	0.659	11(CALC(CIA))
83	DME	Portugal	0.659	11(CALC(CIA))
84	DME	New Zealand	0.658	11(CALC(CIA))
85	SEA	Philippines	0.658	11(CALC(CIA))
86	EEU	Macedonia	0.657	11(CALC(CIA))
87	LAM	Guadeloupe	0.653	11(CALC(WIKI))
88	USR	Russia	0.643	11(CALC(CIA))
89	LAM	Trinidad & Tobago	0.628	11(CALC(CIA))
90	LAM	St. Kitts & Nevis	0.628	11(CALC(CIA))

Table 1.6 Societal Integration Index, Intensity of Open Political Process, 2011

Rank	Region	Country	SCINTX	Source
91	LAM	Uruguay	0.623	11(CALC(CIA))
92	AFR	Nigeria	0.622	11(CALC(CIA))
93	SEA	French Polynesia	0.622	11(CALC(CIA))
94	EEU	Croatia	0.616	11(CALC(CIA))
95	DME	Greece	0.614	11(CALC(CIA))
96	AFR	Sao Tome & Principe	0.614	11(CALC(CIA))
97	DME	Spain	0.614	11(CALC(CIA))
98	DME	United Kingdom	0.612	11(CALC(CIA))
99	SEA	Macao	0.610	11(CALC(CIA))
100	MEA	Bahrain	0.609	11(CALC(CIA))
101	LAM	Sint Maarten	0.604	11(CALC(CIA))
102	AFR	Benin	0.604	11(CALC(CIA))
103	AFR	Rwanda	0.600	11(CALC(CIA))
104	SEA	Thailand	0.598	11(CALC(CIA))
105	AFR	Malawi	0.597	11(CALC(CIA))
106	EEU	Montenegro	0.594	11(CALC(CIA))
107	AFR	Congo, Republic	0.592	11(CALC(CIA))
108	LAM	Guyana	0.586	11(CALC(CIA))
109	DME	Canada	0.585	11(CALC(CIA))
110	MEA	Iran	0.585	11(CALC(CIA))
111	SEA	Korea, South	0.583	11(CALC(CIA))
112	DME	France	0.577	11(CALC(CIA))
113	SEA	Northern Mariana Is.	0.575	11(CALC(CIA))
114	MEA	Turkey	0.575	11(CALC(CIA))
115	LAM	Anguilla	0.571	11(CALC(CIA))
116	AFR	Central African Rep.	0.569	11(CALC(CIA))
117	AFR	Sierra Leone	0.567	11(CALC(CIA))
118	LAM	Honduras	0.566	11(CALC(CIA))
119	SEA	Samoa	0.559	11(CALC(CIA))
120	EEU	Albania	0.553	11(CALC(CIA))
121	SEA	Taiwan	0.552	11(CALC(CIA))
122	SEA	Fiji	0.551	11(CALC(CIA))
123	LAM	Antigua & Barbuda	0.547	11(CALC(CIA))
124	AFR	Burkina Faso	0.546	11(CALC(CIA))
125	AFR	Ghana	0.537	11(CALC(CIA))
126	DME	Liechtenstein	0.534	11(CALC(CIA))
127	LAM	Aruba	0.526	11(CALC(CIA))
128	AFR	South Africa	0.526	11(CALC(CIA))
129	LAM	Cayman Islands	0.524	11(CALC(CIA))
130	DME	Japan	0.523	11(CALC(CIA))
131	AFR	Cape Verde	0.523	11(CALC(CIA))
132	CPA	Mongolia	0.520	11(CALC(CIA))
133	AFR	Zimbabwe	0.517	11(CALC(CIA))

Table 1.6 Societal Integration Index, Intensity of Open Political Process, 2011

Rank	Region	Country	SCINTX	Source
134	SAS	Sri Lanka	0.514	11(CALC(CIA))
135	AFR	Ivory Coast	0.510	11(CALC(CIA))
136	AFR	Togo	0.505	11(CALC(CIA))
137	LAM	Dominican Republic	0.503	11(CALC(CIA))
138	DME	Malta	0.500	11(CALC(CIA))
139	LAM	Virgin Islands, U.S.	0.498	11(CALC(CIA))
140	LAM	St. Vincent	0.498	11(CALC(CIA))
141	EEU	Hungary	0.496	11(CALC(CIA))
142	MEA	Lebanon	0.494	11(CALC(CIA))
143	DME	United States	0.493	11(CALC(CIA))
144	LAM	Bahamas	0.493	11(CALC(CIA))
145	LAM	Venezuela	0.492	11(CALC(CIA))
146	DME	Gibraltar	0.484	11(CALC(CIA))
147	AFR	Uganda	0.482	11(CALC(CIA))
148	SEA	Guam	0.480	11(CALC(CIA))
149	AFR	Mauritius	0.477	11(CALC(CIA))
150	DME	Bermuda	0.475	11(CALC(CIA))
151	AFR	Guinea-Bissau	0.472	11(CALC(CIA))
152	SEA	Malaysia	0.466	11(CALC(CIA))
153	LAM	St. Lucia	0.457	11(CALC(CIA))
154	SEA	Wallis & Futuna	0.455	11(CALC(CIA))
155	LAM	Bolivia	0.454	11(CALC(CIA))
156	LAM	Saint Martin	0.446	11(CALC(CIA))
157	LAM	Nicaragua	0.444	11(CALC(CIA))
159.5	LAM	Barbados	0.444	11(CALC(CIA))
159.5	SEA	Cook Islands	0.444	11(CALC(CIA))
159.5	LAM	Jamaica	0.444	11(CALC(CIA))
159.5	LAM	Montserrat	0.444	11(CALC(CIA))
162	AFR	Chad	0.441	11(CALC(CIA))
163	DME	Andorra	0.439	11(CALC(CIA))
164	AFR	Seychelles	0.438	11(CALC(CIA))
165	AFR	Tanzania	0.430	11(CALC(CIA))
166	LAM	Virgin Islands, Brit.	0.426	11(CALC(CIA))
167	AFR	Sudan	0.426	11(CALC(CIA))
168	AFR	Namibia	0.422	11(CALC(CIA))
169	CPA	Cambodia	0.419	11(CALC(CIA))
170	SEA	Tonga	0.415	11(CALC(CIA))
171	LAM	Puerto Rico	0.398	11(CALC(CIA))
172	SAS	Bangladesh	0.393	11(CALC(CIA))
173	LAM	Grenada	0.391	11(CALC(CIA))
174	AFR	Burundi	0.387	11(CALC(CIA))
175	AFR	Mozambique	0.374	11(CALC(CIA))
176	AFR	Botswana	0.360	11(CALC(CIA))
177	MEA	Yemen	0.350	11(CALC(CIA))

TABLE 1.6 SOCIETAL INTEGRATION INDEX, INTENSITY OF OPEN POLITICAL PROCESS, 2011				
Rank	Region	Country	SCINTX	Source
178	USR	Georgia	0.345	11(CALC(CIA))
179	AFR	Comoros	0.344	11(CALC(CIA))
180	CPA	Burma	0.324	11(CALC(CIA))
181	LAM	Belize	0.312	11(CALC(CIA))
182	DME	St. Pierre & Miquelon	0.277	11(CALC(CIA))
183	AFR	Cameroon	0.254	11(CALC(CIA))
184	LAM	Dominica	0.245	11(CALC(CIA))
185	AFR	Angola	0.239	11(CALC(CIA))
186	USR	Tajikistan	0.234	11(CALC(CIA))
187	LAM	Turks & Caicos Is.	0.231	11(CALC(CIA))
188	AFR	Senegal	0.221	11(CALC(CIA))
189.5	DME	Isle of Man	0.219	11(CALC(CIA))
189.5	DME	Monaco	0.219	11(CALC(CIA))
191	AFR	Gambia	0.207	11(CALC(CIA))
192	AFR	Equatorial Guinea	0.198	11(CALC(CIA))
193	USR	Azerbaijan	0.182	11(CALC(CIA))
194	AFR	Ethiopia	0.165	11(CALC(CIA))
195	SEA	Singapore	0.128	11(CALC(CIA))
196	USR	Belarus	0.120	11(CALC(CIA))
197	AFR	South Sudan	0.108	11(CALC(CIA))
198	AFR	Gabon	0.096	11(CALC(CIA))
199	SAS	Bhutan	0.081	11(CALC(CIA))
200	CPA	Laos	0.059	11(CALC(CIA))
201	AFR	Madagascar	0.016	11(CALC(CIA))
218.5	SEA	Brunei	0.000	11(CALC(CIA))
218.5	CPA	China	0.000	11(CALC(CIA))
218.5	LAM	Cuba	0.000	11(CALC(CIA))
218.5	AFR	Djibouti	0.000	11(CALC(CIA))
218.5	AFR	Eritrea	0.000	11(CALC(CIA))
218.5	DME	Falkland Islands	0.000	11(CALC(CIA))
218.5	MEA	Gaza Strip	0.000	11(CALC(CIA))
218.5	DME	Guernsey	0.000	11(CALC(CIA))
218.5	AFR	Guinea	0.000	11(CALC(CIA))
218.5	DME	Jersey	0.000	11(CALC(CIA))
218.5	MEA	Jordan	0.000	11(CALC(CIA))
218.5	USR	Kazakhstan	0.000	11(CALC(CIA))
218.5	CPA	Korea, North	0.000	11(CALC(CIA))
218.5	MEA	Libya	0.000	11(CALC(CIA))
218.5	SEA	Marshall Islands	0.000	11(CALC(CIA))
218.5	SEA	Micronesia	0.000	11(CALC(CIA))
218.5	SEA	Nauru	0.000	11(CALC(CIA))
218.5	SEA	Niue	0.000	11(CALC(CIA))
218.5	MEA	Oman	0.000	11(CALC(CIA))
218.5	SEA	Palau	0.000	11(CALC(CIA))
218.5	MEA	Qatar	0.000	11(CALC(CIA))
218.5	SEA	Samoa, American	0.000	11(CALC(CIA))

Table 1.6 Societal Integration Index, Intensity of Open Political Process, 2011

Rank	Region	Country	SCINTX	Source
218.5	MEA	Saudi Arabia	0.000	11(CALC(CIA))
218.5	AFR	Somalia	0.000	11(CALC(CIA))
218.5	AFR	St. Helena	0.000	11(CALC(CIA))
218.5	AFR	Swaziland	0.000	11(CALC(CIA))
218.5	MEA	Syria	0.000	11(CALC(CIA))
218.5	SEA	Tokelau	0.000	11(CALC(CIA))
218.5	USR	Turkmenistan	0.000	11(CALC(CIA))
218.5	SEA	Tuvalu	0.000	11(CALC(CIA))
218.5	MEA	United Arab Emirates	0.000	11(CALC(CIA))
218.5	CPA	Vietnam	0.000	11(CALC(CIA))
218.5	MEA	West Bank	0.000	11(CALC(CIA))
218.5	AFR	Western Sahara	0.000	11(CALC(CIA))

Table 1.7 Civil and Political Rights Index, 2011				
Rank	Region	Country	CPRX	Source
41	DME	Andorra	1.0	11(FH)
41	LAM	Anguilla	1.0	11(EST)
41	LAM	Aruba	1.0	11(EST)
41	DME	Australia	1.0	11(FH)
41	DME	Austria	1.0	11(FH)
41	LAM	Bahamas	1.0	11(FH)
41	LAM	Barbados	1.0	11(FH)
41	DME	Belgium	1.0	11(FH)
41	DME	Bermuda	1.0	11(EST)
41	DME	Canada	1.0	11(FH)
41	AFR	Cape Verde	1.0	11(FH)
41	LAM	Cayman Islands	1.0	11(EST)
41	LAM	Chile	1.0	11(FH)
41	SEA	Cook Islands	1.0	11(EST)
41	LAM	Costa Rica	1.0	11(FH)
41	LAM	Curacao	1.0	11(EST)
41	MEA	Cyprus	1.0	11(FH)
41	EEU	Czech Republic	1.0	11(FH)
41	DME	Denmark	1.0	11(FH)
41	LAM	Dominica	1.0	11(FH)
41	USR	Estonia	1.0	11(FH)
41	DME	Falkland Islands	1.0	11(EST)
41	DME	Faroe Islands	1.0	11(EST)
41	DME	Finland	1.0	11(FH)
41	DME	France	1.0	11(FH)
41	SEA	French Polynesia	1.0	11(EST)
41	DME	Germany	1.0	11(FH)
41	DME	Gibraltar	1.0	11(EST)
41	DME	Greenland	1.0	11(EST)
41	LAM	Guadeloupe	1.0	11(EST)
41	SEA	Guam	1.0	11(EST)
41	DME	Guernsey	1.0	11(EST)
41	LAM	Guiana, French	1.0	11(EST)
41	DME	Iceland	1.0	11(FH)
41	DME	Ireland	1.0	11(FH)
41	DME	Isle of Man	1.0	11(EST)
41	DME	Italy	1.0	11(FH)
41	DME	Jersey	1.0	11(EST)
41	SEA	Kiribati	1.0	11(FH)
41	DME	Liechtenstein	1.0	11(FH)
41	USR	Lithuania	1.0	11(FH)
41	DME	Luxembourg	1.0	11(FH)
41	DME	Malta	1.0	11(FH)
41	SEA	Marshall Islands	1.0	11(FH)
41	LAM	Martinique	1.0	11(EST)
41	AFR	Mayotte	1.0	11(EST)
41	SEA	Micronesia	1.0	11(FH)

Table 1.7 Civil and Political Rights Index, 2011				
Rank	Region	Country	CPRX	Source
41	LAM	Montserrat	1.0	11(EST)
41	SEA	Nauru	1.0	11(FH)
41	DME	Netherlands	1.0	11(FH)
41	SEA	New Caledonia	1.0	11(EST)
41	DME	New Zealand	1.0	11(FH)
41	SEA	Niue	1.0	11(EST)
41	DME	Norway	1.0	11(FH)
41	SEA	Palau	1.0	11(FH)
41	EEU	Poland	1.0	11(FH)
41	DME	Portugal	1.0	11(FH)
41	AFR	Reunion	1.0	11(EST)
41	LAM	Saint Martin	1.0	11(EST)
41	SEA	Samoa, American	1.0	11(EST)
41	DME	San Marino	1.0	11(FH)
41	LAM	Sint Maarten	1.0	11(EST)
41	EEU	Slovakia	1.0	11(FH)
41	EEU	Slovenia	1.0	11(FH)
41	DME	Spain	1.0	11(FH)
41	AFR	St. Helena	1.0	11(EST)
41	LAM	St. Kitts & Nevis	1.0	11(FH)
41	LAM	St. Lucia	1.0	11(FH)
41	DME	St. Pierre & Miquelon	1.0	11(EST)
41	LAM	St. Vincent	1.0	11(FH)
41	DME	Sweden	1.0	11(FH)
41	DME	Switzerland	1.0	11(FH)
41	SEA	Tokelau	1.0	11(EST)
41	LAM	Turks & Caicos Is.	1.0	11(EST)
41	SEA	Tuvalu	1.0	11(FH)
41	DME	United Kingdom	1.0	11(FH)
41	DME	United States	1.0	11(FH)
41	LAM	Uruguay	1.0	11(FH)
41	LAM	Virgin Islands, Brit.	1.0	11(EST)
41	LAM	Virgin Islands, U.S.	1.0	11(EST)
41	SEA	Wallis & Futuna	1.0	11(EST)
88	LAM	Belize	1.5	11(FH)
88	EEU	Croatia	1.5	11(FH)
88	AFR	Ghana	1.5	11(FH)
88	LAM	Grenada	1.5	11(FH)
88	EEU	Hungary	1.5	11(FH)
88	DME	Israel	1.5	11(FH)
88	DME	Japan	1.5	11(FH)
88	SEA	Korea, South	1.5	11(FH)
88	AFR	Mauritius	1.5	11(FH)
88	DME	Monaco	1.5	11(FH)
88	LAM	Panama	1.5	11(FH)
88	LAM	Puerto Rico	1.5	11(FH)
88	SEA	Taiwan	1.5	11(FH)

Table 1.7 Civil and Political Rights Index, 2011				
Rank	Region	Country	CPRX	Source
103	LAM	Argentina	2.0	11(FH)
103	AFR	Benin	2.0	11(FH)
103	LAM	Brazil	2.0	11(FH)
103	EEU	Bulgaria	2.0	11(FH)
103	LAM	Dominican Republic	2.0	11(FH)
103	DME	Greece	2.0	11(FH)
103	USR	Latvia	2.0	11(FH)
103	CPA	Mongolia	2.0	11(FH)
103	AFR	Namibia	2.0	11(FH)
103	EEU	Romania	2.0	11(FH)
103	SEA	Samoa	2.0	11(FH)
103	AFR	Sao Tome & Principe	2.0	11(FH)
103	EEU	Serbia	2.0	11(FH)
103	AFR	South Africa	2.0	11(FH)
103	LAM	Suriname	2.0	11(FH)
103	LAM	Trinidad & Tobago	2.0	11(FH)
103	SEA	Vanuatu	2.0	11(FH)
112	SEA	Northern Mariana Is.	2.0	(REG)
117.5	LAM	Antigua & Barbuda	2.5	11(FH)
117.5	AFR	Botswana	2.5	11(FH)
117.5	LAM	El Salvador	2.5	11(FH)
117.5	LAM	Guyana	2.5	11(FH)
117.5	SAS	India	2.5	11(FH)
117.5	SEA	Indonesia	2.5	11(FH)
117.5	LAM	Jamaica	2.5	11(FH)
117.5	AFR	Mali	2.5	11(FH)
117.5	EEU	Montenegro	2.5	11(FH)
117.5	LAM	Peru	2.5	11(FH)
130	EEU	Albania	3.0	11(FH)
130	LAM	Bolivia	3.0	11(FH)
130	LAM	Ecuador	3.0	11(FH)
130	AFR	Lesotho	3.0	11(FH)
130	EEU	Macedonia	3.0	11(FH)
130	LAM	Mexico	3.0	11(FH)
130	USR	Moldova	3.0	11(FH)
130	LAM	Paraguay	3.0	11(FH)
130	SEA	Philippines	3.0	11(FH)
130	AFR	Senegal	3.0	11(FH)
130	AFR	Seychelles	3.0	11(FH)
130	AFR	Sierra Leone	3.0	11(FH)
130	AFR	Tanzania	3.0	11(FH)
130	SEA	Tonga	3.0	11(FH)
130	MEA	Turkey	3.0	11(FH)
147.5	SAS	Bangladesh	3.5	11(FH)
147.5	EEU	Bosnia	3.5	11(FH)

Table 1.7 Civil and Political Rights Index, 2011				
Rank	Region	Country	CPRX	Source
147.5	LAM	Colombia	3.5	11(FH)
147.5	AFR	Comoros	3.5	11(FH)
147.5	SEA	East Timor	3.5	11(FH)
147.5	USR	Georgia	3.5	11(FH)
147.5	LAM	Guatemala	3.5	11(FH)
147.5	SEA	Hong Kong	3.5	11(FH)
147.5	AFR	Kenya	3.5	11(FH)
147.5	AFR	Liberia	3.5	11(FH)
147.5	SEA	Macao	3.5	11(EST)
147.5	AFR	Malawi	3.5	11(FH)
147.5	SAS	Maldives	3.5	11(FH)
147.5	AFR	Mozambique	3.5	11(FH)
147.5	AFR	Niger	3.5	11(FH)
147.5	SEA	Papua New Guinea	3.5	11(FH)
147.5	SEA	Solomon Islands	3.5	11(FH)
147.5	MEA	Tunisia	3.5	11(FH)
147.5	USR	Ukraine	3.5	11(FH)
147.5	AFR	Zambia	3.5	11(FH)
161.5	AFR	Burkina Faso	4.0	11(FH)
161.5	AFR	Guinea-Bissau	4.0	11(FH)
161.5	LAM	Honduras	4.0	11(FH)
161.5	SEA	Malaysia	4.0	11(FH)
161.5	SAS	Nepal	4.0	11(FH)
161.5	AFR	Nigeria	4.0	11(FH)
161.5	SEA	Singapore	4.0	11(FH)
161.5	SEA	Thailand	4.0	11(FH)
171	SAS	Bhutan	4.5	11(FH)
171	LAM	Haiti	4.5	11(FH)
171	EEU	Kosovo	4.5	11(FH)
171	MEA	Kuwait	4.5	11(FH)
171	MEA	Lebanon	4.5	11(FH)
171	MEA	Morocco	4.5	11(FH)
171	LAM	Nicaragua	4.5	11(FH)
171	SAS	Pakistan	4.5	11(FH)
171	SAS	Sri Lanka	4.5	11(FH)
171	AFR	Togo	4.5	11(FH)
171	AFR	Uganda	4.5	11(FH)
180.5	USR	Armenia	5.0	11(FH)
180.5	AFR	Burundi	5.0	11(FH)
180.5	AFR	Central African Rep.	5.0	11(FH)
180.5	SEA	Fiji	5.0	11(FH)
180.5	AFR	Guinea	5.0	11(FH)
180.5	USR	Kyrgyzstan	5.0	11(FH)
180.5	AFR	Madagascar	5.0	11(FH)
180.5	LAM	Venezuela	5.0	11(FH)
194.5	MEA	Algeria	5.5	11(FH)
194.5	AFR	Angola	5.5	11(FH)

Table 1.7 Civil and Political Rights Index, 2011				
Rank	Region	Country	CPRX	Source
194.5	USR	Azerbaijan	5.5	11(FH)
194.5	SEA	Brunei	5.5	11(FH)
194.5	CPA	Cambodia	5.5	11(FH)
194.5	AFR	Congo, Republic	5.5	11(FH)
194.5	AFR	Djibouti	5.5	11(FH)
194.5	MEA	Egypt	5.5	11(FH)
194.5	AFR	Gabon	5.5	11(FH)
194.5	AFR	Gambia	5.5	11(FH)
194.5	MEA	Iraq	5.5	11(FH)
194.5	MEA	Jordan	5.5	11(FH)
194.5	USR	Kazakhstan	5.5	11(FH)
194.5	AFR	Mauritania	5.5	11(FH)
194.5	MEA	Oman	5.5	11(FH)
194.5	MEA	Qatar	5.5	11(FH)
194.5	USR	Russia	5.5	11(FH)
194.5	AFR	Rwanda	5.5	11(FH)
194.5	USR	Tajikistan	5.5	11(FH)
194.5	MEA	West Bank	5.5	11(FH)
211	SAS	Afghanistan	6.0	11(FH)
211	MEA	Bahrain	6.0	11(FH)
211	AFR	Cameroon	6.0	11(FH)
211	AFR	Congo, Dem. Republic	6.0	11(FH)
211	AFR	Ethiopia	6.0	11(FH)
211	MEA	Gaza Strip	6.0	11(FH)
211	MEA	Iran	6.0	11(FH)
211	AFR	Ivory Coast	6.0	11(FH)
211	AFR	Swaziland	6.0	11(FH)
211	MEA	United Arab Emirates	6.0	11(FH)
211	CPA	Vietnam	6.0	11(FH)
211	MEA	Yemen	6.0	11(FH)
211	AFR	Zimbabwe	6.0	11(FH)
221.5	USR	Belarus	6.5	11(FH)
221.5	CPA	Burma	6.5	11(FH)
221.5	AFR	Chad	6.5	11(FH)
221.5	CPA	China	6.5	11(FH)
221.5	LAM	Cuba	6.5	11(FH)
221.5	CPA	Laos	6.5	11(FH)
221.5	MEA	Libya	6.5	11(FH)
221.5	AFR	South Sudan	6.5	11(FH)
230.5	AFR	Equatorial Guinea	7.0	11(FH)
230.5	AFR	Eritrea	7.0	11(FH)
230.5	CPA	Korea, North	7.0	11(FH)
230.5	MEA	Saudi Arabia	7.0	11(FH)
230.5	AFR	Somalia	7.0	11(FH)
230.5	AFR	Sudan	7.0	11(FH)
230.5	MEA	Syria	7.0	11(FH)

Table 1.7 Civil and Political Rights Index, 2011				
Rank	Region	Country	CPRX	Source
230.5	USR	Turkmenistan	7.0	11(FH)
230.5	USR	Uzbekistan	7.0	11(FH)
230.5	AFR	Western Sahara	7.0	11(FH)

Table 1.8 Human Development Index, 2011				
Rank	Region	Country	HDX	Source
1	DME	Monaco	0.998	(REG)
2	DME	Bermuda	0.953	(REG)
3	DME	Norway	0.943	11(UN)
4	DME	Australia	0.929	11(UN)
5	DME	Jersey	0.918	(REG)
6.5	DME	Netherlands	0.910	11(UN)
6.5	DME	United States	0.910	11(UN)
8	SEA	Macao	0.909	(REG)
10	DME	Canada	0.908	11(UN)
10	DME	Ireland	0.908	11(UN)
10	DME	New Zealand	0.908	11(UN)
12.5	DME	Germany	0.905	11(UN)
12.5	DME	Liechtenstein	0.905	11(UN)
14	DME	Sweden	0.904	11(UN)
15	DME	Falkland Islands	0.903	(REG)
16	DME	Guernsey	0.903	(REG)
17	DME	Switzerland	0.903	11(UN)
18	LAM	Cayman Islands	0.901	(REG)
19	DME	Japan	0.901	11(UN)
20.5	SEA	Hong Kong	0.898	11(UN)
20.5	DME	Iceland	0.898	11(UN)
22	SEA	Korea, South	0.897	11(UN)
23	DME	Denmark	0.895	11(UN)
24	DME	Israel	0.888	11(UN)
25	DME	Belgium	0.886	11(UN)
26	DME	Austria	0.885	11(UN)
27	DME	San Marino	0.885	(REG)
28.5	DME	France	0.884	11(UN)
28.5	EEU	Slovenia	0.884	11(UN)
30	DME	Finland	0.882	11(UN)
31	LAM	Virgin Islands, U.S.	0.879	(REG)
32	DME	Gibraltar	0.879	(REG)
33	DME	Spain	0.878	11(UN)
34	DME	Isle of Man	0.878	(REG)
35	DME	Italy	0.874	11(UN)
36	DME	Luxembourg	0.867	11(UN)
37	SEA	Singapore	0.866	11(UN)
38	EEU	Czech Republic	0.865	11(UN)
39	LAM	Virgin Islands, Brit.	0.864	(REG)
40	DME	Faroe Islands	0.864	(REG)
41	SEA	New Caledonia	0.863	(REG)
42	DME	United Kingdom	0.863	11(UN)
43	DME	Greece	0.861	11(UN)
44	LAM	Martinique	0.855	(REG)
45	SEA	Taiwan	0.854	(REG)
46	LAM	Guadeloupe	0.851	(REG)

Table 1.8 Human Development Index, 2011				
Rank	Region	Country	HDX	Source
47	MEA	United Arab Emirates	0.846	11(UN)
48	MEA	Cyprus	0.840	11(UN)
49	AFR	Reunion	0.840	(REG)
50.5	DME	Andorra	0.838	11(UN)
50.5	SEA	Brunei	0.838	11(UN)
52	USR	Estonia	0.835	11(UN)
53	EEU	Slovakia	0.834	11(UN)
54	LAM	Saint Martin	0.832	(REG)
55	DME	Malta	0.832	11(UN)
56	MEA	Qatar	0.831	11(UN)
57	DME	Greenland	0.825	(REG)
58	DME	St. Pierre & Miquelon	0.818	(REG)
59	EEU	Hungary	0.816	11(UN)
60	LAM	Guiana, French	0.815	(REG)
61	EEU	Poland	0.813	11(UN)
62	USR	Lithuania	0.810	11(UN)
63	DME	Portugal	0.809	11(UN)
64	LAM	Aruba	0.808	(REG)
65	LAM	Curacao	0.807	(REG)
66	MEA	Bahrain	0.806	11(UN)
67	SEA	French Polynesia	0.806	(REG)
68.5	LAM	Chile	0.805	11(UN)
68.5	USR	Latvia	0.805	11(UN)
70	LAM	Puerto Rico	0.798	(REG)
71	LAM	Argentina	0.797	11(UN)
72	EEU	Croatia	0.796	11(UN)
73	SEA	Guam	0.794	(REG)
74	LAM	Anguilla	0.793	(REG)
75	LAM	Barbados	0.793	11(UN)
76	LAM	Turks & Caicos Is.	0.790	(REG)
77	LAM	Sint Maarten	0.788	(REG)
78	SEA	Northern Mariana Is.	0.784	(REG)
79	LAM	Uruguay	0.783	11(UN)
80	SEA	Palau	0.782	11(UN)
81	EEU	Romania	0.781	11(UN)
82	LAM	Cuba	0.776	11(UN)
83	AFR	Seychelles	0.773	11(UN)
85	LAM	Bahamas	0.771	11(UN)
85	EEU	Bulgaria	0.771	11(UN)
85	EEU	Montenegro	0.771	11(UN)
87.5	LAM	Mexico	0.770	11(UN)
87.5	MEA	Saudi Arabia	0.770	11(UN)
89	LAM	Panama	0.768	11(UN)
90	EEU	Serbia	0.766	11(UN)
91	LAM	Antigua & Barbuda	0.764	11(UN)

Table 1.8 Human Development Index, 2011				
Rank	Region	Country	HDX	Source
92	SEA	Malaysia	0.761	11(UN)
94	MEA	Kuwait	0.760	11(UN)
94	MEA	Libya	0.760	11(UN)
94	LAM	Trinidad & Tobago	0.760	11(UN)
96	USR	Belarus	0.756	11(UN)
97	USR	Russia	0.755	11(UN)
98	LAM	Grenada	0.748	11(UN)
99	USR	Kazakhstan	0.745	11(UN)
100	LAM	Costa Rica	0.744	11(UN)
101.5	EEU	Albania	0.739	11(UN)
101.5	MEA	Lebanon	0.739	11(UN)
103	SEA	Cook Islands	0.738	(REG)
104.5	LAM	St. Kitts & Nevis	0.735	11(UN)
104.5	LAM	Venezuela	0.735	11(UN)
106.5	EEU	Bosnia	0.733	11(UN)
106.5	USR	Georgia	0.733	11(UN)
108	USR	Ukraine	0.729	11(UN)
109.5	EEU	Macedonia	0.728	11(UN)
109.5	AFR	Mauritius	0.728	11(UN)
111	SEA	Samoa, American	0.728	(REG)
112	LAM	Jamaica	0.727	11(UN)
113	LAM	Peru	0.725	11(UN)
114	LAM	Dominica	0.724	11(UN)
115	AFR	Mayotte	0.723	(REG)
116	LAM	St. Lucia	0.723	11(UN)
117	LAM	Ecuador	0.720	11(UN)
118	LAM	Brazil	0.718	11(UN)
119	LAM	St. Vincent	0.717	11(UN)
120	USR	Armenia	0.716	11(UN)
121	AFR	St. Helena	0.713	(REG)
122	LAM	Colombia	0.710	11(UN)
123	SEA	Wallis & Futuna	0.710	(REG)
124	MEA	Iran	0.707	11(UN)
125	MEA	Oman	0.705	11(UN)
126	SEA	Tonga	0.704	11(UN)
127	USR	Azerbaijan	0.700	11(UN)
128.5	LAM	Belize	0.699	11(UN)
128.5	MEA	Turkey	0.699	11(UN)
131	MEA	Algeria	0.698	11(UN)
131	MEA	Jordan	0.698	11(UN)
131	MEA	Tunisia	0.698	11(UN)
133	SAS	Sri Lanka	0.691	11(UN)
134	LAM	Dominican Republic	0.689	11(UN)
135.5	SEA	Fiji	0.688	11(UN)
135.5	SEA	Samoa	0.688	11(UN)
137	CPA	China	0.687	11(UN)
138	USR	Turkmenistan	0.686	11(UN)

Table 1.8 Human Development Index, 2011

Rank	Region	Country	HDX	Source
139	SEA	Thailand	0.682	11(UN)
140	LAM	Suriname	0.680	11(UN)
141.5	LAM	El Salvador	0.674	11(UN)
141.5	AFR	Gabon	0.674	11(UN)
143	SEA	Niue	0.674	(REG)
144	LAM	Montserrat	0.674	(REG)
145	EEU	Kosovo	0.668	(REG)
146	LAM	Paraguay	0.665	11(UN)
147	LAM	Bolivia	0.663	11(UN)
148	SEA	Tuvalu	0.662	(REG)
149	SEA	Nauru	0.662	(REG)
150	SAS	Maldives	0.661	11(UN)
151	CPA	Mongolia	0.653	11(UN)
152	USR	Moldova	0.649	11(UN)
153.5	MEA	Egypt	0.644	11(UN)
153.5	SEA	Philippines	0.644	11(UN)
155	USR	Uzbekistan	0.641	11(UN)
156	SEA	Micronesia	0.636	11(UN)
157.5	AFR	Botswana	0.633	11(UN)
157.5	LAM	Guyana	0.633	11(UN)
159	MEA	West Bank	0.633	(REG)
160	MEA	Syria	0.632	11(UN)
161.5	LAM	Honduras	0.625	11(UN)
161.5	AFR	Namibia	0.625	11(UN)
163	SEA	Kiribati	0.624	11(UN)
164	AFR	South Africa	0.619	11(UN)
165.5	SEA	Indonesia	0.617	11(UN)
165.5	SEA	Vanuatu	0.617	11(UN)
167	SEA	Marshall Islands	0.615	(REG)
168	USR	Kyrgyzstan	0.615	11(UN)
169	USR	Tajikistan	0.607	11(UN)
170	CPA	Vietnam	0.593	11(UN)
171	MEA	Gaza Strip	0.592	(REG)
172	LAM	Nicaragua	0.589	11(UN)
173	MEA	Morocco	0.582	11(UN)
174	LAM	Guatemala	0.574	11(UN)
175	MEA	Iraq	0.573	11(UN)
176	AFR	Cape Verde	0.568	11(UN)
177	SEA	Tokelau	0.567	(REG)
178	SAS	India	0.547	11(UN)
179	AFR	Ghana	0.541	11(UN)
180	AFR	Equatorial Guinea	0.537	11(UN)
181	AFR	Congo, Republic	0.533	11(UN)
182	CPA	Korea, North	0.532	(REG)
183	CPA	Laos	0.524	11(UN)
184	CPA	Cambodia	0.523	11(UN)
185.5	SAS	Bhutan	0.522	11(UN)
185.5	AFR	Swaziland	0.522	11(UN)

Table 1.8 Human Development Index, 2011				
Rank	Region	Country	HDX	Source
187	SEA	Solomon Islands	0.510	11(UN)
188.5	AFR	Kenya	0.509	11(UN)
188.5	AFR	Sao Tome & Principe	0.509	11(UN)
190	SAS	Pakistan	0.504	11(UN)
191	SAS	Bangladesh	0.500	11(UN)
192	SEA	East Timor	0.495	11(UN)
193	AFR	Angola	0.486	11(UN)
194	AFR	Western Sahara	0.485	(REG)
195	CPA	Burma	0.483	11(UN)
196	AFR	Cameroon	0.482	11(UN)
197	AFR	Madagascar	0.480	11(UN)
198.5	SEA	Papua New Guinea	0.466	11(UN)
198.5	AFR	Tanzania	0.466	11(UN)
200	MEA	Yemen	0.462	11(UN)
201.5	AFR	Nigeria	0.459	11(UN)
201.5	AFR	Senegal	0.459	11(UN)
203	SAS	Nepal	0.458	11(UN)
204	LAM	Haiti	0.454	11(UN)
205	AFR	Mauritania	0.453	11(UN)
206	AFR	Lesotho	0.450	11(UN)
207	AFR	Uganda	0.446	11(UN)
208	AFR	Togo	0.435	11(UN)
209	AFR	Comoros	0.433	11(UN)
210.5	AFR	Djibouti	0.430	11(UN)
210.5	AFR	Zambia	0.430	11(UN)
212	AFR	Rwanda	0.429	11(UN)
213	AFR	Benin	0.427	11(UN)
214	AFR	Gambia	0.420	11(UN)
215	AFR	Sudan	0.408	11(UN)
216.5	AFR	Ivory Coast	0.400	11(UN)
216.5	AFR	Malawi	0.400	11(UN)
218	SAS	Afghanistan	0.398	11(UN)
219	AFR	Zimbabwe	0.376	11(UN)
220	AFR	Ethiopia	0.363	11(UN)
221	AFR	Mali	0.359	11(UN)
222	AFR	Guinea-Bissau	0.353	11(UN)
223	AFR	Eritrea	0.349	11(UN)
224	AFR	Guinea	0.344	11(UN)
225	AFR	Central African Rep.	0.343	11(UN)
226	AFR	Sierra Leone	0.336	11(UN)
227	AFR	Burkina Faso	0.331	11(UN)
228	AFR	Liberia	0.329	11(UN)
229	AFR	Chad	0.328	11(UN)
230	AFR	Mozambique	0.322	11(UN)
231	AFR	Burundi	0.316	11(UN)
232	AFR	South Sudan	0.311	(REG)

Table 1.8 Human Development Index, 2011				
Rank	Region	Country	HDX	Source
233	AFR	Niger	0.295	11(UN)
234	AFR	Congo, Dem. Republic	0.286	11(UN)
235	AFR	Somalia	0.277	(REG)

TABLE 1.9 GINI COEFFICIENT OF INCOME INEQUALITY, 2011				
Rank	Region	Country	GINI	Source
1	DME	Denmark	24.70	11(WB)
2	DME	Japan	24.85	11(WB)
3	DME	Sweden	25.00	11(WB)
4	DME	Norway	25.79	11(WB)
5	EEU	Czech Republic	25.82	11(WB)
6.5	DME	Malta	26.00	07(CIA)
6.5	EEU	Slovakia	26.00	11(WB)
8	USR	Ukraine	26.44	11(WB)
9	DME	Finland	26.88	11(WB)
10	USR	Belarus	27.22	11(WB)
11	EEU	Serbia	27.80	11(WB)
12	SAS	Afghanistan	27.82	11(WB)
13	DME	Iceland	28.00	06(CIA)
14	EEU	Bulgaria	28.19	11(WB)
15	DME	Germany	28.31	11(WB)
16	MEA	Cyprus	29.00	05(CIA)
17	USR	Kazakhstan	29.04	11(WB)
18	DME	Austria	29.15	11(WB)
19	DME	San Marino	29.67	(REG)
20	AFR	Ethiopia	29.83	11(WB)
21	SEA	Wallis & Futuna	29.92	(REG)
22	EEU	Montenegro	29.99	11(WB)
25	LAM	Cuba	30.00	11(GPI)
25	EEU	Kosovo	30.00	06(CIA)
25	MEA	Kuwait	30.00	11(GPI)
25	EEU	Romania	30.00	11(WB)
25	AFR	Somalia	30.00	11(GPI)
28	SAS	Pakistan	30.02	11(WB)
29	DME	Luxembourg	30.76	11(WB)
30	MEA	Egypt	30.77	11(WB)
31	USR	Tajikistan	30.83	11(WB)
32.5	USR	Armenia	30.86	11(WB)
32.5	MEA	Iraq	30.86	11(WB)
34	DME	Netherlands	30.90	11(WB)
35.5	CPA	Korea, North	31.00	11(GPI)
35.5	MEA	United Arab Emirates	31.00	11(GPI)
37	EEU	Slovenia	31.15	11(WB)
38	EEU	Hungary	31.18	11(WB)
39	LAM	Anguilla	31.24	(REG)
40	SEA	Korea, South	31.59	11(WB)
41	SEA	East Timor	31.93	11(WB)
42.5	MEA	Oman	32.00	11(GPI)
42.5	MEA	Saudi Arabia	32.00	11(GPI)
44	SAS	Bangladesh	32.12	11(WB)
45	DME	Canada	32.56	11(WB)
46	SEA	Taiwan	32.60	00(CIA)

TABLE 1.9 GINI COEFFICIENT OF INCOME INEQUALITY, 2011

Rank	Region	Country	GINI	Source
47	DME	France	32.74	11(WB)
48	SAS	Nepal	32.82	11(WB)
49	DME	Belgium	32.97	11(WB)
50	AFR	Mali	33.02	11(WB)
51	USR	Moldova	33.03	11(WB)
52	AFR	Burundi	33.27	11(WB)
53	SAS	India	33.38	11(WB)
54	DME	Andorra	33.42	(REG)
55	EEU	Croatia	33.65	11(WB)
56	DME	Switzerland	33.68	11(WB)
57	USR	Azerbaijan	33.71	11(WB)
58	SEA	Indonesia	34.01	11(WB)
59	EEU	Poland	34.07	11(WB)
60	DME	Greece	34.27	11(WB)
61	DME	Ireland	34.28	11(WB)
62	AFR	Togo	34.41	11(WB)
63	EEU	Albania	34.51	11(WB)
64	AFR	Niger	34.55	11(WB)
65	SEA	Nauru	34.60	(REG)
66	DME	Spain	34.66	11(WB)
67	DME	Liechtenstein	35.06	(REG)
68	DME	Australia	35.19	11(WB)
69	AFR	Sudan	35.29	11(WB)
70	MEA	Algeria	35.33	11(WB)
71	MEA	Jordan	35.43	11(WB)
72.5	MEA	Gaza Strip	35.50	11(WB)
72.5	MEA	West Bank	35.50	11(WB)
74	AFR	Guinea-Bissau	35.52	11(WB)
75	SEA	Vanuatu	35.54	(REG)
76	CPA	Vietnam	35.57	11(WB)
77	SEA	Northern Mariana Is.	35.59	(REG)
78	SEA	Guam	35.61	(REG)
79	MEA	Syria	35.78	11(WB)
80	DME	Guernsey	35.93	(REG)
81	LAM	St. Kitts & Nevis	35.94	(REG)
82	DME	United Kingdom	35.97	11(WB)
84	MEA	Bahrain	36.00	11(GPI)
84	USR	Estonia	36.00	11(WB)
84	MEA	Libya	36.00	11(GPI)
86	DME	Italy	36.03	11(WB)
87	LAM	Sint Maarten	36.15	(REG)
88	DME	New Zealand	36.17	11(WB)
89	USR	Kyrgyzstan	36.19	11(WB)
90	EEU	Bosnia	36.21	11(WB)
91	DME	Bermuda	36.24	(REG)
92	DME	Isle of Man	36.41	(REG)
93	LAM	Antigua & Barbuda	36.48	(REG)

Table 1.9 GINI Coefficient of Income Inequality, 2011				
Rank	Region	Country	GINI	Source
94	CPA	Mongolia	36.52	11(WB)
95	DME	Falkland Islands	36.53	(REG)
96	SEA	Samoa, American	36.54	(REG)
97	USR	Latvia	36.61	11(WB)
98	USR	Uzbekistan	36.72	11(WB)
99	CPA	Laos	36.74	11(WB)
100	SEA	Tonga	36.84	(REG)
101	AFR	Reunion	37.25	(REG)
102	SEA	Solomon Islands	37.32	(REG)
103	SAS	Maldives	37.37	11(WB)
104	DME	Jersey	37.46	(REG)
105	USR	Lithuania	37.57	11(WB)
106	AFR	Tanzania	37.58	11(WB)
107	LAM	Montserrat	37.61	(REG)
108	DME	St. Pierre & Miquelon	37.65	(REG)
109	LAM	Saint Martin	37.68	(REG)
110	MEA	Yemen	37.69	11(WB)
111	SEA	French Polynesia	37.79	(REG)
112	SEA	Samoa	37.79	(REG)
113	LAM	Grenada	37.82	(REG)
114	DME	Faroe Islands	37.84	(REG)
115	CPA	Cambodia	37.85	11(WB)
116	LAM	Puerto Rico	37.89	(REG)
117	AFR	Eritrea	38.05	(REG)
118	SAS	Bhutan	38.06	11(WB)
119	SEA	Marshall Islands	38.08	(REG)
120	AFR	Liberia	38.16	11(WB)
121	LAM	Martinique	38.24	(REG)
122	MEA	Iran	38.28	11(WB)
123	DME	Monaco	38.36	(REG)
124	SEA	New Caledonia	38.41	(REG)
125	DME	Portugal	38.45	11(WB)
126	AFR	Benin	38.62	11(WB)
127	LAM	Dominica	38.72	(REG)
128	AFR	St. Helena	38.80	(REG)
129	AFR	Cameroon	38.91	11(WB)
130	LAM	Curacao	38.93	(REG)
131	SEA	Brunei	38.95	(REG)
132	MEA	Turkey	38.95	11(WB)
133	SEA	Niue	39.00	(REG)
134	AFR	Mauritius	39.00	06(CIA)
135	AFR	Malawi	39.02	11(WB)
136	AFR	Senegal	39.19	11(WB)
137	DME	Israel	39.20	11(WB)
138	AFR	Guinea	39.35	11(WB)
139	LAM	Guadeloupe	39.63	(REG)
140	DME	Gibraltar	39.77	(REG)

TABLE 1.9 GINI COEFFICIENT OF INCOME INEQUALITY, 2011

Rank	Region	Country	GINI	Source
141	AFR	Chad	39.78	11(WB)
142	AFR	Burkina Faso	39.79	11(WB)
143	LAM	Turks & Caicos Is.	39.84	(REG)
144	SEA	Tokelau	39.92	(REG)
145	AFR	Djibouti	39.96	11(WB)
146	CPA	Burma	40.00	11(GPI)
147	SEA	Thailand	40.02	11(WB)
148	USR	Russia	40.11	11(WB)
149	LAM	Virgin Islands, U.S.	40.20	(REG)
150	SAS	Sri Lanka	40.26	11(WB)
151	LAM	Trinidad & Tobago	40.27	11(WB)
152	LAM	Cayman Islands	40.31	(REG)
153	LAM	Guiana, French	40.31	(REG)
154	SEA	Cook Islands	40.41	(REG)
155	AFR	Mauritania	40.46	11(WB)
156	LAM	Nicaragua	40.47	11(WB)
157	SEA	Palau	40.70	(REG)
158	USR	Turkmenistan	40.77	11(WB)
159	DME	United States	40.81	11(WB)
160	MEA	Morocco	40.88	11(WB)
161	MEA	Qatar	41.10	11(WB)
162	SEA	Kiribati	41.20	(REG)
163	USR	Georgia	41.34	11(WB)
164	MEA	Tunisia	41.42	11(WB)
165	AFR	Gabon	41.45	11(WB)
166	AFR	Ivory Coast	41.50	11(WB)
167	SEA	Micronesia	41.67	(REG)
168	DME	Greenland	41.68	(REG)
169	LAM	St. Vincent	41.88	(REG)
170	LAM	Aruba	41.92	(REG)
171	SEA	Tuvalu	42.45	(REG)
172.5	CPA	China	42.48	11(WB)
172.5	SEA	Singapore	42.48	11(WB)
174	AFR	Sierra Leone	42.52	11(WB)
175	LAM	St. Lucia	42.58	11(WB)
176	AFR	Ghana	42.76	11(WB)
177	SEA	Fiji	42.83	11(WB)
178	SEA	Philippines	42.98	11(WB)
179	EEU	Macedonia	43.17	11(WB)
180	LAM	Bahamas	43.33	(REG)
181	SEA	Macao	43.40	03(WB)
182	SEA	Hong Kong	43.44	11(WB)
183	LAM	Barbados	43.81	(REG)
184	AFR	Madagascar	44.11	11(WB)
185	LAM	Virgin Islands, Brit.	44.28	(REG)
186	AFR	Uganda	44.30	11(WB)
187	AFR	Congo, Dem. Republic	44.43	11(WB)

Table 1.9 GINI Coefficient of Income Inequality, 2011				
Rank	Region	Country	GINI	Source
188	LAM	Argentina	44.49	11(WB)
189	LAM	Guyana	44.54	11(WB)
190	AFR	Western Sahara	44.58	(REG)
191	LAM	Venezuela	44.77	11(WB)
192	MEA	Lebanon	45.00	11(GPI)
193	LAM	Uruguay	45.32	11(WB)
194	LAM	Jamaica	45.51	11(WB)
195	AFR	South Sudan	45.53	11(WB)
196	AFR	Mozambique	45.66	11(WB)
197	SEA	Malaysia	46.21	11(WB)
198	LAM	Dominican Republic	47.20	11(WB)
199	AFR	Gambia	47.28	11(WB)
200	AFR	Congo, Republic	47.32	11(WB)
201	AFR	Kenya	47.68	11(WB)
202	LAM	Peru	48.14	11(WB)
203	LAM	Mexico	48.28	11(WB)
204	LAM	El Salvador	48.33	11(WB)
205	AFR	Nigeria	48.83	11(WB)
206	AFR	Mayotte	49.09	(REG)
207	LAM	Ecuador	49.26	11(WB)
208	AFR	Zimbabwe	50.10	11(WB)
209	AFR	Cape Verde	50.52	11(WB)
210	LAM	Costa Rica	50.73	11(WB)
211.5	AFR	Rwanda	50.82	11(WB)
211.5	AFR	Sao Tome & Principe	50.82	11(WB)
213	SEA	Papua New Guinea	50.88	11(WB)
214	AFR	Swaziland	51.49	11(WB)
215	LAM	Panama	51.92	11(WB)
216	LAM	Chile	52.06	11(WB)
217	LAM	Paraguay	52.42	11(WB)
218	AFR	Lesotho	52.50	11(WB)
219	LAM	Suriname	52.88	11(WB)
220	LAM	Belize	53.13	11(WB)
221	AFR	Zambia	54.63	11(WB)
222	LAM	Brazil	54.69	11(WB)
223	LAM	Guatemala	55.89	11(WB)
224	LAM	Colombia	55.91	11(WB)
225	LAM	Bolivia	56.29	11(WB)
226	AFR	Central African Rep.	56.30	11(WB)
227	LAM	Honduras	56.95	11(WB)
228	AFR	Angola	58.64	11(WB)
229	LAM	Haiti	59.21	11(WB)
230	AFR	Botswana	60.96	11(WB)
231	AFR	South Africa	63.14	11(WB)
232	AFR	Namibia	63.90	11(WB)
233	AFR	Comoros	64.30	11(WB)

Table 1.9 GINI Coefficient of Income Inequality, 2011				
Rank	Region	Country	GINI	Source
234	AFR	Equatorial Guinea	65.00	11(GPI)
235	AFR	Seychelles	65.77	11(WB)

Table 1.10 Human Rights Index, Principal Component 1 of the Political Quality-of-Life Indicators, 2011				
Rank	Region	Country	PQLX	Source
1	DME	Norway	1.755	PRIN1(PQL)
2	DME	Denmark	1.730	PRIN1(PQL)
3	DME	Sweden	1.701	PRIN1(PQL)
4	DME	Finland	1.647	PRIN1(PQL)
5	DME	Netherlands	1.639	PRIN1(PQL)
6	DME	Iceland	1.588	PRIN1(PQL)
7	DME	Germany	1.584	PRIN1(PQL)
8	EEU	Czech Republic	1.577	PRIN1(PQL)
9	DME	Belgium	1.554	PRIN1(PQL)
10	DME	Austria	1.529	PRIN1(PQL)
11	DME	Switzerland	1.515	PRIN1(PQL)
12	EEU	Slovenia	1.498	PRIN1(PQL)
13	DME	San Marino	1.496	PRIN1(PQL)
14	EEU	Slovakia	1.463	PRIN1(PQL)
15	DME	Ireland	1.398	PRIN1(PQL)
16	DME	Luxembourg	1.397	PRIN1(PQL)
17	DME	Australia	1.375	PRIN1(PQL)
18	MEA	Cyprus	1.319	PRIN1(PQL)
19	DME	Japan	1.312	PRIN1(PQL)
20	SEA	New Caledonia	1.312	PRIN1(PQL)
21	DME	Canada	1.309	PRIN1(PQL)
22	DME	Faroe Islands	1.293	PRIN1(PQL)
23	DME	New Zealand	1.292	PRIN1(PQL)
24	DME	Israel	1.252	PRIN1(PQL)
25	DME	France	1.234	PRIN1(PQL)
26	DME	Italy	1.225	PRIN1(PQL)
27	AFR	Reunion	1.225	PRIN1(PQL)
28	DME	Bermuda	1.213	PRIN1(PQL)
29	DME	Spain	1.207	PRIN1(PQL)
30	USR	Estonia	1.193	PRIN1(PQL)
31	DME	Malta	1.192	PRIN1(PQL)
32	SEA	Korea, South	1.189	PRIN1(PQL)
33	DME	Liechtenstein	1.182	PRIN1(PQL)
34	USR	Lithuania	1.181	PRIN1(PQL)
35	LAM	Martinique	1.157	PRIN1(PQL)
36	EEU	Poland	1.137	PRIN1(PQL)
37	DME	United Kingdom	1.132	PRIN1(PQL)
38	LAM	Curacao	1.053	PRIN1(PQL)
39	LAM	Guadeloupe	1.048	PRIN1(PQL)
40	LAM	Anguilla	1.031	PRIN1(PQL)
41	LAM	Guiana, French	1.027	PRIN1(PQL)
42	LAM	Cayman Islands	1.025	PRIN1(PQL)
43	SEA	Taiwan	1.019	PRIN1(PQL)
44	EEU	Serbia	1.010	PRIN1(PQL)
45	DME	United States	1.002	PRIN1(PQL)
46	DME	Portugal	0.976	PRIN1(PQL)

Table 1.10 Human Rights Index, Principal Component 1 of the Political Quality-of-Life Indicators, 2011

Rank	Region	Country	PQLX	Source
47	DME	Greenland	0.961	PRIN1(PQL)
48	EEU	Romania	0.960	PRIN1(PQL)
49	EEU	Bulgaria	0.958	PRIN1(PQL)
50	DME	Andorra	0.950	PRIN1(PQL)
51	SEA	French Polynesia	0.945	PRIN1(PQL)
52	DME	Greece	0.945	PRIN1(PQL)
53	LAM	Virgin Islands, U.S.	0.943	PRIN1(PQL)
54	DME	Gibraltar	0.939	PRIN1(PQL)
55	LAM	Sint Maarten	0.923	PRIN1(PQL)
56	USR	Latvia	0.913	PRIN1(PQL)
57	EEU	Croatia	0.908	PRIN1(PQL)
58	EEU	Hungary	0.898	PRIN1(PQL)
59	DME	Monaco	0.891	PRIN1(PQL)
60	LAM	Saint Martin	0.832	PRIN1(PQL)
61	SEA	Guam	0.822	PRIN1(PQL)
62	LAM	St. Kitts & Nevis	0.817	PRIN1(PQL)
63	LAM	Chile	0.789	PRIN1(PQL)
64	LAM	Aruba	0.743	PRIN1(PQL)
65	DME	Isle of Man	0.743	PRIN1(PQL)
66	SEA	Hong Kong	0.728	PRIN1(PQL)
67	SEA	Wallis & Futuna	0.725	PRIN1(PQL)
68	LAM	Virgin Islands, Brit.	0.722	PRIN1(PQL)
69	LAM	Uruguay	0.692	PRIN1(PQL)
70	EEU	Montenegro	0.687	PRIN1(PQL)
71	SEA	Northern Mariana Is.	0.649	PRIN1(PQL)
72	DME	St. Pierre & Miquelon	0.617	PRIN1(PQL)
73	LAM	Costa Rica	0.592	PRIN1(PQL)
74	DME	Guernsey	0.590	PRIN1(PQL)
75	DME	Jersey	0.587	PRIN1(PQL)
76	LAM	Argentina	0.580	PRIN1(PQL)
77	DME	Falkland Islands	0.575	PRIN1(PQL)
78	LAM	Bahamas	0.575	PRIN1(PQL)
79	LAM	Puerto Rico	0.574	PRIN1(PQL)
80	LAM	Barbados	0.568	PRIN1(PQL)
81	SEA	Vanuatu	0.553	PRIN1(PQL)
82	USR	Ukraine	0.552	PRIN1(PQL)
83	LAM	Trinidad & Tobago	0.541	PRIN1(PQL)
84	SEA	Cook Islands	0.515	PRIN1(PQL)
85	SEA	Macao	0.485	PRIN1(PQL)
86	LAM	St. Vincent	0.477	PRIN1(PQL)
87	AFR	Mayotte	0.476	PRIN1(PQL)
88	LAM	Panama	0.476	PRIN1(PQL)

TABLE 1.10 HUMAN RIGHTS INDEX, PRINCIPAL COMPONENT 1 OF THE POLITICAL QUALITY-OF-LIFE INDICATORS, 2011

Rank	Region	Country	PQLX	Source
89	LAM	Antigua & Barbuda	0.450	PRIN1(PQL)
90	AFR	Mauritius	0.445	PRIN1(PQL)
91	SEA	Indonesia	0.441	PRIN1(PQL)
92	LAM	Turks & Caicos Is.	0.439	PRIN1(PQL)
93	LAM	Grenada	0.437	PRIN1(PQL)
94	EEU	Bosnia	0.434	PRIN1(PQL)
95	LAM	St. Lucia	0.432	PRIN1(PQL)
96	SEA	Kiribati	0.426	PRIN1(PQL)
97	LAM	Montserrat	0.420	PRIN1(PQL)
98	SEA	Samoa	0.345	PRIN1(PQL)
99	LAM	Brazil	0.343	PRIN1(PQL)
100	EEU	Albania	0.330	PRIN1(PQL)
101	LAM	Dominica	0.311	PRIN1(PQL)
102	MEA	Kuwait	0.294	PRIN1(PQL)
103	USR	Moldova	0.279	PRIN1(PQL)
104	LAM	Peru	0.258	PRIN1(PQL)
105	CPA	Mongolia	0.247	PRIN1(PQL)
106	SAS	India	0.223	PRIN1(PQL)
107	EEU	Kosovo	0.222	PRIN1(PQL)
108	EEU	Macedonia	0.185	PRIN1(PQL)
109	LAM	Mexico	0.175	PRIN1(PQL)
110	MEA	Tunisia	0.164	PRIN1(PQL)
111	SEA	Palau	0.151	PRIN1(PQL)
112	MEA	Turkey	0.133	PRIN1(PQL)
113	SEA	Samoa, American	0.118	PRIN1(PQL)
114	SAS	Maldives	0.111	PRIN1(PQL)
115	LAM	Suriname	0.068	PRIN1(PQL)
116	USR	Armenia	0.067	PRIN1(PQL)
117	LAM	Ecuador	0.062	PRIN1(PQL)
118	LAM	Dominican Republic	0.043	PRIN1(PQL)
119	SEA	Tonga	0.032	PRIN1(PQL)
120	LAM	El Salvador	0.028	PRIN1(PQL)
121	AFR	St. Helena	0.022	PRIN1(PQL)
122	LAM	Jamaica	0.011	PRIN1(PQL)
123	SEA	Nauru	-0.002	PRIN1(PQL)
124	SEA	Philippines	-0.027	PRIN1(PQL)
125	LAM	Guyana	-0.059	PRIN1(PQL)
126	AFR	Ghana	-0.075	PRIN1(PQL)
127	SEA	Niue	-0.086	PRIN1(PQL)
128	MEA	Algeria	-0.103	PRIN1(PQL)
129	AFR	Cape Verde	-0.108	PRIN1(PQL)
130	SEA	East Timor	-0.121	PRIN1(PQL)
131	SEA	Thailand	-0.143	PRIN1(PQL)
132	LAM	Colombia	-0.155	PRIN1(PQL)

Table 1.10 Human Rights Index, Principal Component 1 of the Political Quality-of-Life Indicators, 2011

Rank	Region	Country	PQLX	Source
133	MEA	Bahrain	-0.161	PRIN1(PQL)
134	LAM	Paraguay	-0.167	PRIN1(PQL)
135	LAM	Belize	-0.173	PRIN1(PQL)
136	USR	Georgia	-0.198	PRIN1(PQL)
137	SEA	Solomon Islands	-0.205	PRIN1(PQL)
138	SEA	Tuvalu	-0.206	PRIN1(PQL)
139	SEA	Marshall Islands	-0.215	PRIN1(PQL)
140	SEA	Singapore	-0.226	PRIN1(PQL)
141	MEA	Egypt	-0.232	PRIN1(PQL)
142	USR	Kyrgyzstan	-0.236	PRIN1(PQL)
143	SEA	Malaysia	-0.239	PRIN1(PQL)
144	AFR	Mali	-0.246	PRIN1(PQL)
145	USR	Russia	-0.250	PRIN1(PQL)
146	SEA	Micronesia	-0.254	PRIN1(PQL)
147	MEA	Morocco	-0.274	PRIN1(PQL)
148	SAS	Pakistan	-0.289	PRIN1(PQL)
149	AFR	Benin	-0.306	PRIN1(PQL)
150	SAS	Sri Lanka	-0.328	PRIN1(PQL)
151	MEA	Iraq	-0.336	PRIN1(PQL)
152	MEA	Lebanon	-0.349	PRIN1(PQL)
153	SAS	Nepal	-0.362	PRIN1(PQL)
154	SEA	Tokelau	-0.389	PRIN1(PQL)
155	AFR	Sao Tome & Principe	-0.401	PRIN1(PQL)
156	LAM	Venezuela	-0.469	PRIN1(PQL)
157	SEA	Fiji	-0.479	PRIN1(PQL)
158	MEA	Iran	-0.503	PRIN1(PQL)
159	SAS	Bangladesh	-0.513	PRIN1(PQL)
160	AFR	Seychelles	-0.519	PRIN1(PQL)
161	AFR	South Africa	-0.529	PRIN1(PQL)
162	LAM	Bolivia	-0.541	PRIN1(PQL)
163	LAM	Guatemala	-0.558	PRIN1(PQL)
164	MEA	United Arab Emirates	-0.570	PRIN1(PQL)
165	AFR	Kenya	-0.578	PRIN1(PQL)
166	AFR	Tanzania	-0.590	PRIN1(PQL)
167	AFR	Namibia	-0.643	PRIN1(PQL)
168	AFR	Liberia	-0.653	PRIN1(PQL)
169	SEA	Papua New Guinea	-0.658	PRIN1(PQL)
170	USR	Kazakhstan	-0.667	PRIN1(PQL)
171	LAM	Nicaragua	-0.673	PRIN1(PQL)
172	SEA	Brunei	-0.684	PRIN1(PQL)
173	USR	Belarus	-0.692	PRIN1(PQL)
174	AFR	Niger	-0.709	PRIN1(PQL)
175	USR	Azerbaijan	-0.714	PRIN1(PQL)
176	USR	Uzbekistan	-0.721	PRIN1(PQL)

TABLE 1.10 HUMAN RIGHTS INDEX, PRINCIPAL COMPONENT 1 OF THE POLITICAL QUALITY-OF-LIFE INDICATORS, 2011

Rank	Region	Country	PQLX	Source
177	AFR	Botswana	-0.725	PRIN1(PQL)
178	AFR	Malawi	-0.736	PRIN1(PQL)
179	AFR	Lesotho	-0.755	PRIN1(PQL)
180	MEA	Qatar	-0.758	PRIN1(PQL)
181	LAM	Honduras	-0.766	PRIN1(PQL)
182	USR	Tajikistan	-0.825	PRIN1(PQL)
183	LAM	Cuba	-0.840	PRIN1(PQL)
184	MEA	Oman	-0.848	PRIN1(PQL)
185	AFR	Togo	-0.850	PRIN1(PQL)
186	SAS	Afghanistan	-0.868	PRIN1(PQL)
187	AFR	Senegal	-0.871	PRIN1(PQL)
188	AFR	Mauritania	-0.882	PRIN1(PQL)
189	AFR	Sierra Leone	-0.912	PRIN1(PQL)
190	AFR	Nigeria	-0.927	PRIN1(PQL)
191	MEA	Jordan	-0.956	PRIN1(PQL)
192	AFR	Zambia	-0.997	PRIN1(PQL)
193	AFR	Guinea-Bissau	-1.014	PRIN1(PQL)
194	MEA	Saudi Arabia	-1.022	PRIN1(PQL)
195	CPA	Cambodia	-1.031	PRIN1(PQL)
196	MEA	Libya	-1.038	PRIN1(PQL)
197	AFR	Congo, Republic	-1.069	PRIN1(PQL)
198	AFR	Gabon	-1.074	PRIN1(PQL)
199	LAM	Haiti	-1.092	PRIN1(PQL)
200	AFR	Burkina Faso	-1.104	PRIN1(PQL)
201	AFR	Uganda	-1.105	PRIN1(PQL)
202	MEA	West Bank	-1.128	PRIN1(PQL)
203	SAS	Bhutan	-1.168	PRIN1(PQL)
204	CPA	Vietnam	-1.346	PRIN1(PQL)
205	MEA	Gaza Strip	-1.348	PRIN1(PQL)
206	AFR	Mozambique	-1.348	PRIN1(PQL)
207	AFR	Burundi	-1.369	PRIN1(PQL)
208	MEA	Yemen	-1.372	PRIN1(PQL)
209	CPA	China	-1.396	PRIN1(PQL)
210	AFR	Rwanda	-1.421	PRIN1(PQL)
211	AFR	Cameroon	-1.454	PRIN1(PQL)
212	AFR	Ivory Coast	-1.463	PRIN1(PQL)
213	USR	Turkmenistan	-1.468	PRIN1(PQL)
214	MEA	Syria	-1.479	PRIN1(PQL)
215	CPA	Burma	-1.519	PRIN1(PQL)
216	AFR	Congo, Dem. Republic	-1.524	PRIN1(PQL)
217	AFR	Comoros	-1.577	PRIN1(PQL)
218	AFR	Sudan	-1.598	PRIN1(PQL)
219	CPA	Laos	-1.608	PRIN1(PQL)
220	CPA	Korea, North	-1.614	PRIN1(PQL)
221	AFR	Madagascar	-1.618	PRIN1(PQL)
222	AFR	Ethiopia	-1.620	PRIN1(PQL)

TABLE 1.10 HUMAN RIGHTS INDEX, PRINCIPAL COMPONENT 1 OF THE POLITICAL QUALITY-OF-LIFE INDICATORS, 2011

Rank	Region	Country	PQLX	Source
223	AFR	Central African Rep.	-1.706	PRIN1(PQL)
224	AFR	Zimbabwe	-1.742	PRIN1(PQL)
225	AFR	Gambia	-1.768	PRIN1(PQL)
226	AFR	Djibouti	-1.770	PRIN1(PQL)
227	AFR	Chad	-1.792	PRIN1(PQL)
228	AFR	Angola	-1.859	PRIN1(PQL)
229	AFR	Guinea	-1.864	PRIN1(PQL)
230	AFR	Swaziland	-1.946	PRIN1(PQL)
231	AFR	Western Sahara	-2.090	PRIN1(PQL)
232	AFR	Somalia	-2.249	PRIN1(PQL)
233	AFR	Eritrea	-2.273	PRIN1(PQL)
234	AFR	Equatorial Guinea	-2.278	PRIN1(PQL)
235	AFR	South Sudan	-2.337	PRIN1(PQL)

Table 1.11 Ecomonico-Political Quality-if-Life Index, Principal Component 1 of the Economic and Political Quality-of-Life Indicators, 2011

Rank	Region	Country	EPQLX	Source
1	DME	Monaco	2.151	PRIN1(EPQL)
2	DME	Liechtenstein	1.734	PRIN1(EPQL)
3	DME	Norway	1.683	PRIN1(EPQL)
4	DME	Bermuda	1.633	PRIN1(EPQL)
5	DME	San Marino	1.605	PRIN1(EPQL)
6	DME	Luxembourg	1.599	PRIN1(EPQL)
7	DME	Sweden	1.586	PRIN1(EPQL)
8	DME	Iceland	1.548	PRIN1(EPQL)
9	DME	Switzerland	1.523	PRIN1(EPQL)
10	DME	Japan	1.474	PRIN1(EPQL)
11	DME	Finland	1.473	PRIN1(EPQL)
12	DME	Denmark	1.472	PRIN1(EPQL)
13	DME	Netherlands	1.455	PRIN1(EPQL)
14	DME	Germany	1.419	PRIN1(EPQL)
15	DME	Austria	1.412	PRIN1(EPQL)
16	DME	Australia	1.396	PRIN1(EPQL)
17	DME	Belgium	1.364	PRIN1(EPQL)
18	DME	Ireland	1.351	PRIN1(EPQL)
19	DME	France	1.335	PRIN1(EPQL)
20	DME	Jersey	1.331	PRIN1(EPQL)
21	DME	Andorra	1.324	PRIN1(EPQL)
22	DME	Italy	1.307	PRIN1(EPQL)
23	DME	Guernsey	1.304	PRIN1(EPQL)
24	DME	Canada	1.304	PRIN1(EPQL)
25	EEU	Slovenia	1.302	PRIN1(EPQL)
26	DME	Spain	1.288	PRIN1(EPQL)
27	SEA	Hong Kong	1.271	PRIN1(EPQL)
28	DME	Falkland Islands	1.268	PRIN1(EPQL)
29	DME	New Zealand	1.235	PRIN1(EPQL)
30	LAM	Cayman Islands	1.230	PRIN1(EPQL)
31	DME	Isle of Man	1.228	PRIN1(EPQL)
32	MEA	Cyprus	1.225	PRIN1(EPQL)
33	DME	Israel	1.224	PRIN1(EPQL)
34	DME	Faroe Islands	1.221	PRIN1(EPQL)
35	SEA	Macao	1.220	PRIN1(EPQL)
36	DME	United Kingdom	1.202	PRIN1(EPQL)
37	SEA	Korea, South	1.161	PRIN1(EPQL)
38	EEU	Czech Republic	1.161	PRIN1(EPQL)
39	DME	Malta	1.140	PRIN1(EPQL)
40	DME	United States	1.133	PRIN1(EPQL)
41	SEA	Singapore	1.132	PRIN1(EPQL)
42	DME	Portugal	1.098	PRIN1(EPQL)
43	LAM	Virgin Islands, U.S.	1.084	PRIN1(EPQL)
44	DME	Greece	1.083	PRIN1(EPQL)

Table 1.11 Ecomonico-Political Quality-if-Life Index, Principal Component 1 of the Economic and Political Quality-of-Life Indicators, 2011

Rank	Region	Country	EPQLX	Source
45	SEA	New Caledonia	1.082	PRIN1(EPQL)
46	DME	Gibraltar	1.078	PRIN1(EPQL)
47	LAM	Martinique	1.041	PRIN1(EPQL)
48	SEA	Taiwan	1.018	PRIN1(EPQL)
49	AFR	Reunion	0.981	PRIN1(EPQL)
50	LAM	Guadeloupe	0.967	PRIN1(EPQL)
51	USR	Estonia	0.960	PRIN1(EPQL)
52	LAM	Anguilla	0.925	PRIN1(EPQL)
53	EEU	Slovakia	0.921	PRIN1(EPQL)
54	LAM	Virgin Islands, Brit.	0.873	PRIN1(EPQL)
55	LAM	Saint Martin	0.865	PRIN1(EPQL)
56	EEU	Poland	0.836	PRIN1(EPQL)
57	LAM	Curacao	0.820	PRIN1(EPQL)
58	EEU	Croatia	0.796	PRIN1(EPQL)
59	MEA	Qatar	0.796	PRIN1(EPQL)
60	SEA	Guam	0.777	PRIN1(EPQL)
61	DME	St. Pierre & Miquelon	0.769	PRIN1(EPQL)
62	SEA	French Polynesia	0.767	PRIN1(EPQL)
63	USR	Lithuania	0.765	PRIN1(EPQL)
64	DME	Greenland	0.743	PRIN1(EPQL)
65	EEU	Hungary	0.742	PRIN1(EPQL)
66	LAM	Sint Maarten	0.735	PRIN1(EPQL)
67	LAM	Guiana, French	0.730	PRIN1(EPQL)
68	LAM	Puerto Rico	0.700	PRIN1(EPQL)
69	MEA	United Arab Emirates	0.683	PRIN1(EPQL)
70	SEA	Brunei	0.674	PRIN1(EPQL)
71	SEA	Northern Mariana Is.	0.672	PRIN1(EPQL)
72	MEA	Kuwait	0.671	PRIN1(EPQL)
73	LAM	Chile	0.654	PRIN1(EPQL)
74	LAM	Aruba	0.631	PRIN1(EPQL)
75	USR	Latvia	0.610	PRIN1(EPQL)
76	LAM	St. Kitts & Nevis	0.608	PRIN1(EPQL)
77	LAM	Bahamas	0.593	PRIN1(EPQL)
78	LAM	Antigua & Barbuda	0.539	PRIN1(EPQL)
79	LAM	Uruguay	0.537	PRIN1(EPQL)
80	LAM	Turks & Caicos Is.	0.536	PRIN1(EPQL)
81	EEU	Serbia	0.522	PRIN1(EPQL)
82	LAM	Barbados	0.516	PRIN1(EPQL)
83	EEU	Romania	0.500	PRIN1(EPQL)
84	EEU	Montenegro	0.480	PRIN1(EPQL)

TABLE 1.11 ECOMONICO-POLITICAL QUALITY-IF-LIFE INDEX, PRINCIPAL COMPONENT 1 OF THE ECONOMIC AND POLITICAL QUALITY-OF-LIFE INDICATORS, 2011

Rank	Region	Country	EPQLX	Source
85	LAM	Costa Rica	0.473	PRIN1(EPQL)
86	EEU	Bulgaria	0.464	PRIN1(EPQL)
87	MEA	Bahrain	0.427	PRIN1(EPQL)
88	LAM	Argentina	0.422	PRIN1(EPQL)
89	SEA	Wallis & Futuna	0.396	PRIN1(EPQL)
90	LAM	Grenada	0.346	PRIN1(EPQL)
91	LAM	Dominica	0.340	PRIN1(EPQL)
92	LAM	Mexico	0.301	PRIN1(EPQL)
93	MEA	Oman	0.292	PRIN1(EPQL)
94	SEA	Cook Islands	0.283	PRIN1(EPQL)
95	LAM	Panama	0.283	PRIN1(EPQL)
96	AFR	Mauritius	0.283	PRIN1(EPQL)
97	SEA	Malaysia	0.277	PRIN1(EPQL)
98	EEU	Bosnia	0.276	PRIN1(EPQL)
99	LAM	Trinidad & Tobago	0.274	PRIN1(EPQL)
100	MEA	Turkey	0.257	PRIN1(EPQL)
101	SEA	Samoa, American	0.247	PRIN1(EPQL)
102	LAM	St. Lucia	0.244	PRIN1(EPQL)
103	LAM	Cuba	0.232	PRIN1(EPQL)
104	MEA	Saudi Arabia	0.211	PRIN1(EPQL)
105	SEA	Palau	0.197	PRIN1(EPQL)
106	EEU	Albania	0.190	PRIN1(EPQL)
107	EEU	Macedonia	0.188	PRIN1(EPQL)
108	LAM	Brazil	0.170	PRIN1(EPQL)
109	SAS	Maldives	0.168	PRIN1(EPQL)
110	USR	Belarus	0.140	PRIN1(EPQL)
111	AFR	Seychelles	0.132	PRIN1(EPQL)
112	MEA	Lebanon	0.131	PRIN1(EPQL)
113	USR	Russia	0.121	PRIN1(EPQL)
114	LAM	St. Vincent	0.116	PRIN1(EPQL)
115	USR	Ukraine	0.107	PRIN1(EPQL)
116	AFR	Mayotte	0.102	PRIN1(EPQL)
117	AFR	St. Helena	0.097	PRIN1(EPQL)
118	LAM	Peru	0.081	PRIN1(EPQL)
119	LAM	Venezuela	0.064	PRIN1(EPQL)
120	MEA	Tunisia	0.027	PRIN1(EPQL)
121	MEA	Libya	0.024	PRIN1(EPQL)
122	SEA	Thailand	-0.010	PRIN1(EPQL)
123	LAM	Jamaica	-0.026	PRIN1(EPQL)
124	EEU	Kosovo	-0.031	PRIN1(EPQL)
125	LAM	Ecuador	-0.036	PRIN1(EPQL)
126	LAM	Dominican Republic	-0.042	PRIN1(EPQL)
127	LAM	Montserrat	-0.051	PRIN1(EPQL)
128	LAM	Belize	-0.053	PRIN1(EPQL)

Table 1.11 Ecomonico-Political Quality-if-Life Index, Principal Component 1 of the Economic and Political Quality-of-Life Indicators, 2011				
Rank	Region	Country	EPQLX	Source
129	SEA	Nauru	-0.053	PRIN1(EPQL)
130	LAM	Colombia	-0.065	PRIN1(EPQL)
131	SEA	Vanuatu	-0.091	PRIN1(EPQL)
132	SEA	Samoa	-0.094	PRIN1(EPQL)
133	SEA	Tonga	-0.097	PRIN1(EPQL)
134	USR	Armenia	-0.098	PRIN1(EPQL)
135	SEA	Niue	-0.101	PRIN1(EPQL)
136	LAM	El Salvador	-0.125	PRIN1(EPQL)
137	LAM	Suriname	-0.139	PRIN1(EPQL)
138	MEA	Iran	-0.150	PRIN1(EPQL)
139	SAS	Sri Lanka	-0.153	PRIN1(EPQL)
140	USR	Kazakhstan	-0.166	PRIN1(EPQL)
141	MEA	Algeria	-0.184	PRIN1(EPQL)
142	USR	Georgia	-0.198	PRIN1(EPQL)
143	SEA	Indonesia	-0.265	PRIN1(EPQL)
144	AFR	Cape Verde	-0.267	PRIN1(EPQL)
145	MEA	Egypt	-0.268	PRIN1(EPQL)
146	USR	Moldova	-0.273	PRIN1(EPQL)
147	SEA	Tuvalu	-0.281	PRIN1(EPQL)
148	LAM	Paraguay	-0.294	PRIN1(EPQL)
149	MEA	Jordan	-0.311	PRIN1(EPQL)
150	CPA	Mongolia	-0.313	PRIN1(EPQL)
151	CPA	China	-0.326	PRIN1(EPQL)
152	SEA	Marshall Islands	-0.330	PRIN1(EPQL)
153	LAM	Guyana	-0.334	PRIN1(EPQL)
154	SEA	Fiji	-0.349	PRIN1(EPQL)
155	USR	Azerbaijan	-0.353	PRIN1(EPQL)
156	SEA	Philippines	-0.402	PRIN1(EPQL)
157	MEA	Syria	-0.435	PRIN1(EPQL)
158	MEA	Morocco	-0.448	PRIN1(EPQL)
159	SEA	Micronesia	-0.459	PRIN1(EPQL)
160	MEA	West Bank	-0.485	PRIN1(EPQL)
161	AFR	Botswana	-0.488	PRIN1(EPQL)
162	AFR	Gabon	-0.524	PRIN1(EPQL)
163	LAM	Nicaragua	-0.537	PRIN1(EPQL)
164	LAM	Honduras	-0.537	PRIN1(EPQL)
165	LAM	Guatemala	-0.538	PRIN1(EPQL)
166	SEA	Kiribati	-0.542	PRIN1(EPQL)
167	MEA	Iraq	-0.573	PRIN1(EPQL)
168	AFR	Namibia	-0.587	PRIN1(EPQL)
169	AFR	South Africa	-0.604	PRIN1(EPQL)
170	SAS	India	-0.637	PRIN1(EPQL)
171	CPA	Vietnam	-0.639	PRIN1(EPQL)
172	SEA	Solomon Islands	-0.639	PRIN1(EPQL)
173	LAM	Bolivia	-0.661	PRIN1(EPQL)
174	USR	Kyrgyzstan	-0.696	PRIN1(EPQL)

Table 1.11 Ecomonico-Political Quality-if-Life Index, Principal Component 1 of the Economic and Political Quality-of-Life Indicators, 2011				
Rank	Region	Country	EPQLX	Source
175	USR	Turkmenistan	-0.702	PRIN1(EPQL)
176	MEA	Gaza Strip	-0.714	PRIN1(EPQL)
177	SEA	Tokelau	-0.728	PRIN1(EPQL)
178	SAS	Bhutan	-0.795	PRIN1(EPQL)
179	USR	Uzbekistan	-0.808	PRIN1(EPQL)
180	SEA	East Timor	-0.826	PRIN1(EPQL)
181	AFR	Ghana	-0.830	PRIN1(EPQL)
182	SAS	Bangladesh	-0.880	PRIN1(EPQL)
183	SAS	Pakistan	-0.897	PRIN1(EPQL)
184	USR	Tajikistan	-0.945	PRIN1(EPQL)
185	AFR	Sao Tome & Principe	-0.959	PRIN1(EPQL)
186	AFR	Equatorial Guinea	-0.989	PRIN1(EPQL)
187	SAS	Nepal	-1.007	PRIN1(EPQL)
188	SEA	Papua New Guinea	-1.010	PRIN1(EPQL)
189	CPA	Korea, North	-1.050	PRIN1(EPQL)
190	CPA	Laos	-1.054	PRIN1(EPQL)
191	CPA	Cambodia	-1.080	PRIN1(EPQL)
192	AFR	Congo, Republic	-1.088	PRIN1(EPQL)
193	AFR	Senegal	-1.120	PRIN1(EPQL)
194	AFR	Kenya	-1.174	PRIN1(EPQL)
195	AFR	Benin	-1.186	PRIN1(EPQL)
196	AFR	Tanzania	-1.188	PRIN1(EPQL)
197	MEA	Yemen	-1.199	PRIN1(EPQL)
198	AFR	Mauritania	-1.262	PRIN1(EPQL)
199	AFR	Swaziland	-1.283	PRIN1(EPQL)
200	AFR	Nigeria	-1.317	PRIN1(EPQL)
201	AFR	Sudan	-1.325	PRIN1(EPQL)
202	AFR	Angola	-1.334	PRIN1(EPQL)
203	AFR	Lesotho	-1.348	PRIN1(EPQL)
204	AFR	Djibouti	-1.367	PRIN1(EPQL)
205	AFR	Western Sahara	-1.387	PRIN1(EPQL)
206	AFR	Madagascar	-1.388	PRIN1(EPQL)
207	LAM	Haiti	-1.395	PRIN1(EPQL)
208	AFR	Zambia	-1.397	PRIN1(EPQL)
209	CPA	Burma	-1.404	PRIN1(EPQL)
210	AFR	Mali	-1.409	PRIN1(EPQL)
211	AFR	Togo	-1.418	PRIN1(EPQL)
212	AFR	Cameroon	-1.422	PRIN1(EPQL)
213	AFR	Uganda	-1.470	PRIN1(EPQL)
214	AFR	Malawi	-1.471	PRIN1(EPQL)
215	AFR	Rwanda	-1.498	PRIN1(EPQL)
216	AFR	Ivory Coast	-1.502	PRIN1(EPQL)
217	AFR	Comoros	-1.510	PRIN1(EPQL)

Table 1.11 Ecomonico-Political Quality-if-Life Index, Principal Component 1 of the Economic and Political Quality-of-Life Indicators, 2011

Rank	Region	Country	EPQLX	Source
218	AFR	Gambia	-1.545	PRIN1(EPQL)
219	AFR	Burkina Faso	-1.546	PRIN1(EPQL)
220	AFR	Liberia	-1.556	PRIN1(EPQL)
221	SAS	Afghanistan	-1.562	PRIN1(EPQL)
222	AFR	Ethiopia	-1.571	PRIN1(EPQL)
223	AFR	Niger	-1.578	PRIN1(EPQL)
224	AFR	Guinea-Bissau	-1.605	PRIN1(EPQL)
225	AFR	Sierra Leone	-1.686	PRIN1(EPQL)
226	AFR	Mozambique	-1.706	PRIN1(EPQL)
227	AFR	Guinea	-1.751	PRIN1(EPQL)
228	AFR	Eritrea	-1.775	PRIN1(EPQL)
229	AFR	Zimbabwe	-1.776	PRIN1(EPQL)
230	AFR	Chad	-1.779	PRIN1(EPQL)
231	AFR	Burundi	-1.868	PRIN1(EPQL)
232	AFR	Central African Rep.	-1.947	PRIN1(EPQL)
233	AFR	Somalia	-2.108	PRIN1(EPQL)
234	AFR	Congo, Dem. Republic	-2.152	PRIN1(EPQL)
235	AFR	South Sudan	-2.178	PRIN1(EPQL)

Balance of Powers

Table 2.1 Population, Thousands, 2011				
Rank	Region	Country	POP	Source
1	CPA	China	1,342,274	11(E)
2	SAS	India	1,216,728	11(E)
3	DME	United States	313,387	11(E)
4	SEA	Indonesia	241,343	11(E)
5	LAM	Brazil	192,813	11(E)
6	SAS	Pakistan	187,343	11(E)
7	AFR	Nigeria	162,471	11(E)
8	SAS	Bangladesh	142,875	11(E)
9	USR	Russia	142,707	11(E)
10	DME	Japan	127,937	11(E)
11	LAM	Mexico	114,492	11(E)
12	SEA	Philippines	95,849	11(E)
13	CPA	Vietnam	88,145	11(E)
14	MEA	Egypt	82,537	11(E)
15	AFR	Ethiopia	82,102	11(E)
16	DME	Germany	81,604	11(E)
17	MEA	Iran	75,276	11(E)
18	MEA	Turkey	74,306	11(E)
19	AFR	Congo, Dem. Republic	67,758	11(E)
20	SEA	Thailand	65,856	11(E)
21	DME	France	63,278	11(E)
22	DME	United Kingdom	62,675	11(E)
23	DME	Italy	60,769	11(E)
24	CPA	Burma	54,000	11(E)
25	AFR	South Africa	50,587	11(E)
26	SEA	Korea, South	48,755	11(E)
27	DME	Spain	47,215	11(E)
28	USR	Ukraine	45,672	11(E)
29	AFR	Tanzania	45,030	11(E)
30	LAM	Colombia	44,726	11(E)
31	AFR	Kenya	40,770	11(E)
32	LAM	Argentina	40,365	11(E)
33	EEU	Poland	38,216	11(E)
34	AFR	Sudan	36,787	11(E)
35	MEA	Algeria	36,649	11(E)
36	AFR	Uganda	34,509	11(E)
37	DME	Canada	34,447	11(E)
38	MEA	Iraq	32,665	11(E)
39	MEA	Morocco	31,968	11(E)
40	LAM	Venezuela	29,437	11(E)
41	LAM	Peru	29,249	11(E)
42	MEA	Saudi Arabia	28,572	11(E)
43	SEA	Malaysia	28,161	11(E)
44	USR	Uzbekistan	28,129	11(E)
45	SAS	Nepal	26,629	11(E)
46	SAS	Afghanistan	26,442	11(E)
47	MEA	Yemen	24,800	11(E)

Table 2.1 Population, Thousands, 2011				
Rank	Region	Country	POP	Source
48	AFR	Ghana	24,661	11(E)
49	CPA	Korea, North	24,336	11(E)
50	SEA	Taiwan	23,190	11(E)
51	AFR	Mozambique	22,949	11(E)
52	DME	Australia	22,651	11(E)
53	AFR	Ivory Coast	21,504	11(E)
54	EEU	Romania	21,393	11(E)
55	AFR	Madagascar	21,307	11(E)
56	SAS	Sri Lanka	21,045	11(E)
57	MEA	Syria	20,766	11(E)
58	AFR	Cameroon	20,073	11(E)
59	AFR	Angola	19,618	11(E)
60	LAM	Chile	17,270	11(E)
61	AFR	Burkina Faso	16,968	11(E)
62	DME	Netherlands	16,683	11(E)
63	USR	Kazakhstan	16,560	11(E)
64	AFR	Niger	16,469	11(E)
65	AFR	Mali	15,525	11(E)
66	AFR	Malawi	15,381	11(E)
67	LAM	Guatemala	14,729	11(E)
68	CPA	Cambodia	14,702	11(E)
69	LAM	Ecuador	14,650	11(E)
70	AFR	Zambia	13,306	11(E)
71	AFR	Senegal	12,644	11(E)
72	AFR	Zimbabwe	12,084	11(E)
73	AFR	Chad	12,018	11(E)
74	DME	Greece	11,372	11(E)
75	LAM	Cuba	11,240	11(E)
76	DME	Belgium	10,971	11(E)
77	AFR	Rwanda	10,943	11(E)
78	MEA	Tunisia	10,594	11(E)
79	DME	Portugal	10,555	11(E)
80	EEU	Czech Republic	10,551	11(E)
81	AFR	Guinea	10,222	11(E)
82	LAM	Bolivia	10,088	11(E)
83	EEU	Hungary	9,972	11(E)
84	AFR	Somalia	9,926	11(E)
85	LAM	Haiti	9,720	11(E)
86	USR	Belarus	9,472	11(E)
87	DME	Sweden	9,451	11(E)
88	LAM	Dominican Republic	9,440	11(E)
89.5	USR	Azerbaijan	9,150	11(E)
89.5	AFR	South Sudan	9,150	11(E)
91	AFR	Benin	9,100	11(E)
92	AFR	Burundi	8,575	11(E)
93	DME	Austria	8,419	11(E)
94	DME	Switzerland	7,913	11(E)

Table 2.1 Population, Thousands, 2011				
Rank	Region	Country	POP	Source
95	MEA	United Arab Emirates	7,891	11(E)
96	LAM	Honduras	7,755	11(E)
97	USR	Tajikistan	7,681	11(E)
98	DME	Israel	7,431	11(E)
99	EEU	Bulgaria	7,333	11(E)
100	EEU	Serbia	7,262	11(E)
101	SEA	Hong Kong	7,125	11(E)
102	LAM	Paraguay	6,459	11(E)
103	MEA	Libya	6,423	11(E)
104	CPA	Laos	6,392	11(E)
105	SEA	Papua New Guinea	6,188	11(E)
106	MEA	Jordan	6,180	11(E)
107	LAM	El Salvador	6,072	11(E)
108	AFR	Sierra Leone	5,997	11(E)
109	LAM	Nicaragua	5,870	11(E)
110	AFR	Togo	5,830	11(E)
111	DME	Denmark	5,574	11(E)
112	EEU	Slovakia	5,440	11(E)
113	AFR	Eritrea	5,415	11(E)
114	DME	Finland	5,387	11(E)
115	SEA	Singapore	5,182	11(E)
116	USR	Kyrgyzstan	5,168	11(E)
117	USR	Turkmenistan	4,998	11(E)
118	DME	Norway	4,953	11(E)
119	AFR	Central African Rep.	4,950	11(E)
120	DME	Ireland	4,606	11(E)
121	LAM	Costa Rica	4,577	11(E)
122	USR	Georgia	4,474	11(E)
123	DME	New Zealand	4,407	11(E)
124	EEU	Croatia	4,287	11(E)
125	MEA	Lebanon	4,143	11(E)
126	AFR	Liberia	3,953	11(E)
127	USR	Moldova	3,927	11(E)
128	AFR	Congo, Republic	3,920	11(E)
129	EEU	Bosnia	3,843	11(E)
130	LAM	Puerto Rico	3,716	11(E)
131	MEA	Kuwait	3,650	11(E)
132	LAM	Panama	3,643	11(E)
133	LAM	Uruguay	3,380	11(E)
134	AFR	Mauritania	3,282	11(E)
135	USR	Lithuania	3,218	11(E)
136	EEU	Albania	3,196	11(E)
137	USR	Armenia	3,100	11(E)
138	MEA	Oman	2,810	11(E)
139	CPA	Mongolia	2,765	11(E)

TABLE 2.1 POPULATION, THOUSANDS, 2011				
Rank	Region	Country	POP	Source
140	LAM	Jamaica	2,709	11(E)
141	MEA	West Bank	2,551	11(E)
142	AFR	Namibia	2,324	11(E)
143	USR	Latvia	2,217	11(E)
144	EEU	Macedonia	2,060	11(E)
145	EEU	Slovenia	2,052	11(E)
146	AFR	Botswana	2,033	11(E)
147	AFR	Lesotho	1,925	11(E)
148	EEU	Kosovo	1,826	11(E)
149	AFR	Gambia	1,776	11(E)
150	MEA	Qatar	1,624	11(E)
151	AFR	Guinea-Bissau	1,606	11(E)
152	MEA	Gaza Strip	1,574	11(E)
153	AFR	Gabon	1,534	11(E)
154	USR	Estonia	1,340	11(E)
155.5	MEA	Bahrain	1,325	11(E)
155.5	LAM	Trinidad & Tobago	1,325	11(E)
157	AFR	Mauritius	1,288	11(E)
158	AFR	Swaziland	1,203	11(E)
159	MEA	Cyprus	1,118	11(E)
160	SEA	East Timor	1,092	11(E)
161.5	SEA	Fiji	852	11(E)
161.5	AFR	Reunion	852	11(E)
163	AFR	Djibouti	840	11(E)
164	LAM	Guyana	756	11(E)
165	AFR	Comoros	754	11(E)
166	AFR	Equatorial Guinea	720	11(E)
167	SAS	Bhutan	701	11(E)
168	EEU	Montenegro	620	11(E)
169	SEA	Macao	561	11(E)
170	SEA	Solomon Islands	535	11(E)
171	LAM	Suriname	529	11(E)
172	DME	Luxembourg	517	11(E)
173	AFR	Western Sahara	507	11(E)
174	AFR	Cape Verde	498	11(E)
175	SEA	Brunei	422	11(E)
176	DME	Malta	419	11(E)
177	LAM	Guadeloupe	407	11(E)
178	LAM	Martinique	401	11(E)
179	LAM	Bahamas	360	11(E)
180	SAS	Maldives	325	11(E)
181	LAM	Belize	322	11(E)
182	DME	Iceland	319	11(E)
183	LAM	Barbados	277	11(E)
184	SEA	French Polynesia	272	11(E)
185	SEA	New Caledonia	255	11(E)
186	SEA	Vanuatu	251	11(E)

Table 2.1 Population, Thousands, 2011				
Rank	Region	Country	POP	Source
187	LAM	Guiana, French	243	11(E)
188	AFR	Mayotte	210	11(E)
189	SEA	Samoa	184	11(E)
190	AFR	Sao Tome & Principe	169	11(E)
191	LAM	St. Lucia	167	11(E)
192	SEA	Guam	160	11(E)
193	LAM	Curacao	143	11(E)
194	LAM	Virgin Islands, U.S.	119	11(E)
195	LAM	Grenada	108	11(E)
196	SEA	Tonga	104	11(E)
197.5	LAM	Aruba	102	11(E)
197.5	SEA	Micronesia	102	11(E)
199.5	SEA	Kiribati	101	11(E)
199.5	LAM	St. Vincent	101	11(E)
201	DME	Jersey	94	11(E)
202	AFR	Seychelles	92	11(E)
203	LAM	Antigua & Barbuda	91	11(E)
204	DME	Andorra	86	11(E)
205	DME	Isle of Man	85	11(E)
206	LAM	Dominica	73	11(E)
207	SEA	Samoa, American	67	11(E)
208.5	DME	Bermuda	65	11(E)
208.5	DME	Guernsey	65	11(E)
210	DME	Greenland	57	11(E)
211	LAM	Cayman Islands	56	11(E)
212	SEA	Marshall Islands	55	11(E)
213	LAM	St. Kitts & Nevis	50	11(E)
214	DME	Faroe Islands	49	11(E)
215	SEA	Northern Mariana Is.	46	11(E)
216	LAM	Turks & Caicos Is.	45	11(CIA)
217	LAM	Sint Maarten	38	11(E)
218	DME	Liechtenstein	36	11(E)
219	DME	Monaco	36	11(E)
220	DME	San Marino	32	11(E)
221	LAM	Saint Martin	31	11(CIA)
222	DME	Gibraltar	29	11(CIA)
223	LAM	Virgin Islands, Brit.	25	11(CIA)
224	SEA	Palau	21	11(E)
225	SEA	Wallis & Futuna	15	11(CIA)
226	LAM	Anguilla	15	11(CIA)
227	SEA	Tuvalu	11	11(E)
228	SEA	Cook Islands	11	11(CIA)
229	SEA	Nauru	9	11(E)
230	AFR	St. Helena	8	11(CIA)

Table 2.1 Population, Thousands, 2011				
Rank	Region	Country	POP	Source
231	DME	St. Pierre & Miquelon	6	11(CIA)
232	LAM	Montserrat	5	11(CIA)
233	DME	Falkland Islands	3	08(CIA)
234	SEA	Tokelau	1	11(CIA)
235	SEA	Niue	1	11(CIA)

TABLE 2.2 GDP AT PURCHASING POWER PARITIES, MILLIONS OF DOLLARS, 2011				
Rank	Region	Country	GDPPPP	Source
1	DME	United States	15,077,675	POP*GPCPPP
2	CPA	China	11,275,102	POP*GPCPPP
3	SAS	India	4,441,057	POP*GPCPPP
4	DME	Japan	4,307,383	POP*GPCPPP
5	DME	Germany	3,219,767	POP*GPCPPP
6	USR	Russia	3,128,280	POP*GPCPPP
7	LAM	Brazil	2,244,343	POP*GPCPPP
8	DME	United Kingdom	2,231,105	POP*GPCPPP
9	DME	France	2,230,360	POP*GPCPPP
10	DME	Italy	1,985,445	POP*GPCPPP
11	LAM	Mexico	1,899,193	POP*GPCPPP
12	DME	Spain	1,514,988	POP*GPCPPP
13	SEA	Korea, South	1,454,557	POP*GPCPPP
14	DME	Canada	1,392,348	POP*GPCPPP
15	MEA	Turkey	1,271,376	POP*GPCPPP
16	SEA	Indonesia	1,118,866	POP*GPCPPP
17	DME	Australia	950,753	POP*GPCPPP
18	MEA	Iran	918,367	POP*GPCPPP
19	SEA	Taiwan	878,901	POP*GPCPPP
20	EEU	Poland	805,784	POP*GPCPPP
21	DME	Netherlands	713,682	POP*GPCPPP
22	LAM	Argentina	696,296	POP*GPCPPP
23	MEA	Saudi Arabia	693,385	POP*GPCPPP
24	SEA	Thailand	569,391	POP*GPCPPP
25	AFR	South Africa	554,434	POP*GPCPPP
26	MEA	Egypt	518,415	POP*GPCPPP
27	SAS	Pakistan	514,257	POP*GPCPPP
28	SEA	Malaysia	452,012	POP*GPCPPP
29	LAM	Colombia	448,736	POP*GPCPPP
30	DME	Belgium	424,830	POP*GPCPPP
31	AFR	Nigeria	411,539	POP*GPCPPP
32	DME	Switzerland	405,359	POP*GPCPPP
33	SEA	Philippines	394,802	POP*GPCPPP
34	DME	Sweden	392,065	POP*GPCPPP
35	MEA	United Arab Emirates	377,924	POP*GPCPPP
36	LAM	Venezuela	375,292	POP*GPCPPP
37	SEA	Hong Kong	359,905	POP*GPCPPP
38	DME	Austria	355,046	POP*GPCPPP
39	EEU	Romania	341,924	POP*GPCPPP
40	USR	Ukraine	329,204	POP*GPCPPP
41	MEA	Algeria	317,197	POP*GPCPPP
42	SEA	Singapore	314,485	POP*GPCPPP
43	CPA	Vietnam	300,751	POP*GPCPPP
44	LAM	Peru	299,334	POP*GPCPPP

TABLE 2.2 GDP AT PURCHASING POWER PARITIES, MILLIONS OF DOLLARS, 2011

Rank	Region	Country	GDPPPP	Source
45	DME	Norway	299,122	POP*GPCPPP
46	LAM	Chile	298,253	POP*GPCPPP
47	DME	Greece	294,057	POP*GPCPPP
48	EEU	Czech Republic	277,829	POP*GPCPPP
49	DME	Portugal	269,828	POP*GPCPPP
50	SAS	Bangladesh	253,889	POP*GPCPPP
51	DME	Denmark	228,161	POP*GPCPPP
52	USR	Kazakhstan	216,919	POP*GPCPPP
53	EEU	Hungary	216,003	POP*GPCPPP
54	DME	Israel	214,080	POP*GPCPPP
55	DME	Finland	201,770	POP*GPCPPP
56	DME	Ireland	188,238	POP*GPCPPP
57	MEA	Morocco	158,306	POP*GPCPPP
58	MEA	Kuwait	148,555	POP*GPCPPP
59	MEA	Qatar	143,422	POP*GPCPPP
60	USR	Belarus	141,493	POP*GPCPPP
61	DME	New Zealand	136,978	POP*GPCPPP
62	EEU	Slovakia	131,077	POP*GPCPPP
63	LAM	Ecuador	127,001	POP*GPCPPP
64	MEA	Iraq	126,218	POP*GPCPPP
65	SAS	Sri Lanka	117,473	POP*GPCPPP
66	AFR	Angola	116,139	POP*GPCPPP
67	LAM	Cuba	114,862	POP*GPCPPP
68	EEU	Bulgaria	110,604	POP*GPCPPP
69	MEA	Syria	107,609	POP*GPCPPP
70	MEA	Tunisia	98,704	POP*GPCPPP
71	MEA	Libya	93,480	POP*GPCPPP
72	LAM	Dominican Republic	92,474	POP*GPCPPP
73	USR	Uzbekistan	92,460	POP*GPCPPP
74	USR	Azerbaijan	92,067	POP*GPCPPP
75	AFR	Ethiopia	91,051	POP*GPCPPP
76	EEU	Serbia	86,323	POP*GPCPPP
77	AFR	Sudan	85,530	POP*GPCPPP
78	EEU	Croatia	83,541	POP*GPCPPP
79	MEA	Oman	80,602	POP*GPCPPP
80	LAM	Guatemala	72,585	POP*GPCPPP
81	CPA	Burma	70,200	POP*GPCPPP
82	AFR	Kenya	69,717	POP*GPCPPP
83	USR	Lithuania	69,123	POP*GPCPPP
84	AFR	Tanzania	68,085	POP*GPCPPP
85	LAM	Puerto Rico	66,929	POP*GPCPPP
86	MEA	Lebanon	60,525	POP*GPCPPP
87	MEA	Yemen	57,858	POP*GPCPPP
88	LAM	Panama	56,791	POP*GPCPPP
89	LAM	Costa Rica	55,643	POP*GPCPPP

TABLE 2.2 GDP AT PURCHASING POWER PARITIES, MILLIONS OF DOLLARS, 2011				
Rank	Region	Country	GDPPPP	Source
90	EEU	Slovenia	55,287	POP*GPCPPP
91	LAM	Bolivia	51,439	POP*GPCPPP
92	LAM	Uruguay	50,964	POP*GPCPPP
93	AFR	Cameroon	47,352	POP*GPCPPP
94	USR	Turkmenistan	47,081	POP*GPCPPP
95	AFR	Uganda	46,415	POP*GPCPPP
96	AFR	Ghana	46,141	POP*GPCPPP
97	DME	Luxembourg	45,908	POP*GPCPPP
98	CPA	Korea, North	43,805	POP*GPCPPP
99	SEA	Macao	43,241	POP*GPCPPP
100	USR	Latvia	42,014	POP*GPCPPP
101	LAM	El Salvador	41,478	POP*GPCPPP
102	AFR	Ivory Coast	38,471	POP*GPCPPP
103	MEA	Jordan	36,870	POP*GPCPPP
104	MEA	Bahrain	36,173	POP*GPCPPP
105	MEA	Cyprus	36,060	POP*GPCPPP
106	LAM	Paraguay	35,531	POP*GPCPPP
107	EEU	Bosnia	34,879	POP*GPCPPP
108	CPA	Cambodia	34,667	POP*GPCPPP
109	SAS	Nepal	33,340	POP*GPCPPP
110	LAM	Trinidad & Tobago	33,223	POP*GPCPPP
111	LAM	Honduras	31,384	POP*GPCPPP
112	SAS	Afghanistan	30,117	POP*GPCPPP
113	AFR	Botswana	29,979	POP*GPCPPP
114	USR	Estonia	29,476	POP*GPCPPP
115	EEU	Albania	28,336	POP*GPCPPP
116	AFR	Equatorial Guinea	26,065	POP*GPCPPP
117	AFR	Congo, Dem. Republic	25,274	POP*GPCPPP
118	AFR	Senegal	24,871	POP*GPCPPP
119	USR	Georgia	24,450	POP*GPCPPP
120	AFR	Gabon	24,317	POP*GPCPPP
121	AFR	Reunion	24,034	POP*GPCPPP
122	EEU	Macedonia	23,816	POP*GPCPPP
123	LAM	Nicaragua	22,376	POP*GPCPPP
124	AFR	Mozambique	22,375	POP*GPCPPP
125	AFR	Burkina Faso	22,092	POP*GPCPPP
126	SEA	Brunei	21,843	POP*GPCPPP
127	AFR	Zambia	21,569	POP*GPCPPP
128	LAM	Jamaica	21,049	POP*GPCPPP
129	AFR	Madagascar	20,583	POP*GPCPPP
130	AFR	Mauritius	18,573	POP*GPCPPP
131	AFR	Chad	18,003	POP*GPCPPP
132	USR	Armenia	17,946	POP*GPCPPP
133	USR	Tajikistan	17,851	POP*GPCPPP

Table 2.2 GDP at Purchasing Power Parities, Millions of Dollars, 2011				
Rank	Region	Country	GDPPPP	Source
134	CPA	Laos	17,834	POP*GPCPPP
135	AFR	Congo, Republic	17,091	POP*GPCPPP
136	AFR	Mali	16,938	POP*GPCPPP
137	SEA	Papua New Guinea	16,559	POP*GPCPPP
138	AFR	Namibia	15,806	POP*GPCPPP
139	AFR	Benin	14,733	POP*GPCPPP
140	AFR	Rwanda	14,029	POP*GPCPPP
141	AFR	Malawi	13,735	POP*GPCPPP
142	USR	Moldova	13,230	POP*GPCPPP
143	CPA	Mongolia	13,112	POP*GPCPPP
144	LAM	Martinique	12,783	POP*GPCPPP
145	LAM	Guadeloupe	12,506	POP*GPCPPP
146	USR	Kyrgyzstan	12,414	POP*GPCPPP
147	AFR	Niger	11,973	POP*GPCPPP
148	EEU	Kosovo	11,869	POP*GPCPPP
149	DME	Iceland	11,638	POP*GPCPPP
150	DME	Malta	11,524	POP*GPCPPP
151	LAM	Bahamas	11,512	POP*GPCPPP
152	AFR	Guinea	11,490	POP*GPCPPP
153	LAM	Haiti	11,382	POP*GPCPPP
154	SEA	New Caledonia	10,749	POP*GPCPPP
155	MEA	West Bank	9,258	POP*GPCPPP
156	EEU	Montenegro	8,328	POP*GPCPPP
157	AFR	Mauritania	8,310	POP*GPCPPP
158	DME	Bermuda	7,461	POP*GPCPPP
159	AFR	Swaziland	7,282	POP*GPCPPP
160	AFR	Sierra Leone	6,783	POP*GPCPPP
161	LAM	Barbados	6,537	POP*GPCPPP
162	AFR	Somalia	6,144	POP*GPCPPP
163	AFR	Togo	6,116	POP*GPCPPP
164	DME	Jersey	6,070	POP*GPCPPP
165	AFR	Zimbabwe	6,042	POP*GPCPPP
166	SEA	French Polynesia	5,846	POP*GPCPPP
167	LAM	Guiana, French	5,776	POP*GPCPPP
168	LAM	Guyana	5,670	POP*GPCPPP
169	LAM	Virgin Islands, U.S.	5,443	POP*GPCPPP
170	DME	Liechtenstein	5,402	POP*GPCPPP
171	AFR	Burundi	5,179	POP*GPCPPP
172	DME	Monaco	4,731	POP*GPCPPP
173	LAM	Suriname	4,420	POP*GPCPPP
174	SAS	Bhutan	4,098	POP*GPCPPP

Table 2.2 GDP at Purchasing Power Parities, Millions of Dollars, 2011				
Rank	Region	Country	GDPPPP	Source
175	SEA	Fiji	4,053	POP*GPCPPP
176	AFR	Central African Rep.	4,010	POP*GPCPPP
177	MEA	Gaza Strip	3,808	POP*GPCPPP
178	DME	Isle of Man	3,355	POP*GPCPPP
179	DME	Guernsey	3,296	POP*GPCPPP
180	AFR	Lesotho	3,255	POP*GPCPPP
181	AFR	Gambia	3,213	POP*GPCPPP
182	DME	Andorra	3,184	POP*GPCPPP
183	AFR	Eritrea	3,168	POP*GPCPPP
184	LAM	Cayman Islands	3,154	POP*GPCPPP
185	LAM	Curacao	2,956	POP*GPCPPP
186	SAS	Maldives	2,883	POP*GPCPPP
187	AFR	Mayotte	2,765	POP*GPCPPP
188	SEA	Guam	2,716	POP*GPCPPP
189	AFR	South Sudan	2,716	POP*GPCPPP
190	LAM	Aruba	2,507	POP*GPCPPP
191	AFR	Seychelles	2,372	POP*GPCPPP
192	AFR	Liberia	2,313	POP*GPCPPP
193	AFR	Djibouti	2,184	POP*GPCPPP
194	LAM	Belize	2,148	POP*GPCPPP
195	DME	Greenland	2,133	POP*GPCPPP
196	AFR	Guinea-Bissau	2,040	POP*GPCPPP
197	AFR	Cape Verde	2,039	POP*GPCPPP
198	LAM	St. Lucia	1,937	POP*GPCPPP
199	SEA	East Timor	1,723	POP*GPCPPP
200	LAM	Antigua & Barbuda	1,690	POP*GPCPPP
201	SEA	Solomon Islands	1,564	POP*GPCPPP
202	DME	Faroe Islands	1,525	POP*GPCPPP
203	DME	Gibraltar	1,357	POP*GPCPPP
204	AFR	Western Sahara	1,316	POP*GPCPPP
205	LAM	Grenada	1,170	POP*GPCPPP
206	LAM	Virgin Islands, Brit.	1,167	POP*GPCPPP
207	DME	San Marino	1,136	POP*GPCPPP
208	SEA	Vanuatu	1,099	POP*GPCPPP
209	LAM	St. Vincent	1,082	POP*GPCPPP
210	LAM	Dominica	963	POP*GPCPPP
211	LAM	St. Kitts & Nevis	866	POP*GPCPPP
212	AFR	Comoros	837	POP*GPCPPP
213	SEA	Samoa	823	POP*GPCPPP
214	LAM	Saint Martin	798	POP*GPCPPP

Table 2.2 GDP at Purchasing Power Parities, Millions of Dollars, 2011

Rank	Region	Country	GDPPPP	Source
215	SEA	Northern Mariana Is.	790	POP*GPCPPP
216	LAM	Turks & Caicos Is.	673	POP*GPCPPP
217	LAM	Sint Maarten	607	POP*GPCPPP
218	SEA	Samoa, American	554	POP*GPCPPP
219	SEA	Tonga	508	POP*GPCPPP
220	AFR	Sao Tome & Principe	351	POP*GPCPPP
221	SEA	Micronesia	348	POP*GPCPPP
222	SEA	Palau	283	POP*GPCPPP
223	SEA	Kiribati	236	POP*GPCPPP
224	LAM	Anguilla	186	POP*GPCPPP
225	DME	Falkland Islands	173	POP*GPCPPP
226	SEA	Marshall Islands	141	POP*GPCPPP
227	DME	St. Pierre & Miquelon	115	POP*GPCPPP
228	SEA	Cook Islands	115	POP*GPCPPP
229	SEA	Tuvalu	86	POP*GPCPPP
230	SEA	Wallis & Futuna	70	POP*GPCPPP
231	SEA	Nauru	53	POP*GPCPPP
232	AFR	St. Helena	45	POP*GPCPPP
233	LAM	Montserrat	24	POP*GPCPPP
234	SEA	Niue	10	POP*GPCPPP
235	SEA	Tokelau	3	POP*GPCPPP

Table 2.3 GNI at Market Exchange Rates, Millions of Dollars, 2011				
Rank	Region	Country	GDP	Source
1	DME	United States	15,236,876	POP*GPC
2	CPA	China	6,630,834	POP*GPC
3	DME	Japan	5,744,371	POP*GPC
4	DME	Germany	3,609,345	POP*GPC
5	DME	France	2,684,253	POP*GPC
6	DME	United Kingdom	2,367,862	POP*GPC
7	DME	Italy	2,146,361	POP*GPC
8	LAM	Brazil	2,066,955	POP*GPC
9	SAS	India	1,727,754	POP*GPC
10	DME	Canada	1,569,061	POP*GPC
11	USR	Russia	1,519,830	POP*GPC
12	DME	Spain	1,460,360	POP*GPC
13	DME	Australia	1,127,793	POP*GPC
14	LAM	Mexico	1,078,515	POP*GPC
15	SEA	Korea, South	1,017,517	POP*GPC
16	DME	Netherlands	828,478	POP*GPC
17	MEA	Turkey	773,525	POP*GPC
18	SEA	Indonesia	709,548	POP*GPC
19	DME	Switzerland	604,158	POP*GPC
20	MEA	Saudi Arabia	509,153	POP*GPC
21	SEA	Taiwan	504,591	POP*GPC
22	DME	Belgium	503,898	POP*GPC
23	DME	Sweden	502,510	POP*GPC
24	MEA	Iran	480,336	POP*GPC
25	EEU	Poland	473,114	POP*GPC
26	DME	Norway	440,173	POP*GPC
27	DME	Austria	405,543	POP*GPC
28	LAM	Argentina	393,155	POP*GPC
29	AFR	South Africa	352,086	POP*GPC
30	LAM	Venezuela	347,945	POP*GPC
31	DME	Denmark	335,332	POP*GPC
32	MEA	United Arab Emirates	321,637	POP*GPC
33	SEA	Thailand	292,401	POP*GPC
34	DME	Greece	278,500	POP*GPC
35	LAM	Colombia	271,487	POP*GPC
36	DME	Finland	257,283	POP*GPC
37	SEA	Hong Kong	256,571	POP*GPC
38	SEA	Malaysia	246,972	POP*GPC
39	DME	Portugal	225,560	POP*GPC
40	SEA	Singapore	222,463	POP*GPC
41	DME	Israel	214,979	POP*GPC
42	MEA	Egypt	214,596	POP*GPC
43	LAM	Chile	212,076	POP*GPC
44	SEA	Philippines	211,826	POP*GPC
45	SAS	Pakistan	209,824	POP*GPC
46	AFR	Nigeria	207,963	POP*GPC

Table 2.3 GNI at Market Exchange Rates, Millions of Dollars, 2011				
Rank	Region	Country	GDP	Source
47	EEU	Czech Republic	197,304	POP*GPC
48	DME	Ireland	180,325	POP*GPC
49	EEU	Romania	174,139	POP*GPC
50	MEA	Kuwait	171,101	POP*GPC
51	DME	New Zealand	168,801	POP*GPC
52	MEA	Algeria	163,821	POP*GPC
53	LAM	Peru	150,632	POP*GPC
54	USR	Ukraine	142,953	POP*GPC
55	USR	Kazakhstan	136,786	POP*GPC
56	MEA	Qatar	130,635	POP*GPC
57	EEU	Hungary	126,944	POP*GPC
58	CPA	Vietnam	111,944	POP*GPC
59	SAS	Bangladesh	111,443	POP*GPC
60	MEA	Morocco	94,945	POP*GPC
61	EEU	Slovakia	88,074	POP*GPC
62	MEA	Iraq	86,236	POP*GPC
63	MEA	Libya	79,510	POP*GPC
64	AFR	Angola	75,137	POP*GPC
65	MEA	Oman	66,799	POP*GPC
66	MEA	Syria	64,707	POP*GPC
67	LAM	Puerto Rico	63,176	POP*GPC
68	LAM	Ecuador	61,530	POP*GPC
69	LAM	Cuba	59,021	POP*GPC
70	EEU	Croatia	58,046	POP*GPC
71	USR	Belarus	55,222	POP*GPC
72	SAS	Sri Lanka	54,296	POP*GPC
73	LAM	Dominican Republic	49,466	POP*GPC
74	EEU	Bulgaria	48,691	POP*GPC
75	EEU	Slovenia	48,427	POP*GPC
76	USR	Azerbaijan	48,404	POP*GPC
77	AFR	Sudan	48,191	POP*GPC
78	MEA	Tunisia	42,588	POP*GPC
79	USR	Uzbekistan	42,475	POP*GPC
80	LAM	Guatemala	42,272	POP*GPC
81	USR	Lithuania	41,770	POP*GPC
82	EEU	Serbia	41,321	POP*GPC
83	LAM	Uruguay	40,087	POP*GPC
84	DME	Luxembourg	40,011	POP*GPC
85	MEA	Lebanon	37,867	POP*GPC
86	LAM	Costa Rica	34,968	POP*GPC
87	AFR	Ghana	34,772	POP*GPC
88	AFR	Kenya	33,431	POP*GPC
89	AFR	Ethiopia	30,378	POP*GPC
90	USR	Latvia	29,530	POP*GPC
91	LAM	Panama	27,213	POP*GPC
92	MEA	Jordan	27,068	POP*GPC
93	MEA	Yemen	26,536	POP*GPC

Table 2.3 GNI at Market Exchange Rates, Millions of Dollars, 2011				
Rank	Region	Country	GDP	Source
94	MEA	Bahrain	26,401	POP*GPC
95	SEA	Macao	26,181	POP*GPC
96	MEA	Cyprus	25,699	POP*GPC
97	AFR	Tanzania	24,316	POP*GPC
98	AFR	Cameroon	24,288	POP*GPC
99	CPA	Korea, North	24,263	POP*GPC
100	USR	Turkmenistan	23,990	POP*GPC
101	AFR	Ivory Coast	23,439	POP*GPC
102	CPA	Burma	21,708	POP*GPC
103	LAM	El Salvador	21,131	POP*GPC
104	AFR	Reunion	20,503	POP*GPC
105	USR	Estonia	20,448	POP*GPC
106	LAM	Bolivia	20,378	POP*GPC
107	LAM	Trinidad & Tobago	19,928	POP*GPC
108	LAM	Paraguay	19,506	POP*GPC
109	EEU	Bosnia	18,370	POP*GPC
110	AFR	Uganda	17,600	POP*GPC
111	SEA	Brunei	15,600	POP*GPC
112	AFR	Zambia	15,435	POP*GPC
113	LAM	Honduras	15,355	POP*GPC
114	AFR	Botswana	15,187	POP*GPC
115	SAS	Nepal	14,380	POP*GPC
116	AFR	Senegal	13,529	POP*GPC
117	LAM	Jamaica	13,491	POP*GPC
118	AFR	Congo, Dem. Republic	12,874	POP*GPC
119	USR	Georgia	12,796	POP*GPC
120	EEU	Albania	12,720	POP*GPC
121	SAS	Afghanistan	12,428	POP*GPC
122	AFR	Gabon	12,395	POP*GPC
123	CPA	Cambodia	12,056	POP*GPC
124	AFR	Equatorial Guinea	11,282	POP*GPC
125	LAM	Martinique	11,202	POP*GPC
126	DME	Iceland	11,108	POP*GPC
127	AFR	Namibia	10,923	POP*GPC
128	LAM	Guadeloupe	10,871	POP*GPC
129	AFR	Mozambique	10,557	POP*GPC
130	USR	Armenia	10,416	POP*GPC
131	AFR	Mauritius	10,356	POP*GPC
132	SEA	New Caledonia	10,017	POP*GPC
133	EEU	Macedonia	9,909	POP*GPC
134	AFR	Burkina Faso	9,841	POP*GPC
135	AFR	Mali	9,470	POP*GPC
136	AFR	Madagascar	9,162	POP*GPC
137	SEA	Papua New Guinea	9,158	POP*GPC
138	LAM	Nicaragua	8,864	POP*GPC

Table 2.3 GNI at Market Exchange Rates, Millions of Dollars, 2011				
Rank	Region	Country	GDP	Source
139	AFR	Congo, Republic	8,820	POP*GPC
140	DME	Bermuda	8,657	POP*GPC
141	AFR	Chad	8,653	POP*GPC
142	LAM	Bahamas	8,100	POP*GPC
143	DME	Malta	8,009	POP*GPC
144	AFR	Zimbabwe	7,975	POP*GPC
145	USR	Moldova	7,775	POP*GPC
146	CPA	Laos	7,223	POP*GPC
147	AFR	Benin	7,098	POP*GPC
148	SEA	French Polynesia	6,947	POP*GPC
149	LAM	Haiti	6,804	POP*GPC
150	USR	Tajikistan	6,682	POP*GPC
151	EEU	Kosovo	6,409	POP*GPC
152	CPA	Mongolia	6,387	POP*GPC
153	AFR	Rwanda	6,238	POP*GPC
154	DME	Jersey	6,220	POP*GPC
155	AFR	Niger	5,929	POP*GPC
156	DME	Isle of Man	5,668	POP*GPC
157	DME	Monaco	5,661	POP*GPC
158	AFR	Malawi	5,537	POP*GPC
159	DME	Liechtenstein	5,265	POP*GPC
160	LAM	Curacao	5,220	POP*GPC
161	LAM	Virgin Islands, U.S.	5,164	POP*GPC
162	LAM	Guiana, French	4,746	POP*GPC
163	MEA	West Bank	4,735	POP*GPC
164	USR	Kyrgyzstan	4,651	POP*GPC
165	EEU	Montenegro	4,427	POP*GPC
166	LAM	Barbados	4,400	POP*GPC
167	AFR	Guinea	4,395	POP*GPC
168	AFR	Swaziland	4,174	POP*GPC
169	LAM	Suriname	4,147	POP*GPC
170	SEA	Guam	4,139	POP*GPC
171	DME	Andorra	3,628	POP*GPC
172	AFR	Mauritania	3,380	POP*GPC
173	AFR	Togo	3,323	POP*GPC
174	SEA	Fiji	3,169	POP*GPC
175	LAM	Cayman Islands	3,143	POP*GPC
176	DME	Guernsey	3,113	POP*GPC
177	SEA	East Timor	3,061	POP*GPC
178	AFR	Sierra Leone	2,759	POP*GPC
179	LAM	Aruba	2,498	POP*GPC
180	AFR	Somalia	2,432	POP*GPC
181	AFR	Central African Rep.	2,376	POP*GPC
182	DME	Faroe Islands	2,356	POP*GPC
183	AFR	Lesotho	2,329	POP*GPC
184	AFR	Eritrea	2,328	POP*GPC
185	LAM	Guyana	2,215	POP*GPC

Table 2.3 GNI at Market Exchange Rates, Millions of Dollars, 2011				
Rank	Region	Country	GDP	Source
186	DME	Greenland	2,160	POP*GPC
187	AFR	Burundi	2,144	POP*GPC
188	MEA	Gaza Strip	1,949	POP*GPC
189	SAS	Maldives	1,859	POP*GPC
190	AFR	Cape Verde	1,763	POP*GPC
191	DME	San Marino	1,611	POP*GPC
192	AFR	Mayotte	1,605	POP*GPC
193	SAS	Bhutan	1,493	POP*GPC
194	AFR	Liberia	1,304	POP*GPC
195	AFR	Djibouti	1,300	POP*GPC
196	DME	Gibraltar	1,205	POP*GPC
197	LAM	Belize	1,195	POP*GPC
198	LAM	Virgin Islands, Brit.	1,176	POP*GPC
199	LAM	St. Lucia	1,139	POP*GPC
200	LAM	Antigua & Barbuda	1,091	POP*GPC
201	AFR	Seychelles	1,037	POP*GPC
202	AFR	Guinea-Bissau	964	POP*GPC
203	AFR	Gambia	888	POP*GPC
204	AFR	South Sudan	851	POP*GPC
205	LAM	Sint Maarten	821	POP*GPC
206	LAM	Grenada	794	POP*GPC
207	AFR	Western Sahara	706	POP*GPC
208	SEA	Vanuatu	685	POP*GPC
209	SEA	Northern Mariana Is.	678	POP*GPC
210	LAM	Saint Martin	669	POP*GPC
211	LAM	St. Kitts & Nevis	634	POP*GPC
212	LAM	St. Vincent	613	POP*GPC
213	SEA	Solomon Islands	594	POP*GPC
214	SEA	Samoa	581	POP*GPC
215	AFR	Comoros	581	POP*GPC
216	SEA	Samoa, American	539	POP*GPC
217	LAM	Dominica	510	POP*GPC
218	LAM	Turks & Caicos Is.	485	POP*GPC
219	SEA	Tonga	397	POP*GPC
220	SEA	Micronesia	292	POP*GPC
221	AFR	Sao Tome & Principe	228	POP*GPC
222	SEA	Marshall Islands	215	POP*GPC
223	SEA	Kiribati	205	POP*GPC
224	LAM	Anguilla	186	POP*GPC
225	DME	Falkland Islands	172	POP*GPC
226	SEA	Palau	134	POP*GPC
227	SEA	Cook Islands	110	POP*GPC
228	DME	St. Pierre & Miquelon	87	POP*GPC

Table 2.3 GNI at Market Exchange Rates, Millions of Dollars, 2011

Rank	Region	Country	GDP	Source
229	SEA	Tuvalu	55	POP*GPC
230	SEA	Nauru	52	POP*GPC
231	SEA	Wallis & Futuna	41	POP*GPC
232	AFR	St. Helena	28	POP*GPC
233	LAM	Montserrat	14	POP*GPC
234	SEA	Niue	10	POP*GPC
235	SEA	Tokelau	1	POP*GPC

Table 2.4 Armed Forces Personnel, Thousands, 2011				
Rank	Region	Country	Army	Source
1	CPA	China	2945.0	11(WB)
2	SAS	India	2647.2	11(WB)
3	DME	United States	1520.1	11(WB)
4	CPA	Korea, North	1379.0	11(WB)
5	USR	Russia	1364.0	11(WB)
6	SAS	Pakistan	946.0	11(WB)
7	MEA	Egypt	835.5	11(WB)
8	MEA	Iraq	802.4	11(WB)
9	LAM	Brazil	713.5	11(WB)
10	SEA	Indonesia	676.5	11(WB)
11	SEA	Korea, South	659.5	11(WB)
12	MEA	Turkey	612.8	11(WB)
13	MEA	Iran	563.0	11(WB)
14	CPA	Vietnam	522.0	11(WB)
15	CPA	Burma	513.3	11(WB)
16	SEA	Thailand	474.6	11(WB)
17	LAM	Colombia	440.2	11(WB)
18	DME	Italy	367.6	11(WB)
19	SAS	Afghanistan	340.4	11(WB)
20	DME	France	332.3	11(WB)
21	LAM	Mexico	329.8	11(WB)
22	MEA	Algeria	317.2	11(WB)
23	SEA	Taiwan	290.0	11(IISS)
24	AFR	Sudan	264.3	11(WB)
25	DME	Japan	260.1	11(WB)
26	MEA	Saudi Arabia	249.0	11(WB)
27	MEA	Morocco	245.8	11(WB)
28	SAS	Sri Lanka	223.1	11(WB)
29	SAS	Bangladesh	221.0	11(WB)
30	DME	Spain	215.7	11(WB)
31	USR	Ukraine	214.9	11(WB)
32	AFR	South Sudan	210.0	11(WB)
33	AFR	Eritrea	201.8	11(WB)
34	DME	Germany	196.0	11(WB)
35	LAM	Peru	192.0	11(WB)
36	CPA	Cambodia	191.3	11(WB)
37	DME	Israel	184.6	11(WB)
38	MEA	Syria	178.0	11(WB)
39	DME	United Kingdom	165.7	11(WB)
40	SEA	Philippines	165.5	11(WB)
41	AFR	Nigeria	162.0	11(WB)
42	USR	Belarus	158.0	11(WB)
43	SAS	Nepal	157.8	11(WB)
44	EEU	Romania	151.3	11(WB)
45	DME	Greece	148.4	11(WB)
46	SEA	Singapore	147.6	11(WB)

Table 2.4 Armed Forces Personnel, Thousands, 2011				
Rank	Region	Country	Army	Source
47	AFR	Ethiopia	138.0	11(WB)
48	MEA	Yemen	137.9	11(WB)
49	AFR	Congo, Dem. Republic	134.3	11(WB)
50	SEA	Malaysia	133.6	11(WB)
51	CPA	Laos	129.1	11(WB)
52	EEU	Poland	118.1	11(WB)
53	AFR	Angola	117.0	11(WB)
54	LAM	Venezuela	115.0	11(WB)
55	MEA	Jordan	110.5	11(WB)
56	LAM	Argentina	104.4	11(WB)
57	LAM	Chile	103.8	11(WB)
58	DME	Portugal	90.3	11(WB)
59	LAM	Bolivia	83.2	11(WB)
60	USR	Azerbaijan	82.0	11(WB)
61	MEA	Lebanon	80.0	11(WB)
62	AFR	South Africa	77.6	11(WB)
63	MEA	Libya	76.0	10(E)
64	LAM	Cuba	75.5	11(WB)
65	USR	Kazakhstan	70.5	11(WB)
66	USR	Uzbekistan	68.0	11(WB)
67	DME	Canada	65.7	11(WB)
68	LAM	Ecuador	59.0	11(WB)
69	DME	Australia	57.1	11(WB)
70	USR	Armenia	55.5	11(WB)
71	AFR	Burundi	51.1	11(WB)
72	MEA	United Arab Emirates	51.0	11(WB)
73	AFR	Zimbabwe	50.8	11(WB)
74	MEA	Tunisia	47.8	11(WB)
75	EEU	Bulgaria	47.3	11(WB)
76	MEA	Oman	47.0	11(WB)
77	AFR	Uganda	46.8	11(WB)
78	DME	Netherlands	43.3	11(WB)
79	LAM	Guatemala	42.3	11(WB)
80	LAM	Dominican Republic	39.5	11(WB)
81	EEU	Hungary	38.5	11(WB)
82	AFR	Rwanda	35.0	11(WB)
83	AFR	Chad	34.9	11(WB)
84	MEA	West Bank	34.6	11(WB)
85	DME	Belgium	34.1	11(WB)
86	USR	Georgia	32.4	11(WB)
87	LAM	El Salvador	32.3	11(WB)
88	AFR	Kenya	29.1	11(WB)
89	AFR	Tanzania	28.4	11(WB)
90	EEU	Serbia	28.2	11(WB)
91	EEU	Czech Republic	26.8	11(WB)

Table 2.4 Armed Forces Personnel, Thousands, 2011				
Rank	Region	Country	Army	Source
92.5	LAM	Paraguay	25.5	11(WB)
92.5	LAM	Uruguay	25.5	11(WB)
94	DME	Finland	25.0	11(WB)
95	DME	Norway	24.5	11(WB)
96	USR	Lithuania	23.4	11(WB)
97	DME	Austria	23.3	11(WB)
98.5	AFR	Cameroon	23.1	11(WB)
98.5	DME	Switzerland	23.1	11(WB)
100	MEA	Kuwait	22.6	11(WB)
101	USR	Turkmenistan	22.0	11(WB)
102.5	EEU	Croatia	21.6	11(WB)
102.5	AFR	Madagascar	21.6	11(WB)
104	MEA	Gaza Strip	21.4	11(WB)
105	DME	Sweden	21.3	11(WB)
106	AFR	Mauritania	20.9	11(WB)
107	USR	Kyrgyzstan	20.4	11(WB)
108	LAM	Honduras	20.0	11(WB)
109	MEA	Bahrain	19.5	11(WB)
110	AFR	Senegal	18.6	11(WB)
111	CPA	Mongolia	17.2	11(WB)
112	AFR	Ivory Coast	17.0	11(IISS)
113.5	DME	Denmark	16.5	11(WB)
113.5	AFR	Zambia	16.5	11(WB)
115	USR	Tajikistan	16.3	11(WB)
116	EEU	Slovakia	15.9	11(WB)
117	AFR	Ghana	15.5	11(WB)
118	AFR	Namibia	15.2	11(WB)
119	EEU	Albania	14.8	11(WB)
120	AFR	Djibouti	13.0	11(WB)
121	MEA	Cyprus	12.8	11(WB)
122	AFR	Guinea	12.3	11(WB)
123.5	AFR	Mali	12.2	11(WB)
123.5	EEU	Montenegro	12.2	11(WB)
125	EEU	Slovenia	12.1	11(WB)
127	AFR	Congo, Republic	12.0	11(WB)
127	LAM	Nicaragua	12.0	11(WB)
127	LAM	Panama	12.0	11(WB)
129	MEA	Qatar	11.8	11(WB)
130	AFR	Burkina Faso	11.5	11(WB)
131	AFR	Mozambique	11.2	11(WB)
132	AFR	Niger	10.7	11(WB)
133	EEU	Bosnia	10.6	11(WB)
134.5	AFR	Botswana	10.5	11(WB)
134.5	AFR	Sierra Leone	10.5	11(WB)
136	LAM	Costa Rica	9.8	11(WB)
137	AFR	Benin	9.5	11(WB)
138.5	SEA	Brunei	9.3	11(WB)

Table 2.4 Armed Forces Personnel, Thousands, 2011				
Rank	Region	Country	Army	Source
138.5	AFR	Togo	9.3	11(WB)
140	DME	Ireland	8.9	11(WB)
141	DME	New Zealand	8.6	11(WB)
142.5	SAS	Bhutan	8.0	09(E)
142.5	EEU	Macedonia	8.0	11(WB)
144	USR	Moldova	7.8	11(WB)
145	AFR	Malawi	6.8	11(WB)
146	AFR	Gabon	6.7	11(WB)
147	AFR	Guinea-Bissau	6.5	11(WB)
148	USR	Estonia	5.8	11(WB)
149	USR	Latvia	5.4	11(WB)
150	LAM	Trinidad & Tobago	4.1	11(WB)
151	SEA	Fiji	3.5	11(WB)
152.5	AFR	Central African Rep.	3.2	11(WB)
152.5	AFR	Somalia	3.2	11(WB)
154	SEA	Papua New Guinea	3.1	11(WB)
155	AFR	Swaziland	3.0	06(E)
156	LAM	Jamaica	2.8	11(WB)
157	AFR	Mauritius	2.5	11(WB)
158.5	AFR	Liberia	2.1	11(WB)
158.5	DME	Malta	2.1	11(WB)
160.5	AFR	Lesotho	2.0	11(WB)
160.5	SAS	Maldives	2.0	06(E)
162	LAM	Suriname	1.8	11(WB)
163	DME	Luxembourg	1.5	11(WB)
164.5	SEA	East Timor	1.3	11(WB)
164.5	AFR	Equatorial Guinea	1.3	11(WB)
166	AFR	Cape Verde	1.2	11(WB)
168	LAM	Belize	1.1	11(WB)
168	AFR	Comoros	1.1	09(E)
168	LAM	Guyana	1.1	11(WB)
170.5	LAM	Bahamas	0.9	11(WB)
170.5	AFR	Seychelles	0.9	11(WB)
172	AFR	Gambia	0.8	11(WB)
173	LAM	Barbados	0.6	11(WB)
174.5	AFR	Sao Tome & Principe	0.5	05(E)
174.5	SEA	Tonga	0.5	09(E)
176.5	LAM	Antigua & Barbuda	0.2	11(WB)
176.5	DME	Iceland	0.2	11(WB)
178	LAM	Haiti	0.1	11(WB)
207	DME	Andorra	0.0	11(CIA)
207	LAM	Anguilla	0.0	11(CIA)

Table 2.4 Armed Forces Personnel, Thousands, 2011				
Rank	Region	Country	Army	Source
207	LAM	Aruba	0.0	11(CIA)
207	DME	Bermuda	0.0	11(CIA)
207	LAM	Cayman Islands	0.0	11(CIA)
207	SEA	Cook Islands	0.0	11(CIA)
207	LAM	Curacao	0.0	11(CIA)
207	LAM	Dominica	0.0	11(CIA)
207	DME	Falkland Islands	0.0	11(CIA)
207	DME	Faroe Islands	0.0	11(CIA)
207	SEA	French Polynesia	0.0	11(CIA)
207	DME	Gibraltar	0.0	11(CIA)
207	DME	Greenland	0.0	11(CIA)
207	LAM	Grenada	0.0	11(CIA)
207	LAM	Guadeloupe	0.0	11(CIA)
207	SEA	Guam	0.0	11(CIA)
207	DME	Guernsey	0.0	11(CIA)
207	LAM	Guiana, French	0.0	11(CIA)
207	SEA	Hong Kong	0.0	11(CIA)
207	DME	Isle of Man	0.0	11(CIA)
207	DME	Jersey	0.0	11(CIA)
207	SEA	Kiribati	0.0	11(CIA)
207	EEU	Kosovo	0.0	11(CIA)
207	DME	Liechtenstein	0.0	11(CIA)
207	SEA	Macao	0.0	11(CIA)
207	SEA	Marshall Islands	0.0	11(CIA)
207	LAM	Martinique	0.0	11(CIA)
207	AFR	Mayotte	0.0	11(CIA)
207	SEA	Micronesia	0.0	11(CIA)
207	DME	Monaco	0.0	11(CIA)
207	LAM	Montserrat	0.0	11(CIA)
207	SEA	Nauru	0.0	11(CIA)
207	SEA	New Caledonia	0.0	11(CIA)
207	SEA	Niue	0.0	11(CIA)
207	SEA	Northern Mariana Is.	0.0	11(CIA)
207	SEA	Palau	0.0	11(CIA)
207	LAM	Puerto Rico	0.0	11(CIA)
207	AFR	Reunion	0.0	11(CIA)
207	LAM	Saint Martin	0.0	11(CIA)
207	SEA	Samoa	0.0	11(CIA)
207	SEA	Samoa, American	0.0	11(CIA)
207	DME	San Marino	0.0	11(CIA)
207	LAM	Sint Maarten	0.0	11(CIA)
207	SEA	Solomon Islands	0.0	11(CIA)

Table 2.4 Armed Forces Personnel, Thousands, 2011				
Rank	Region	Country	Army	Source
207	AFR	St. Helena	0.0	11(CIA)
207	LAM	St. Kitts & Nevis	0.0	11(CIA)
207	LAM	St. Lucia	0.0	11(CIA)
207	DME	St. Pierre & Miquelon	0.0	11(CIA)
207	LAM	St. Vincent	0.0	11(CIA)
207	SEA	Tokelau	0.0	11(CIA)
207	LAM	Turks & Caicos Is.	0.0	11(CIA)
207	SEA	Tuvalu	0.0	11(CIA)
207	SEA	Vanuatu	0.0	11(CIA)
207	LAM	Virgin Islands, Brit.	0.0	11(CIA)
207	LAM	Virgin Islands, U.S.	0.0	11(CIA)
207	SEA	Wallis & Futuna	0.0	11(CIA)
207	AFR	Western Sahara	0.0	11(CIA)

Table 2.5 Military Expenditures as Percentage of GDP, 2011				
Rank	Region	Country	MILGDP	Source
1	CPA	Korea, North	25.000	02(IISS)
2	MEA	Saudi Arabia	8.413	11(WB)
3	DME	Israel	6.768	11(WB)
4.5	MEA	Gaza Strip	6.003	11(WB)
4.5	MEA	West Bank	6.003	11(WB)
6	MEA	Oman	5.978	11(WB)
7	MEA	Iran	5.460	11(IISS)
8	MEA	Iraq	5.066	11(WB)
9	USR	Azerbaijan	4.897	11(WB)
10	DME	United States	4.746	11(WB)
11	MEA	Jordan	4.742	11(WB)
12	SAS	Afghanistan	4.706	11(WB)
13	CPA	Burma	4.690	11(IISS)
14	MEA	Algeria	4.585	11(WB)
15	MEA	Lebanon	4.374	11(WB)
16	MEA	Yemen	4.040	11(IISS)
17	USR	Armenia	4.034	11(WB)
18	AFR	Somalia	4.000	02(IISS)
19	SAS	Maldives	3.960	09(IISS)
20	MEA	Syria	3.946	10(WB)
21	USR	Russia	3.869	11(WB)
22	AFR	Mauritania	3.790	09(WB)
23	MEA	Bahrain	3.710	11(IISS)
24	AFR	Eritrea	3.690	10(IISS)
25	USR	Uzbekistan	3.650	10(IISS)
26	SEA	Singapore	3.647	11(WB)
27	MEA	Libya	3.620	10(IISS)
28	LAM	Ecuador	3.500	11(WB)
29	AFR	Angola	3.497	11(WB)
30	AFR	Namibia	3.411	11(WB)
31	LAM	Cuba	3.345	09(WB)
32	MEA	Morocco	3.335	11(WB)
33	LAM	Colombia	3.280	11(WB)
34	LAM	Chile	3.235	11(WB)
35	MEA	Kuwait	3.195	11(WB)
36	AFR	Swaziland	3.014	11(WB)
37	SAS	Pakistan	3.011	11(WB)
38	USR	Georgia	2.963	11(WB)
39	AFR	South Sudan	2.949	11(WB)
40	DME	Greece	2.808	11(WB)
41	SEA	Korea, South	2.757	11(WB)
42	MEA	United Arab Emirates	2.730	11(IISS)
43	AFR	Burundi	2.680	11(IISS)
44	SAS	Sri Lanka	2.629	11(WB)
45	AFR	Central African Rep.	2.597	10(WB)

Table 2.5 Military Expenditures as Percentage of GDP, 2011				
Rank	Region	Country	MILGDP	Source
46	SEA	East Timor	2.590	11(WB)
47	DME	United Kingdom	2.580	11(WB)
48	SAS	India	2.545	11(WB)
49	SEA	Brunei	2.532	11(WB)
50	USR	Ukraine	2.468	11(WB)
51	AFR	Lesotho	2.350	11(WB)
52	MEA	Turkey	2.306	11(WB)
53	AFR	Chad	2.283	11(WB)
54	USR	Tajikistan	2.250	11(IISS)
55	DME	France	2.249	11(WB)
56	CPA	Vietnam	2.174	11(WB)
57	MEA	Cyprus	2.168	11(WB)
58	AFR	Botswana	2.140	11(WB)
59.5	AFR	Guinea-Bissau	2.080	11(IISS)
59.5	SEA	Taiwan	2.080	11(IISS)
61	EEU	Serbia	2.071	11(WB)
62	MEA	Qatar	1.990	11(IISS)
63	DME	Portugal	1.962	11(WB)
64	CPA	China	1.952	11(WB)
65	EEU	Montenegro	1.951	11(WB)
66	LAM	Uruguay	1.931	11(WB)
67	EEU	Poland	1.886	11(WB)
68	MEA	Egypt	1.862	11(WB)
69	DME	Australia	1.852	11(WB)
70	AFR	Sudan	1.820	11(IISS)
71	AFR	Mali	1.795	11(WB)
72	USR	Kyrgyzstan	1.750	11(IISS)
73	EEU	Croatia	1.746	11(WB)
74	LAM	Trinidad & Tobago	1.680	11(IISS)
75	USR	Estonia	1.668	11(WB)
76	AFR	Uganda	1.634	11(WB)
77	AFR	Togo	1.630	11(WB)
78	LAM	Panama	1.610	11(IISS)
79	DME	Norway	1.595	11(WB)
80	SEA	Thailand	1.594	11(WB)
81	SEA	Malaysia	1.593	11(WB)
82	AFR	Zambia	1.592	11(WB)
83	AFR	Gabon	1.590	11(IISS)
84	AFR	Zimbabwe	1.584	11(WB)
85	DME	Italy	1.568	11(WB)
86	AFR	Kenya	1.535	11(WB)
87	AFR	Congo, Dem. Republic	1.525	11(WB)
88	EEU	Albania	1.519	11(WB)
89	DME	Finland	1.508	11(WB)
90	CPA	Cambodia	1.500	11(WB)
91	AFR	Ivory Coast	1.488	11(WB)
92	SEA	Tonga	1.480	07(WB)

Table 2.5 Military Expenditures as Percentage of GDP, 2011				
Rank	Region	Country	MILGDP	Source
93	EEU	Bulgaria	1.477	11(WB)
94	LAM	Bolivia	1.468	11(WB)
95	DME	Denmark	1.456	11(WB)
96	AFR	Senegal	1.450	11(IISS)
97	EEU	Slovenia	1.442	11(WB)
98	LAM	Brazil	1.430	11(WB)
99	DME	Canada	1.425	11(WB)
100	SAS	Nepal	1.409	11(WB)
101	DME	Netherlands	1.405	11(WB)
102	AFR	Cameroon	1.377	11(WB)
103	EEU	Bosnia	1.360	11(WB)
104	AFR	Burkina Faso	1.339	11(WB)
105	SAS	Bangladesh	1.335	11(WB)
106	MEA	Tunisia	1.322	11(WB)
107	LAM	Suriname	1.310	11(IISS)
108	DME	Germany	1.295	11(WB)
109	AFR	Liberia	1.290	11(IISS)
110	EEU	Macedonia	1.269	11(WB)
111	DME	Sweden	1.263	11(WB)
112	AFR	South Africa	1.252	11(WB)
113	AFR	Rwanda	1.212	11(WB)
114	AFR	Sao Tome & Principe	1.200	07(E)
115	LAM	Peru	1.187	11(WB)
116	LAM	Guyana	1.161	11(WB)
117	EEU	Czech Republic	1.142	11(WB)
118	EEU	Romania	1.130	11(WB)
119	DME	New Zealand	1.119	11(WB)
120	AFR	Congo, Republic	1.113	10(WB)
121	EEU	Slovakia	1.101	11(WB)
122	DME	Belgium	1.086	11(WB)
123.5	USR	Belarus	1.085	11(WB)
123.5	LAM	Belize	1.085	11(WB)
125	AFR	Ethiopia	1.084	11(WB)
126	SEA	Philippines	1.075	11(WB)
127	AFR	Tanzania	1.071	11(WB)
128	LAM	Honduras	1.062	11(WB)
129	LAM	Paraguay	1.057	11(WB)
130	USR	Latvia	1.045	11(WB)
131	AFR	Djibouti	1.040	10(IISS)
132	USR	Lithuania	1.038	11(WB)
133	AFR	Guinea	1.030	10(IISS)
134	DME	Spain	1.025	11(WB)
135	DME	Japan	1.021	11(WB)
136	AFR	Benin	1.010	11(IISS)
137.5	SAS	Bhutan	1.000	05(E)
137.5	USR	Turkmenistan	1.000	10(IISS)
139	EEU	Hungary	0.989	11(WB)

Table 2.5 Military Expenditures as Percentage of GDP, 2011

Rank	Region	Country	MILGDP	Source
140	AFR	Nigeria	0.977	11(WB)
141	LAM	El Salvador	0.963	11(WB)
142	LAM	Jamaica	0.960	11(IISS)
143	USR	Kazakhstan	0.954	11(WB)
144	CPA	Mongolia	0.929	11(WB)
145	AFR	Sierra Leone	0.894	11(WB)
146	AFR	Seychelles	0.884	11(WB)
147	DME	Austria	0.857	11(WB)
148	DME	Switzerland	0.823	11(WB)
149	AFR	Niger	0.820	11(IISS)
150	AFR	Malawi	0.760	11(IISS)
151	LAM	Venezuela	0.754	11(WB)
152	LAM	Argentina	0.735	11(WB)
153	AFR	Madagascar	0.727	11(WB)
154	SEA	Fiji	0.720	11(IISS)
155	DME	Malta	0.713	11(WB)
156	LAM	Barbados	0.700	11(IISS)
157	SEA	Indonesia	0.673	11(WB)
158.5	LAM	Costa Rica	0.660	11(IISS)
158.5	AFR	Gambia	0.660	11(IISS)
160	LAM	Bahamas	0.650	11(IISS)
161	AFR	Mozambique	0.640	10(IISS)
162	LAM	Dominican Republic	0.614	11(WB)
163	DME	Ireland	0.598	11(WB)
164	LAM	Nicaragua	0.587	11(WB)
165	LAM	Antigua & Barbuda	0.530	11(IISS)
166	LAM	Mexico	0.521	11(WB)
167	AFR	Cape Verde	0.509	11(WB)
168	SEA	Papua New Guinea	0.473	11(WB)
169	DME	Luxembourg	0.470	11(IISS)
170	LAM	Guatemala	0.426	11(WB)
171	USR	Moldova	0.298	11(WB)
172	AFR	Ghana	0.251	11(WB)
173	CPA	Laos	0.230	11(IISS)
174	AFR	Comoros	0.200	00(IISS)
175	AFR	Mauritius	0.090	11(WB)
176	DME	Iceland	0.082	09(WB)
177	AFR	Equatorial Guinea	0.040	11(IISS)
178	LAM	Haiti	0.020	11(IISS)
207	DME	Andorra	0.000	11(CIA)
207	LAM	Anguilla	0.000	11(CIA)
207	LAM	Aruba	0.000	11(CIA)
207	DME	Bermuda	0.000	11(CIA)
207	LAM	Cayman Islands	0.000	11(CIA)
207	SEA	Cook Islands	0.000	11(CIA)
207	LAM	Curacao	0.000	11(CIA)
207	LAM	Dominica	0.000	11(CIA)

Table 2.5 Military Expenditures as Percentage of GDP, 2011				
Rank	Region	Country	MILGDP	Source
207	DME	Falkland Islands	0.000	11(CIA)
207	DME	Faroe Islands	0.000	11(CIA)
207	SEA	French Polynesia	0.000	11(CIA)
207	DME	Gibraltar	0.000	11(CIA)
207	DME	Greenland	0.000	11(CIA)
207	LAM	Grenada	0.000	11(CIA)
207	LAM	Guadeloupe	0.000	11(CIA)
207	SEA	Guam	0.000	11(CIA)
207	DME	Guernsey	0.000	11(CIA)
207	LAM	Guiana, French	0.000	11(CIA)
207	SEA	Hong Kong	0.000	11(CIA)
207	DME	Isle of Man	0.000	11(CIA)
207	DME	Jersey	0.000	11(CIA)
207	SEA	Kiribati	0.000	11(CIA)
207	EEU	Kosovo	0.000	11(CIA)
207	DME	Liechtenstein	0.000	11(CIA)
207	SEA	Macao	0.000	11(CIA)
207	SEA	Marshall Islands	0.000	11(CIA)
207	LAM	Martinique	0.000	11(CIA)
207	AFR	Mayotte	0.000	11(CIA)
207	SEA	Micronesia	0.000	11(CIA)
207	DME	Monaco	0.000	11(CIA)
207	LAM	Montserrat	0.000	11(CIA)
207	SEA	Nauru	0.000	11(CIA)
207	SEA	New Caledonia	0.000	11(CIA)
207	SEA	Niue	0.000	11(CIA)
207	SEA	Northern Mariana Is.	0.000	11(CIA)
207	SEA	Palau	0.000	11(CIA)
207	LAM	Puerto Rico	0.000	11(CIA)
207	AFR	Reunion	0.000	11(CIA)
207	LAM	Saint Martin	0.000	11(CIA)
207	SEA	Samoa	0.000	11(CIA)
207	SEA	Samoa, American	0.000	11(CIA)
207	DME	San Marino	0.000	11(CIA)
207	LAM	Sint Maarten	0.000	11(CIA)
207	SEA	Solomon Islands	0.000	11(CIA)
207	AFR	St. Helena	0.000	11(CIA)
207	LAM	St. Kitts & Nevis	0.000	11(CIA)
207	LAM	St. Lucia	0.000	11(CIA)
207	DME	St. Pierre & Miquelon	0.000	11(CIA)
207	LAM	St. Vincent	0.000	11(CIA)
207	SEA	Tokelau	0.000	11(CIA)
207	LAM	Turks & Caicos Is.	0.000	11(CIA)
207	SEA	Tuvalu	0.000	11(CIA)
207	SEA	Vanuatu	0.000	11(CIA)
207	LAM	Virgin Islands, Brit.	0.000	11(CIA)

Table 2.5 Military Expenditures as Percentage of GDP, 2011

Rank	Region	Country	MILGDP	Source
207	LAM	Virgin Islands, U.S.	0.000	11(CIA)
207	SEA	Wallis & Futuna	0.000	11(CIA)
207	AFR	Western Sahara	0.000	11(CIA)

Table 2.6 Foreign Military Aid, Millions of Dollars, 2011				
Rank	Region	Country	MILAID	Source
1	SAS	Afghanistan	10265.4	11(USAID)
2	DME	Israel	2995.1	11(USAID)
3	MEA	Egypt	1298.7	11(USAID)
4	MEA	Iraq	963.7	11(USAID)
5	SAS	Pakistan	673.2	11(USAID)
6	MEA	Jordan	319.2	11(USAID)
7	LAM	Colombia	160.0	11(USAID)
8	LAM	Mexico	93.7	11(USAID)
9	MEA	Lebanon	79.6	11(USAID)
10	AFR	Somalia	75.3	11(USAID)
11	AFR	South Sudan	42.6	11(USAID)
12	USR	Russia	41.6	11(USAID)
13	EEU	Poland	36.0	11(USAID)
14	SEA	Philippines	26.3	11(USAID)
15	SEA	Indonesia	23.3	11(USAID)
16	AFR	Congo, Dem. Republic	22.0	11(USAID)
17	MEA	Yemen	21.1	11(USAID)
18	LAM	Guatemala	20.0	11(USAID)
19	MEA	Tunisia	19.1	11(USAID)
20	USR	Georgia	18.0	11(USAID)
21	USR	Kyrgyzstan	16.2	11(USAID)
22	MEA	Bahrain	15.9	11(USAID)
23	EEU	Romania	15.4	11(USAID)
24	MEA	Morocco	15.1	11(USAID)
25	MEA	Oman	14.6	11(USAID)
26	LAM	Belize	13.5	11(USAID)
27	AFR	Liberia	13.2	11(USAID)
28	LAM	Peru	13.0	11(USAID)
29	EEU	Bulgaria	11.3	11(USAID)
30	USR	Ukraine	11.2	11(USAID)
31	AFR	Nigeria	10.9	11(USAID)
32	LAM	Panama	10.8	11(USAID)
33	LAM	Honduras	10.3	11(USAID)
34	LAM	El Salvador	10.2	11(USAID)
35	LAM	Dominican Republic	8.5	11(USAID)
36	USR	Tajikistan	8.3	11(USAID)
37	EEU	Czech Republic	8.0	11(USAID)
38	LAM	Ecuador	7.2	11(USAID)
39.5	EEU	Kosovo	5.7	11(USAID)
39.5	EEU	Macedonia	5.7	11(USAID)
41	EEU	Bosnia	5.5	11(USAID)
42.5	LAM	Bahamas	5.2	11(USAID)
42.5	USR	Uzbekistan	5.2	11(USAID)
44.5	EEU	Albania	5.1	11(USAID)
44.5	USR	Kazakhstan	5.1	11(USAID)

Table 2.6 Foreign Military Aid, Millions of Dollars, 2011				
Rank	Region	Country	MILAID	Source
46	MEA	Turkey	4.8	11(USAID)
47.5	AFR	Senegal	4.7	11(USAID)
47.5	SEA	Thailand	4.7	11(USAID)
49	EEU	Croatia	4.4	11(USAID)
50.5	USR	Lithuania	4.1	11(USAID)
50.5	LAM	Nicaragua	4.1	11(USAID)
53	SAS	Bangladesh	4.0	11(USAID)
53	LAM	Jamaica	4.0	11(USAID)
53	CPA	Mongolia	4.0	11(USAID)
55.5	USR	Azerbaijan	3.9	11(USAID)
55.5	USR	Latvia	3.9	11(USAID)
57	USR	Estonia	3.8	11(USAID)
58	LAM	Costa Rica	3.5	11(USAID)
59.5	USR	Armenia	3.4	11(USAID)
59.5	CPA	Vietnam	3.4	11(USAID)
61	USR	Turkmenistan	3.3	11(USAID)
62	SEA	Malaysia	2.9	11(USAID)
64	AFR	Ghana	2.8	11(USAID)
64	EEU	Serbia	2.8	11(USAID)
64	DME	United Kingdom	2.8	11(USAID)
66.5	CPA	Cambodia	2.7	11(USAID)
66.5	AFR	Djibouti	2.7	11(USAID)
68.5	AFR	Kenya	2.6	11(USAID)
68.5	LAM	Suriname	2.6	11(USAID)
70	USR	Moldova	2.4	11(USAID)
71	EEU	Slovakia	2.3	11(USAID)
72	EEU	Hungary	2.1	11(USAID)
73	SAS	Sri Lanka	2.0	11(USAID)
75	LAM	Haiti	1.9	11(USAID)
75	EEU	Montenegro	1.9	11(USAID)
75	SAS	Nepal	1.9	11(USAID)
77	AFR	Cape Verde	1.8	11(USAID)
78.5	AFR	Mozambique	1.7	11(USAID)
78.5	AFR	South Africa	1.7	11(USAID)
81	LAM	Brazil	1.6	11(USAID)
81	SAS	India	1.6	11(USAID)
81	AFR	Sierra Leone	1.6	11(USAID)
83	EEU	Slovenia	1.5	11(USAID)
85	LAM	Chile	1.4	11(USAID)
85	DME	Germany	1.4	11(USAID)
85	AFR	Mauritania	1.4	11(USAID)
87	LAM	Paraguay	1.2	11(USAID)
89	AFR	Botswana	1.1	11(USAID)
89	AFR	Cameroon	1.1	11(USAID)
89	LAM	Uruguay	1.1	11(USAID)
91.5	MEA	Algeria	1.0	11(USAID)
91.5	AFR	Tanzania	1.0	11(USAID)
94.5	DME	Italy	0.9	11(USAID)

Table 2.6 Foreign Military Aid, Millions of Dollars, 2011				
Rank	Region	Country	MILAID	Source
94.5	AFR	Rwanda	0.9	11(USAID)
94.5	LAM	Trinidad & Tobago	0.9	11(USAID)
94.5	AFR	Uganda	0.9	11(USAID)
97.5	AFR	Chad	0.8	11(USAID)
97.5	LAM	Guyana	0.8	11(USAID)
100	LAM	Argentina	0.7	11(USAID)
100	AFR	Ethiopia	0.7	11(USAID)
100	AFR	Togo	0.7	11(USAID)
103.5	AFR	Benin	0.6	11(USAID)
103.5	AFR	Mali	0.6	11(USAID)
103.5	DME	Malta	0.6	11(USAID)
103.5	AFR	Seychelles	0.6	11(USAID)
107	LAM	Barbados	0.5	11(USAID)
107	AFR	Gabon	0.5	11(USAID)
107	AFR	Mauritius	0.5	11(USAID)
113	AFR	Angola	0.4	11(USAID)
113	LAM	Antigua & Barbuda	0.4	11(USAID)
113	AFR	Burundi	0.4	11(USAID)
113	AFR	Gambia	0.4	11(USAID)
113	LAM	Grenada	0.4	11(USAID)
113	AFR	Malawi	0.4	11(USAID)
113	LAM	St. Kitts & Nevis	0.4	11(USAID)
113	LAM	St. Lucia	0.4	11(USAID)
113	AFR	Zambia	0.4	11(USAID)
122	LAM	Bolivia	0.3	11(USAID)
122	AFR	Burkina Faso	0.3	11(USAID)
122	LAM	Dominica	0.3	11(USAID)
122	SEA	East Timor	0.3	11(USAID)
122	SAS	Maldives	0.3	11(USAID)
122	AFR	Sao Tome & Principe	0.3	11(USAID)
122	LAM	St. Vincent	0.3	11(USAID)
122	SEA	Tonga	0.3	11(USAID)
122	LAM	Venezuela	0.3	11(USAID)
130	CPA	China	0.2	11(USAID)
130	AFR	Comoros	0.2	11(USAID)
130	CPA	Laos	0.2	11(USAID)
130	AFR	Lesotho	0.2	11(USAID)
130	AFR	Namibia	0.2	11(USAID)
130	SEA	Papua New Guinea	0.2	11(USAID)
130	AFR	Swaziland	0.2	11(USAID)
137.5	AFR	Congo, Republic	0.1	11(USAID)
137.5	DME	Greece	0.1	11(USAID)
137.5	AFR	Ivory Coast	0.1	11(USAID)
137.5	SEA	Micronesia	0.1	11(USAID)

TABLE 2.6 FOREIGN MILITARY AID, MILLIONS OF DOLLARS, 2011

Rank	Region	Country	MILAID	Source
137.5	AFR	Niger	0.1	11(USAID)
137.5	DME	Portugal	0.1	11(USAID)
137.5	SEA	Samoa	0.1	11(USAID)
137.5	SEA	Vanuatu	0.1	11(USAID)
188.5	DME	Andorra	0.0	11(USAID)
188.5	LAM	Anguilla	0.0	11(USAID)
188.5	LAM	Aruba	0.0	11(USAID)
188.5	DME	Australia	0.0	11(USAID)
188.5	DME	Austria	0.0	11(USAID)
188.5	USR	Belarus	0.0	11(USAID)
188.5	DME	Belgium	0.0	11(USAID)
188.5	DME	Bermuda	0.0	11(USAID)
188.5	SAS	Bhutan	0.0	11(USAID)
188.5	SEA	Brunei	0.0	11(USAID)
188.5	CPA	Burma	0.0	11(USAID)
188.5	DME	Canada	0.0	11(USAID)
188.5	LAM	Cayman Islands	0.0	11(USAID)
188.5	AFR	Central African Rep.	0.0	11(USAID)
188.5	SEA	Cook Islands	0.0	11(USAID)
188.5	LAM	Cuba	0.0	11(USAID)
188.5	LAM	Curacao	0.0	11(USAID)
188.5	MEA	Cyprus	0.0	11(USAID)
188.5	DME	Denmark	0.0	11(USAID)
188.5	AFR	Equatorial Guinea	0.0	11(USAID)
188.5	AFR	Eritrea	0.0	11(USAID)
188.5	DME	Falkland Islands	0.0	11(USAID)
188.5	DME	Faroe Islands	0.0	11(USAID)
188.5	SEA	Fiji	0.0	11(USAID)
188.5	DME	Finland	0.0	11(USAID)
188.5	DME	France	0.0	11(USAID)
188.5	SEA	French Polynesia	0.0	11(USAID)
188.5	MEA	Gaza Strip	0.0	11(USAID)
188.5	DME	Gibraltar	0.0	11(USAID)
188.5	DME	Greenland	0.0	11(USAID)
188.5	LAM	Guadeloupe	0.0	11(USAID)
188.5	SEA	Guam	0.0	11(USAID)
188.5	DME	Guernsey	0.0	11(USAID)
188.5	LAM	Guiana, French	0.0	11(USAID)
188.5	AFR	Guinea	0.0	11(USAID)
188.5	AFR	Guinea-Bissau	0.0	11(USAID)
188.5	SEA	Hong Kong	0.0	11(USAID)
188.5	DME	Iceland	0.0	11(USAID)
188.5	MEA	Iran	0.0	11(USAID)
188.5	DME	Ireland	0.0	11(USAID)
188.5	DME	Isle of Man	0.0	11(USAID)
188.5	DME	Japan	0.0	11(USAID)

Rank	Region	Country	MILAID	Source
188.5	DME	Jersey	0.0	11(USAID)
188.5	SEA	Kiribati	0.0	11(USAID)
188.5	CPA	Korea, North	0.0	11(USAID)
188.5	SEA	Korea, South	0.0	11(USAID)
188.5	MEA	Kuwait	0.0	11(USAID)
188.5	MEA	Libya	0.0	11(USAID)
188.5	DME	Liechtenstein	0.0	11(USAID)
188.5	DME	Luxembourg	0.0	11(USAID)
188.5	SEA	Macao	0.0	11(USAID)
188.5	AFR	Madagascar	0.0	11(USAID)
188.5	SEA	Marshall Islands	0.0	11(USAID)
188.5	LAM	Martinique	0.0	11(USAID)
188.5	AFR	Mayotte	0.0	11(USAID)
188.5	DME	Monaco	0.0	11(USAID)
188.5	LAM	Montserrat	0.0	11(USAID)
188.5	SEA	Nauru	0.0	11(USAID)
188.5	DME	Netherlands	0.0	11(USAID)
188.5	SEA	New Caledonia	0.0	11(USAID)
188.5	DME	New Zealand	0.0	11(USAID)
188.5	SEA	Niue	0.0	11(USAID)
188.5	SEA	Northern Mariana Is.	0.0	11(USAID)
188.5	DME	Norway	0.0	11(USAID)
188.5	SEA	Palau	0.0	11(USAID)
188.5	LAM	Puerto Rico	0.0	11(USAID)
188.5	MEA	Qatar	0.0	11(USAID)
188.5	AFR	Reunion	0.0	11(USAID)
188.5	LAM	Saint Martin	0.0	11(USAID)
188.5	SEA	Samoa, American	0.0	11(USAID)
188.5	DME	San Marino	0.0	11(USAID)
188.5	MEA	Saudi Arabia	0.0	11(USAID)
188.5	SEA	Singapore	0.0	11(USAID)
188.5	LAM	Sint Maarten	0.0	11(USAID)
188.5	SEA	Solomon Islands	0.0	11(USAID)
188.5	DME	Spain	0.0	11(USAID)
188.5	AFR	St. Helena	0.0	11(USAID)
188.5	DME	St. Pierre & Miquelon	0.0	11(USAID)
188.5	AFR	Sudan	0.0	11(USAID)
188.5	DME	Sweden	0.0	11(USAID)
188.5	DME	Switzerland	0.0	11(USAID)
188.5	MEA	Syria	0.0	11(USAID)
188.5	SEA	Taiwan	0.0	11(USAID)
188.5	SEA	Tokelau	0.0	11(USAID)
188.5	LAM	Turks & Caicos Is.	0.0	11(USAID)
188.5	SEA	Tuvalu	0.0	11(USAID)

Table 2.6 Foreign Military Aid, Millions of Dollars, 2011

Table 2.6 Foreign Military Aid, Millions of Dollars, 2011				
Rank	Region	Country	MILAID	Source
188.5	MEA	United Arab Emirates	0.0	11(USAID)
188.5	DME	United States	0.0	11(USAID)
188.5	LAM	Virgin Islands, Brit.	0.0	11(USAID)
188.5	LAM	Virgin Islands, U.S.	0.0	11(USAID)
188.5	SEA	Wallis & Futuna	0.0	11(USAID)
188.5	MEA	West Bank	0.0	11(USAID)
188.5	AFR	Western Sahara	0.0	11(USAID)
188.5	AFR	Zimbabwe	0.0	11(USAID)

Table 2.7 Military Expenditures at Purchasing Power Parities Plus Foreign Military Aid, Millions of Dollars, 2011				
Rank	Region	Country	MILXPP	Source
1	DME	United States	715,586	GDPPPP*MILGDP+MILAID
2	CPA	China	220,090	GDPPPP*MILGDP+MILAID
3	USR	Russia	121,075	GDPPPP*MILGDP+MILAID
4	SAS	India	113,027	GDPPPP*MILGDP+MILAID
5	MEA	Saudi Arabia	58,335	GDPPPP*MILGDP+MILAID
6	DME	United Kingdom	57,565	GDPPPP*MILGDP+MILAID
7	DME	France	50,161	GDPPPP*MILGDP+MILAID
8	MEA	Iran	50,143	GDPPPP*MILGDP+MILAID
9	DME	Japan	43,978	GDPPPP*MILGDP+MILAID
10	DME	Germany	41,697	GDPPPP*MILGDP+MILAID
11	SEA	Korea, South	40,102	GDPPPP*MILGDP+MILAID
12	LAM	Brazil	32,096	GDPPPP*MILGDP+MILAID
13	DME	Italy	31,133	GDPPPP*MILGDP+MILAID
14	MEA	Turkey	29,323	GDPPPP*MILGDP+MILAID
15	DME	Canada	19,841	GDPPPP*MILGDP+MILAID
16	SEA	Taiwan	18,281	GDPPPP*MILGDP+MILAID
17	DME	Australia	17,608	GDPPPP*MILGDP+MILAID
18	DME	Israel	17,484	GDPPPP*MILGDP+MILAID
19	SAS	Pakistan	16,157	GDPPPP*MILGDP+MILAID
20	DME	Spain	15,529	GDPPPP*MILGDP+MILAID
21	EEU	Poland	15,233	GDPPPP*MILGDP+MILAID
22	LAM	Colombia	14,879	GDPPPP*MILGDP+MILAID
23	MEA	Algeria	14,544	GDPPPP*MILGDP+MILAID
24	SAS	Afghanistan	11,683	GDPPPP*MILGDP+MILAID
25	SEA	Singapore	11,469	GDPPPP*MILGDP+MILAID
26	MEA	Egypt	10,952	GDPPPP*MILGDP+MILAID
27	CPA	Korea, North	10,951	GDPPPP*MILGDP+MILAID
28	MEA	United Arab Emirates	10,317	GDPPPP*MILGDP+MILAID
29	DME	Netherlands	10,027	GDPPPP*MILGDP+MILAID
30	LAM	Mexico	9,988	GDPPPP*MILGDP+MILAID
31	LAM	Chile	9,650	GDPPPP*MILGDP+MILAID
32	SEA	Thailand	9,081	GDPPPP*MILGDP+MILAID
33	DME	Greece	8,257	GDPPPP*MILGDP+MILAID
34	USR	Ukraine	8,136	GDPPPP*MILGDP+MILAID
35	SEA	Indonesia	7,553	GDPPPP*MILGDP+MILAID
36	MEA	Iraq	7,358	GDPPPP*MILGDP+MILAID
37	SEA	Malaysia	7,203	GDPPPP*MILGDP+MILAID
38	AFR	South Africa	6,943	GDPPPP*MILGDP+MILAID
39	CPA	Vietnam	6,542	GDPPPP*MILGDP+MILAID
40	MEA	Morocco	5,295	GDPPPP*MILGDP+MILAID
41	DME	Portugal	5,294	GDPPPP*MILGDP+MILAID
42	LAM	Argentina	5,118	GDPPPP*MILGDP+MILAID
43	DME	Sweden	4,952	GDPPPP*MILGDP+MILAID
44	MEA	Oman	4,833	GDPPPP*MILGDP+MILAID

Table 2.7 Military Expenditures at Purchasing Power Parities Plus Foreign Military Aid, Millions of Dollars, 2011

Rank	Region	Country	MILXPP	Source
45	DME	Norway	4,771	GDPPPP*MILGDP+MILAID
46	MEA	Kuwait	4,746	GDPPPP*MILGDP+MILAID
47	DME	Belgium	4,614	GDPPPP*MILGDP+MILAID
48	USR	Azerbaijan	4,512	GDPPPP*MILGDP+MILAID
49	LAM	Ecuador	4,452	GDPPPP*MILGDP+MILAID
50	SEA	Philippines	4,270	GDPPPP*MILGDP+MILAID
51	MEA	Syria	4,246	GDPPPP*MILGDP+MILAID
52	AFR	Angola	4,062	GDPPPP*MILGDP+MILAID
53	AFR	Nigeria	4,032	GDPPPP*MILGDP+MILAID
54	EEU	Romania	3,879	GDPPPP*MILGDP+MILAID
55	LAM	Cuba	3,842	GDPPPP*MILGDP+MILAID
56	LAM	Peru	3,566	GDPPPP*MILGDP+MILAID
57	SAS	Bangladesh	3,393	GDPPPP*MILGDP+MILAID
58	MEA	Libya	3,384	GDPPPP*MILGDP+MILAID
59	USR	Uzbekistan	3,380	GDPPPP*MILGDP+MILAID
60	DME	Switzerland	3,336	GDPPPP*MILGDP+MILAID
61	DME	Denmark	3,322	GDPPPP*MILGDP+MILAID
62	CPA	Burma	3,292	GDPPPP*MILGDP+MILAID
63	EEU	Czech Republic	3,181	GDPPPP*MILGDP+MILAID
64	SAS	Sri Lanka	3,090	GDPPPP*MILGDP+MILAID
65	DME	Austria	3,043	GDPPPP*MILGDP+MILAID
66	DME	Finland	3,043	GDPPPP*MILGDP+MILAID
67	MEA	Qatar	2,854	GDPPPP*MILGDP+MILAID
68	LAM	Venezuela	2,830	GDPPPP*MILGDP+MILAID
69	MEA	Lebanon	2,727	GDPPPP*MILGDP+MILAID
70	MEA	Yemen	2,359	GDPPPP*MILGDP+MILAID
71	EEU	Hungary	2,138	GDPPPP*MILGDP+MILAID
72	USR	Kazakhstan	2,075	GDPPPP*MILGDP+MILAID
73	MEA	Jordan	2,068	GDPPPP*MILGDP+MILAID
74	EEU	Serbia	1,791	GDPPPP*MILGDP+MILAID
75	EEU	Bulgaria	1,645	GDPPPP*MILGDP+MILAID
76	AFR	Sudan	1,557	GDPPPP*MILGDP+MILAID
77	USR	Belarus	1,535	GDPPPP*MILGDP+MILAID
78	DME	New Zealand	1,533	GDPPPP*MILGDP+MILAID
79	EEU	Croatia	1,463	GDPPPP*MILGDP+MILAID
80	EEU	Slovakia	1,445	GDPPPP*MILGDP+MILAID
81	MEA	Bahrain	1,358	GDPPPP*MILGDP+MILAID
82	MEA	Tunisia	1,324	GDPPPP*MILGDP+MILAID
83	DME	Ireland	1,126	GDPPPP*MILGDP+MILAID
84	AFR	Kenya	1,073	GDPPPP*MILGDP+MILAID
85	AFR	Ethiopia	988	GDPPPP*MILGDP+MILAID
86	LAM	Uruguay	985	GDPPPP*MILGDP+MILAID
87	LAM	Panama	925	GDPPPP*MILGDP+MILAID
88	EEU	Slovenia	799	GDPPPP*MILGDP+MILAID
89	MEA	Cyprus	782	GDPPPP*MILGDP+MILAID
90	AFR	Uganda	759	GDPPPP*MILGDP+MILAID

Table 2.7 Military Expenditures at Purchasing Power Parities Plus Foreign Military Aid, Millions of Dollars, 2011				
Rank	Region	Country	MILXPP	Source
91	LAM	Bolivia	755	GDPPPP*MILGDP+MILAID
92	USR	Georgia	742	GDPPPP*MILGDP+MILAID
93	AFR	Tanzania	730	GDPPPP*MILGDP+MILAID
94	USR	Armenia	727	GDPPPP*MILGDP+MILAID
95	USR	Lithuania	722	GDPPPP*MILGDP+MILAID
96	AFR	Cameroon	653	GDPPPP*MILGDP+MILAID
97	AFR	Botswana	643	GDPPPP*MILGDP+MILAID
98	LAM	Dominican Republic	576	GDPPPP*MILGDP+MILAID
99	AFR	Ivory Coast	573	GDPPPP*MILGDP+MILAID
100	LAM	Trinidad & Tobago	559	GDPPPP*MILGDP+MILAID
101	MEA	West Bank	556	GDPPPP*MILGDP+MILAID
102	SEA	Brunei	553	GDPPPP*MILGDP+MILAID
103	AFR	Namibia	539	GDPPPP*MILGDP+MILAID
104	CPA	Cambodia	523	GDPPPP*MILGDP+MILAID
105	USR	Estonia	495	GDPPPP*MILGDP+MILAID
106	EEU	Bosnia	480	GDPPPP*MILGDP+MILAID
107	USR	Turkmenistan	474	GDPPPP*MILGDP+MILAID
108	SAS	Nepal	472	GDPPPP*MILGDP+MILAID
109	USR	Latvia	443	GDPPPP*MILGDP+MILAID
110	EEU	Albania	436	GDPPPP*MILGDP+MILAID
111	AFR	Chad	412	GDPPPP*MILGDP+MILAID
112	USR	Tajikistan	410	GDPPPP*MILGDP+MILAID
113	LAM	El Salvador	410	GDPPPP*MILGDP+MILAID
114	AFR	Congo, Dem. Republic	407	GDPPPP*MILGDP+MILAID
115	AFR	Gabon	387	GDPPPP*MILGDP+MILAID
116	LAM	Paraguay	377	GDPPPP*MILGDP+MILAID
117	LAM	Costa Rica	371	GDPPPP*MILGDP+MILAID
118	AFR	Senegal	365	GDPPPP*MILGDP+MILAID
119	AFR	Zambia	344	GDPPPP*MILGDP+MILAID
120	LAM	Honduras	344	GDPPPP*MILGDP+MILAID
121	LAM	Guatemala	329	GDPPPP*MILGDP+MILAID
122	AFR	Somalia	321	GDPPPP*MILGDP+MILAID
123	AFR	Mauritania	316	GDPPPP*MILGDP+MILAID
124	EEU	Macedonia	308	GDPPPP*MILGDP+MILAID
125	AFR	Mali	305	GDPPPP*MILGDP+MILAID
126	AFR	Burkina Faso	296	GDPPPP*MILGDP+MILAID
127	USR	Kyrgyzstan	233	GDPPPP*MILGDP+MILAID
128	MEA	Gaza Strip	229	GDPPPP*MILGDP+MILAID
129	AFR	Swaziland	220	GDPPPP*MILGDP+MILAID
130	DME	Luxembourg	216	GDPPPP*MILGDP+MILAID
131	LAM	Jamaica	206	GDPPPP*MILGDP+MILAID
132	AFR	Congo, Republic	190	GDPPPP*MILGDP+MILAID
133	AFR	Rwanda	171	GDPPPP*MILGDP+MILAID

TABLE 2.7 MILITARY EXPENDITURES AT PURCHASING POWER PARITIES PLUS FOREIGN MILITARY AID, MILLIONS OF DOLLARS, 2011

Rank	Region	Country	MILXPP	Source
134	EEU	Montenegro	164	GDPPPP*MILGDP+MILAID
135	AFR	Madagascar	150	GDPPPP*MILGDP+MILAID
136	AFR	Benin	149	GDPPPP*MILGDP+MILAID
137	AFR	Mozambique	145	GDPPPP*MILGDP+MILAID
138	AFR	Burundi	139	GDPPPP*MILGDP+MILAID
139	LAM	Nicaragua	135	GDPPPP*MILGDP+MILAID
140	CPA	Mongolia	126	GDPPPP*MILGDP+MILAID
141	AFR	South Sudan	123	GDPPPP*MILGDP+MILAID
142	AFR	Ghana	119	GDPPPP*MILGDP+MILAID
143	AFR	Guinea	118	GDPPPP*MILGDP+MILAID
144	AFR	Eritrea	117	GDPPPP*MILGDP+MILAID
145	SAS	Maldives	114	GDPPPP*MILGDP+MILAID
146	AFR	Malawi	105	GDPPPP*MILGDP+MILAID
147	AFR	Central African Rep.	104	GDPPPP*MILGDP+MILAID
148	AFR	Togo	100	GDPPPP*MILGDP+MILAID
149	AFR	Niger	98	GDPPPP*MILGDP+MILAID
150	AFR	Zimbabwe	96	GDPPPP*MILGDP+MILAID
151	DME	Malta	83	GDPPPP*MILGDP+MILAID
152	LAM	Bahamas	80	GDPPPP*MILGDP+MILAID
153	SEA	Papua New Guinea	79	GDPPPP*MILGDP+MILAID
154	AFR	Lesotho	77	GDPPPP*MILGDP+MILAID
155	LAM	Guyana	67	GDPPPP*MILGDP+MILAID
156	AFR	Sierra Leone	62	GDPPPP*MILGDP+MILAID
157	LAM	Suriname	60	GDPPPP*MILGDP+MILAID
158	LAM	Barbados	46	GDPPPP*MILGDP+MILAID
159	SEA	East Timor	45	GDPPPP*MILGDP+MILAID
160	AFR	Liberia	43	GDPPPP*MILGDP+MILAID
161	AFR	Guinea-Bissau	42	GDPPPP*MILGDP+MILAID
162	USR	Moldova	42	GDPPPP*MILGDP+MILAID
163	CPA	Laos	41	GDPPPP*MILGDP+MILAID
164	SAS	Bhutan	41	GDPPPP*MILGDP+MILAID
165	LAM	Belize	37	GDPPPP*MILGDP+MILAID
166	SEA	Fiji	29	GDPPPP*MILGDP+MILAID
167	AFR	Djibouti	25	GDPPPP*MILGDP+MILAID
168	AFR	Gambia	22	GDPPPP*MILGDP+MILAID
169	AFR	Seychelles	22	GDPPPP*MILGDP+MILAID
170	AFR	Mauritius	17	GDPPPP*MILGDP+MILAID
171	AFR	Cape Verde	12	GDPPPP*MILGDP+MILAID
172	AFR	Equatorial Guinea	10	GDPPPP*MILGDP+MILAID
173	DME	Iceland	10	GDPPPP*MILGDP+MILAID
174	LAM	Antigua & Barbuda	9	GDPPPP*MILGDP+MILAID
175	SEA	Tonga	8	GDPPPP*MILGDP+MILAID
176	EEU	Kosovo	6	GDPPPP*MILGDP+MILAID

Table 2.7 Military Expenditures at Purchasing Power Parities Plus Foreign Military Aid, Millions of Dollars, 2011				
Rank	Region	Country	MILXPP	Source
177	AFR	Sao Tome & Principe	5	GDPPPP*MILGDP+MILAID
178	LAM	Haiti	4	GDPPPP*MILGDP+MILAID
179	AFR	Comoros	2	GDPPPP*MILGDP+MILAID
181	LAM	Grenada	0	GDPPPP*MILGDP+MILAID
181	LAM	St. Kitts & Nevis	0	GDPPPP*MILGDP+MILAID
181	LAM	St. Lucia	0	GDPPPP*MILGDP+MILAID
183.5	LAM	Dominica	0	GDPPPP*MILGDP+MILAID
183.5	LAM	St. Vincent	0	GDPPPP*MILGDP+MILAID
186	SEA	Micronesia	0	GDPPPP*MILGDP+MILAID
186	SEA	Samoa	0	GDPPPP*MILGDP+MILAID
186	SEA	Vanuatu	0	GDPPPP*MILGDP+MILAID
211.5	DME	Andorra	0	GDPPPP*MILGDP+MILAID
211.5	LAM	Anguilla	0	GDPPPP*MILGDP+MILAID
211.5	LAM	Aruba	0	GDPPPP*MILGDP+MILAID
211.5	DME	Bermuda	0	GDPPPP*MILGDP+MILAID
211.5	LAM	Cayman Islands	0	GDPPPP*MILGDP+MILAID
211.5	SEA	Cook Islands	0	GDPPPP*MILGDP+MILAID
211.5	LAM	Curacao	0	GDPPPP*MILGDP+MILAID
211.5	DME	Falkland Islands	0	GDPPPP*MILGDP+MILAID
211.5	DME	Faroe Islands	0	GDPPPP*MILGDP+MILAID
211.5	SEA	French Polynesia	0	GDPPPP*MILGDP+MILAID
211.5	DME	Gibraltar	0	GDPPPP*MILGDP+MILAID
211.5	DME	Greenland	0	GDPPPP*MILGDP+MILAID
211.5	LAM	Guadeloupe	0	GDPPPP*MILGDP+MILAID
211.5	SEA	Guam	0	GDPPPP*MILGDP+MILAID
211.5	DME	Guernsey	0	GDPPPP*MILGDP+MILAID
211.5	LAM	Guiana, French	0	GDPPPP*MILGDP+MILAID
211.5	SEA	Hong Kong	0	GDPPPP*MILGDP+MILAID
211.5	DME	Isle of Man	0	GDPPPP*MILGDP+MILAID
211.5	DME	Jersey	0	GDPPPP*MILGDP+MILAID
211.5	SEA	Kiribati	0	GDPPPP*MILGDP+MILAID
211.5	DME	Liechtenstein	0	GDPPPP*MILGDP+MILAID
211.5	SEA	Macao	0	GDPPPP*MILGDP+MILAID
211.5	SEA	Marshall Islands	0	GDPPPP*MILGDP+MILAID
211.5	LAM	Martinique	0	GDPPPP*MILGDP+MILAID
211.5	AFR	Mayotte	0	GDPPPP*MILGDP+MILAID
211.5	DME	Monaco	0	GDPPPP*MILGDP+MILAID
211.5	LAM	Montserrat	0	GDPPPP*MILGDP+MILAID
211.5	SEA	Nauru	0	GDPPPP*MILGDP+MILAID

TABLE 2.7 MILITARY EXPENDITURES AT PURCHASING POWER PARITIES PLUS FOREIGN MILITARY AID, MILLIONS OF DOLLARS, 2011

Rank	Region	Country	MILXPP	Source
211.5	SEA	New Caledonia	0	GDPPPP*MILGDP+MILAID
211.5	SEA	Niue	0	GDPPPP*MILGDP+MILAID
211.5	SEA	Northern Mariana Is.	0	GDPPPP*MILGDP+MILAID
211.5	SEA	Palau	0	GDPPPP*MILGDP+MILAID
211.5	LAM	Puerto Rico	0	GDPPPP*MILGDP+MILAID
211.5	AFR	Reunion	0	GDPPPP*MILGDP+MILAID
211.5	LAM	Saint Martin	0	GDPPPP*MILGDP+MILAID
211.5	SEA	Samoa, American	0	GDPPPP*MILGDP+MILAID
211.5	DME	San Marino	0	GDPPPP*MILGDP+MILAID
211.5	LAM	Sint Maarten	0	GDPPPP*MILGDP+MILAID
211.5	SEA	Solomon Islands	0	GDPPPP*MILGDP+MILAID
211.5	AFR	St. Helena	0	GDPPPP*MILGDP+MILAID
211.5	DME	St. Pierre & Miquelon	0	GDPPPP*MILGDP+MILAID
211.5	SEA	Tokelau	0	GDPPPP*MILGDP+MILAID
211.5	LAM	Turks & Caicos Is.	0	GDPPPP*MILGDP+MILAID
211.5	SEA	Tuvalu	0	GDPPPP*MILGDP+MILAID
211.5	LAM	Virgin Islands, Brit.	0	GDPPPP*MILGDP+MILAID
211.5	LAM	Virgin Islands, U.S.	0	GDPPPP*MILGDP+MILAID
211.5	SEA	Wallis & Futuna	0	GDPPPP*MILGDP+MILAID
211.5	AFR	Western Sahara	0	GDPPPP*MILGDP+MILAID

Table 2.8 Military Expenditures at Market Exchange Rates Plus Foreign Military Aid, Millions of Dollars, 2011				
Rank	Region	Country	MILEXP	Source
1	DME	United States	723,142	GDP*MILGDP+MILAID
2	CPA	China	129,434	GDP*MILGDP+MILAID
3	DME	United Kingdom	61,094	GDP*MILGDP+MILAID
4	DME	France	60,369	GDP*MILGDP+MILAID
5	USR	Russia	58,844	GDP*MILGDP+MILAID
6	DME	Japan	58,650	GDP*MILGDP+MILAID
7	DME	Germany	46,742	GDP*MILGDP+MILAID
8	SAS	India	43,973	GDP*MILGDP+MILAID
9	MEA	Saudi Arabia	42,835	GDP*MILGDP+MILAID
10	DME	Italy	33,656	GDP*MILGDP+MILAID
11	LAM	Brazil	29,559	GDP*MILGDP+MILAID
12	SEA	Korea, South	28,053	GDP*MILGDP+MILAID
13	MEA	Iran	26,226	GDP*MILGDP+MILAID
14	DME	Canada	22,359	GDP*MILGDP+MILAID
15	DME	Australia	20,887	GDP*MILGDP+MILAID
16	MEA	Turkey	17,842	GDP*MILGDP+MILAID
17	DME	Israel	17,545	GDP*MILGDP+MILAID
18	DME	Spain	14,969	GDP*MILGDP+MILAID
19	DME	Netherlands	11,640	GDP*MILGDP+MILAID
20	SAS	Afghanistan	10,850	GDP*MILGDP+MILAID
21	SEA	Taiwan	10,495	GDP*MILGDP+MILAID
22	LAM	Colombia	9,065	GDP*MILGDP+MILAID
23	EEU	Poland	8,959	GDP*MILGDP+MILAID
24	MEA	United Arab Emirates	8,781	GDP*MILGDP+MILAID
25	SEA	Singapore	8,113	GDP*MILGDP+MILAID
26	DME	Greece	7,820	GDP*MILGDP+MILAID
27	MEA	Algeria	7,512	GDP*MILGDP+MILAID
28	DME	Norway	7,021	GDP*MILGDP+MILAID
29	SAS	Pakistan	6,991	GDP*MILGDP+MILAID
30	LAM	Chile	6,862	GDP*MILGDP+MILAID
31	DME	Sweden	6,347	GDP*MILGDP+MILAID
32	CPA	Korea, North	6,066	GDP*MILGDP+MILAID
33	LAM	Mexico	5,713	GDP*MILGDP+MILAID
34	DME	Belgium	5,472	GDP*MILGDP+MILAID
35	MEA	Kuwait	5,467	GDP*MILGDP+MILAID
36	MEA	Iraq	5,332	GDP*MILGDP+MILAID
37	MEA	Egypt	5,294	GDP*MILGDP+MILAID
38	DME	Switzerland	4,972	GDP*MILGDP+MILAID
39	DME	Denmark	4,882	GDP*MILGDP+MILAID
40	SEA	Indonesia	4,799	GDP*MILGDP+MILAID
41	SEA	Thailand	4,666	GDP*MILGDP+MILAID
42	DME	Portugal	4,426	GDP*MILGDP+MILAID
43	AFR	South Africa	4,410	GDP*MILGDP+MILAID
44	MEA	Oman	4,008	GDP*MILGDP+MILAID

TABLE 2.8 MILITARY EXPENDITURES AT MARKET EXCHANGE RATES PLUS FOREIGN MILITARY AID, MILLIONS OF DOLLARS, 2011

Rank	Region	Country	MILEXP	Source
45	SEA	Malaysia	3,937	GDP*MILGDP+MILAID
46	DME	Finland	3,880	GDP*MILGDP+MILAID
47	USR	Ukraine	3,539	GDP*MILGDP+MILAID
48	DME	Austria	3,476	GDP*MILGDP+MILAID
49	MEA	Morocco	3,182	GDP*MILGDP+MILAID
50	LAM	Argentina	2,890	GDP*MILGDP+MILAID
51	MEA	Libya	2,878	GDP*MILGDP+MILAID
52	AFR	Angola	2,628	GDP*MILGDP+MILAID
53	LAM	Venezuela	2,624	GDP*MILGDP+MILAID
54	MEA	Qatar	2,600	GDP*MILGDP+MILAID
55	MEA	Syria	2,553	GDP*MILGDP+MILAID
56	CPA	Vietnam	2,437	GDP*MILGDP+MILAID
57	USR	Azerbaijan	2,374	GDP*MILGDP+MILAID
58	SEA	Philippines	2,303	GDP*MILGDP+MILAID
59	EEU	Czech Republic	2,261	GDP*MILGDP+MILAID
60	LAM	Ecuador	2,161	GDP*MILGDP+MILAID
61	AFR	Nigeria	2,043	GDP*MILGDP+MILAID
62	EEU	Romania	1,983	GDP*MILGDP+MILAID
63	LAM	Cuba	1,974	GDP*MILGDP+MILAID
64	DME	New Zealand	1,889	GDP*MILGDP+MILAID
65	LAM	Peru	1,801	GDP*MILGDP+MILAID
66	MEA	Lebanon	1,736	GDP*MILGDP+MILAID
67	MEA	Jordan	1,603	GDP*MILGDP+MILAID
68	USR	Uzbekistan	1,556	GDP*MILGDP+MILAID
69	SAS	Bangladesh	1,492	GDP*MILGDP+MILAID
70	SAS	Sri Lanka	1,429	GDP*MILGDP+MILAID
71	USR	Kazakhstan	1,310	GDP*MILGDP+MILAID
72	EEU	Hungary	1,258	GDP*MILGDP+MILAID
73	MEA	Yemen	1,093	GDP*MILGDP+MILAID
74	DME	Ireland	1,078	GDP*MILGDP+MILAID
75	CPA	Burma	1,018	GDP*MILGDP+MILAID
76	EEU	Croatia	1,018	GDP*MILGDP+MILAID
77	MEA	Bahrain	995	GDP*MILGDP+MILAID
78	EEU	Slovakia	972	GDP*MILGDP+MILAID
79	AFR	Sudan	877	GDP*MILGDP+MILAID
80	EEU	Serbia	859	GDP*MILGDP+MILAID
81	LAM	Uruguay	775	GDP*MILGDP+MILAID
82	EEU	Bulgaria	730	GDP*MILGDP+MILAID
83	EEU	Slovenia	700	GDP*MILGDP+MILAID
84	USR	Belarus	599	GDP*MILGDP+MILAID
85	MEA	Tunisia	582	GDP*MILGDP+MILAID
86	MEA	Cyprus	557	GDP*MILGDP+MILAID
87	AFR	Kenya	516	GDP*MILGDP+MILAID
88	LAM	Panama	449	GDP*MILGDP+MILAID
89	USR	Lithuania	438	GDP*MILGDP+MILAID
90	USR	Armenia	424	GDP*MILGDP+MILAID

Table 2.8 Military Expenditures at Market Exchange Rates Plus Foreign Military Aid, Millions of Dollars, 2011				
Rank	Region	Country	MILEXP	Source
91	USR	Georgia	397	GDP*MILGDP+MILAID
92	SEA	Brunei	395	GDP*MILGDP+MILAID
93	AFR	Namibia	373	GDP*MILGDP+MILAID
94	AFR	Ivory Coast	349	GDP*MILGDP+MILAID
95	USR	Estonia	345	GDP*MILGDP+MILAID
96	LAM	Trinidad & Tobago	336	GDP*MILGDP+MILAID
97	AFR	Cameroon	336	GDP*MILGDP+MILAID
98	AFR	Ethiopia	330	GDP*MILGDP+MILAID
99	AFR	Botswana	326	GDP*MILGDP+MILAID
100	USR	Latvia	312	GDP*MILGDP+MILAID
101	LAM	Dominican Republic	312	GDP*MILGDP+MILAID
102	LAM	Bolivia	299	GDP*MILGDP+MILAID
103	AFR	Uganda	288	GDP*MILGDP+MILAID
104	MEA	West Bank	284	GDP*MILGDP+MILAID
105	AFR	Tanzania	261	GDP*MILGDP+MILAID
106	EEU	Bosnia	255	GDP*MILGDP+MILAID
107	AFR	Zambia	246	GDP*MILGDP+MILAID
108	USR	Turkmenistan	243	GDP*MILGDP+MILAID
109	LAM	Costa Rica	234	GDP*MILGDP+MILAID
110	AFR	Congo, Dem. Republic	218	GDP*MILGDP+MILAID
111	LAM	El Salvador	214	GDP*MILGDP+MILAID
112	LAM	Paraguay	207	GDP*MILGDP+MILAID
113	SAS	Nepal	205	GDP*MILGDP+MILAID
114	AFR	Senegal	201	GDP*MILGDP+MILAID
115	LAM	Guatemala	200	GDP*MILGDP+MILAID
116	AFR	Chad	198	GDP*MILGDP+MILAID
117	EEU	Albania	198	GDP*MILGDP+MILAID
118	AFR	Gabon	198	GDP*MILGDP+MILAID
119	DME	Luxembourg	188	GDP*MILGDP+MILAID
120	CPA	Cambodia	184	GDP*MILGDP+MILAID
121	LAM	Honduras	173	GDP*MILGDP+MILAID
122	AFR	Somalia	173	GDP*MILGDP+MILAID
123	AFR	Mali	171	GDP*MILGDP+MILAID
124	USR	Tajikistan	159	GDP*MILGDP+MILAID
125	LAM	Jamaica	134	GDP*MILGDP+MILAID
126	AFR	Burkina Faso	132	GDP*MILGDP+MILAID
127	EEU	Macedonia	131	GDP*MILGDP+MILAID
128	AFR	Mauritania	130	GDP*MILGDP+MILAID
129	AFR	Zimbabwe	126	GDP*MILGDP+MILAID
130	AFR	Swaziland	126	GDP*MILGDP+MILAID
131	MEA	Gaza Strip	117	GDP*MILGDP+MILAID
132	AFR	Congo, Republic	98	GDP*MILGDP+MILAID
133	USR	Kyrgyzstan	98	GDP*MILGDP+MILAID

TABLE 2.8 MILITARY EXPENDITURES AT MARKET EXCHANGE RATES PLUS FOREIGN MILITARY AID, MILLIONS OF DOLLARS, 2011

Rank	Region	Country	MILEXP	Source
134	AFR	Ghana	90	GDP*MILGDP+MILAID
135	EEU	Montenegro	88	GDP*MILGDP+MILAID
136	AFR	Eritrea	86	GDP*MILGDP+MILAID
137	SEA	East Timor	80	GDP*MILGDP+MILAID
138	AFR	Rwanda	76	GDP*MILGDP+MILAID
139	SAS	Maldives	74	GDP*MILGDP+MILAID
140	AFR	Benin	72	GDP*MILGDP+MILAID
141	AFR	Mozambique	69	GDP*MILGDP+MILAID
142	AFR	South Sudan	68	GDP*MILGDP+MILAID
143	AFR	Madagascar	67	GDP*MILGDP+MILAID
144	CPA	Mongolia	63	GDP*MILGDP+MILAID
145	AFR	Central African Rep.	62	GDP*MILGDP+MILAID
146	AFR	Burundi	58	GDP*MILGDP+MILAID
147	LAM	Bahamas	58	GDP*MILGDP+MILAID
148	DME	Malta	58	GDP*MILGDP+MILAID
149	LAM	Suriname	57	GDP*MILGDP+MILAID
150	LAM	Nicaragua	56	GDP*MILGDP+MILAID
151	AFR	Lesotho	55	GDP*MILGDP+MILAID
152	AFR	Togo	55	GDP*MILGDP+MILAID
153	AFR	Niger	49	GDP*MILGDP+MILAID
154	AFR	Guinea	45	GDP*MILGDP+MILAID
155	SEA	Papua New Guinea	44	GDP*MILGDP+MILAID
156	AFR	Malawi	42	GDP*MILGDP+MILAID
157	LAM	Barbados	31	GDP*MILGDP+MILAID
158	AFR	Liberia	30	GDP*MILGDP+MILAID
159	LAM	Guyana	27	GDP*MILGDP+MILAID
160	LAM	Belize	26	GDP*MILGDP+MILAID
161	AFR	Sierra Leone	26	GDP*MILGDP+MILAID
162	USR	Moldova	26	GDP*MILGDP+MILAID
163	SEA	Fiji	23	GDP*MILGDP+MILAID
164	AFR	Guinea-Bissau	20	GDP*MILGDP+MILAID
165	CPA	Laos	17	GDP*MILGDP+MILAID
166	AFR	Djibouti	16	GDP*MILGDP+MILAID
167	SAS	Bhutan	15	GDP*MILGDP+MILAID
168	AFR	Cape Verde	11	GDP*MILGDP+MILAID
169	AFR	Mauritius	10	GDP*MILGDP+MILAID
170	AFR	Seychelles	10	GDP*MILGDP+MILAID
171	DME	Iceland	9	GDP*MILGDP+MILAID
172	AFR	Gambia	6	GDP*MILGDP+MILAID
173	LAM	Antigua & Barbuda	6	GDP*MILGDP+MILAID
174	SEA	Tonga	6	GDP*MILGDP+MILAID
175	EEU	Kosovo	6	GDP*MILGDP+MILAID
176	AFR	Equatorial Guinea	5	GDP*MILGDP+MILAID

Table 2.8 Military Expenditures at Market Exchange Rates Plus Foreign Military Aid, Millions of Dollars, 2011				
Rank	Region	Country	MILEXP	Source
177	LAM	Haiti	3	GDP*MILGDP+MILAID
178	AFR	Sao Tome & Principe	3	GDP*MILGDP+MILAID
179	AFR	Comoros	1	GDP*MILGDP+MILAID
181	LAM	Grenada	0	GDP*MILGDP+MILAID
181	LAM	St. Kitts & Nevis	0	GDP*MILGDP+MILAID
181	LAM	St. Lucia	0	GDP*MILGDP+MILAID
183.5	LAM	Dominica	0	GDP*MILGDP+MILAID
183.5	LAM	St. Vincent	0	GDP*MILGDP+MILAID
186	SEA	Micronesia	0	GDP*MILGDP+MILAID
186	SEA	Samoa	0	GDP*MILGDP+MILAID
186	SEA	Vanuatu	0	GDP*MILGDP+MILAID
211.5	DME	Andorra	0	GDP*MILGDP+MILAID
211.5	LAM	Anguilla	0	GDP*MILGDP+MILAID
211.5	LAM	Aruba	0	GDP*MILGDP+MILAID
211.5	DME	Bermuda	0	GDP*MILGDP+MILAID
211.5	LAM	Cayman Islands	0	GDP*MILGDP+MILAID
211.5	SEA	Cook Islands	0	GDP*MILGDP+MILAID
211.5	LAM	Curacao	0	GDP*MILGDP+MILAID
211.5	DME	Falkland Islands	0	GDP*MILGDP+MILAID
211.5	DME	Faroe Islands	0	GDP*MILGDP+MILAID
211.5	SEA	French Polynesia	0	GDP*MILGDP+MILAID
211.5	DME	Gibraltar	0	GDP*MILGDP+MILAID
211.5	DME	Greenland	0	GDP*MILGDP+MILAID
211.5	LAM	Guadeloupe	0	GDP*MILGDP+MILAID
211.5	SEA	Guam	0	GDP*MILGDP+MILAID
211.5	DME	Guernsey	0	GDP*MILGDP+MILAID
211.5	LAM	Guiana, French	0	GDP*MILGDP+MILAID
211.5	SEA	Hong Kong	0	GDP*MILGDP+MILAID
211.5	DME	Isle of Man	0	GDP*MILGDP+MILAID
211.5	DME	Jersey	0	GDP*MILGDP+MILAID
211.5	SEA	Kiribati	0	GDP*MILGDP+MILAID
211.5	DME	Liechtenstein	0	GDP*MILGDP+MILAID
211.5	SEA	Macao	0	GDP*MILGDP+MILAID
211.5	SEA	Marshall Islands	0	GDP*MILGDP+MILAID
211.5	LAM	Martinique	0	GDP*MILGDP+MILAID
211.5	AFR	Mayotte	0	GDP*MILGDP+MILAID
211.5	DME	Monaco	0	GDP*MILGDP+MILAID
211.5	LAM	Montserrat	0	GDP*MILGDP+MILAID
211.5	SEA	Nauru	0	GDP*MILGDP+MILAID

Table 2.8 Military Expenditures at Market Exchange Rates Plus Foreign Military Aid, Millions of Dollars, 2011

Rank	Region	Country	MILEXP	Source
211.5	SEA	New Caledonia	0	GDP*MILGDP+MILAID
211.5	SEA	Niue	0	GDP*MILGDP+MILAID
211.5	SEA	Northern Mariana Is.	0	GDP*MILGDP+MILAID
211.5	SEA	Palau	0	GDP*MILGDP+MILAID
211.5	LAM	Puerto Rico	0	GDP*MILGDP+MILAID
211.5	AFR	Reunion	0	GDP*MILGDP+MILAID
211.5	LAM	Saint Martin	0	GDP*MILGDP+MILAID
211.5	SEA	Samoa, American	0	GDP*MILGDP+MILAID
211.5	DME	San Marino	0	GDP*MILGDP+MILAID
211.5	LAM	Sint Maarten	0	GDP*MILGDP+MILAID
211.5	SEA	Solomon Islands	0	GDP*MILGDP+MILAID
211.5	AFR	St. Helena	0	GDP*MILGDP+MILAID
211.5	DME	St. Pierre & Miquelon	0	GDP*MILGDP+MILAID
211.5	SEA	Tokelau	0	GDP*MILGDP+MILAID
211.5	LAM	Turks & Caicos Is.	0	GDP*MILGDP+MILAID
211.5	SEA	Tuvalu	0	GDP*MILGDP+MILAID
211.5	LAM	Virgin Islands, Brit.	0	GDP*MILGDP+MILAID
211.5	LAM	Virgin Islands, U.S.	0	GDP*MILGDP+MILAID
211.5	SEA	Wallis & Futuna	0	GDP*MILGDP+MILAID
211.5	AFR	Western Sahara	0	GDP*MILGDP+MILAID

TABLE 2.9 OPERATIONAL NUCLEAR DELIVERY SYSTEMS, 2012-2013							
NAME/DESIGNATION	AKA	NUMBER OF SYSTEMS Active+Spares	YEAR FIRST DEPLOYED	WARHEAD TYPE	NUMBER OF WARHEADS x YIELD (kilotons)	RANGE (km)	TOTAL NUMBER OF WARHEADS Active+Spares
LAND BALLISTIC MISSILES							
UNITED STATES							
ICBM							
LGM-30G	Minuteman III					13,000	
	MK-12	0	1970	Single	1 x 170		0
	MK-12A	250	1979	MIRV, Single	1-3 x 335		250
	MK-21 SERV	250	2006 (1986)	Single	1 x 300		250
TOTAL 12(SIPRI) 12(BULL) 11(SIPRI)		450					500
SRBM							
ATACMS Block I		Some	1991	Single	1 x 560kg payload	165	Some
ATACMS Block IA		Some	1998	Single	1 x 160kg payload	300	Some
ATACMS Block II		Some	2002	Single	1 x 270kg payload	140	Some
TOTAL 08(WIKI)		Some					Some
RUSSIA							
ICBM							
SS-18	Satan	50	1992	MIRV	10 x 500-800	11,000-15,000	500
SS-19	Stiletto	48	1980	MIRV	6 x 400	10,000	288
SS-25	Sickle	135	1985	Single	1 x 800	10,500	135
SS-27	Topol-M1 (SILO)	56	1997	Single	1 x 800	10,500	56
SS-27	Topol-M1 (MOBILE)	18	2006	Single	1 x (800)?	10,500	18
SS-27	Topol-M2 (RS-24) (MOBILE)	15	2010	MIRV	6 x 100?	10,500	90
SS-27	Topol-M2 (RS-24) (SILO)		(2012)	MIRV	6 x 100?	?	

Table 2.9 Operational Nuclear Delivery Systems, 2012-2013

NAME/DESIGNATION	AKA	NUMBER OF SYSTEMS Active+Spares	YEAR FIRST DEPLOYED	WARHEAD TYPE	NUMBER OF WARHEADS x YIELD (kilotons)	RANGE (km)	TOTAL NUMBER OF WARHEADS Active+Spares
TOTAL 12(SIPRI) 12(BULL) 11(SIPRI) 11(BULL)		322					1,087
SRBM							
SS-1c Mod 1	Scud-B	Some	1964	Single	1 x 1,000kg payload	300	Some
SS-1c Mod 2	Scud-B	Some	1964	Single	1 x 950kg payload	240	Some
SS-21 Scarab	Tochka	150	1981	Single	1 x 10?	120	150?
SS-26 Stone	Iskander	24	2005	Single	1 x 10?	500	24?
TOTAL 12(SIPRI) 12(BULL) 08(WIKI)		164					164?
CHINA							
ICBM							
CSS-4	DF-5A	20	1981	Single	1 x 4,000-5,000	13,000	20
CSS-X-10	DF-31	10-20	2006			>7,200	10-20
				Single	1 x 200-300		
				MIRV	3 x 50-100		
?	DF-31A	10-20	2007			>11,200	10-20
				Single	1 x 200-300		
				MIRV	3-5 x 20-150		
TOTAL 12(SIPRI) 11(SIPRI) 11(BULL)		40-60					40-60
IRBM							
CSS-2	DF-3A	16	1971	Single	1 x 3,300	3,100	16
CSS-3	DF-4	12	1980	Single	1 x 3,300	5,500	12
CSS-5	DF-21, DF-21A	60	1991	Single	1 x 200-300	1,800-3,000	60
TOTAL 12(SIPRI) 11(SIPRI) 11(BULL) 11(WIKI)		88					88

TABLE 2.9 OPERATIONAL NUCLEAR DELIVERY SYSTEMS, 2012-2013							
NAME/DESIGNATION	AKA	NUMBER OF SYSTEMS Active+Spares	YEAR FIRST DEPLOYED	WARHEAD TYPE	NUMBER OF WARHEADS x YIELD (kilotons)	RANGE (km)	TOTAL NUMBER OF WARHEADS Active+Spares
SRBM							
CSS-6	DF-15/M-9	24	1989	Single	1 x 50-350	600	Some
CSS-7	DF-11/M-11	32	1999	Single	1 x 0.5	300	Some
CSS-8	DF-7	30	?	Single	1 x 500kg payload	150	?
TOTAL 11(SIPRI) 04(IISS)		96					Some
INDIA							
IRBM							
Agni II		Some	2004	Single	1 x 15-250	2,000	Some
Agni III		Some	2010-2011	Single	1 x 15-250	3,000	Some
Agni IV		Some	2010		1,000kg	3,500	Some
Agni V		Some	2012	Single	1 x 1,000kg payload	>5,000	Some
TOTAL 12(SIPRI) 12(BULL) 12(JDW) 11(SIPRI) 11(WIKI)		Some					Some
SRBM							
Agni I		Some	2007	Single	1 x 1,000kg payload	700+	Some
Prithvi I		<50	1998	Single	1 x 1,000kg payload	150	Some
Prithvi II		Some	2004	Single	1 x 500kg payload	250	Some
Prithvi III		30	2004	Single	1 x 10-20	350-600	Some
TOTAL 11(SIPRI) 11(BULL)		Some					Some
PAKISTAN							
IRBM							
Ghauri-1	Haft 5	<50	2003	Single	1 x 700-1,000kg payload	>1,200	Some
Ghauri-2	Haft 5A	Some	2003	Single	1 x 1,200kg payload	2,500	Some

TABLE 2.9 OPERATIONAL NUCLEAR DELIVERY SYSTEMS, 2012-2013							
NAME/DESIGNATION	AKA	NUMBER OF SYSTEMS Active+Spares	YEAR FIRST DEPLOYED	WARHEAD TYPE	NUMBER OF WARHEADS x YIELD (kilotons)	RANGE (km)	TOTAL NUMBER OF WARHEADS Active+Spares
Ghauri-3		Some	(>2011)	Single		3,000-3,500	Some
Shaheen-2	Haft 6	Some	2007	Single	1 x 1,000+kg payload	2,500	Some
Shaheen-3		Some	(>2011)	Single		4,000-4,500	Some
TOTAL 12(SIPRI) 11(SIPRI) 11(WIKI)		Some					Some
SRBM							
Abdali	Haft 2	Some	2006	Single	1 x 200-400kg payload	180	Some
Ghaznavi	Haft 3	<50	2004	Single	1 x 500kg payload	290	Some
Shaheen-1	Haft 4	<50	2008	Single	1 x 750-1,000kg payload	650	Some
Nasr	Haft 9		(2011)			60	
TOTAL 12(SIPRI) 11(SIPRI)		Some					Some
ISRAEL							
ICBM							
Jericho 3		2-5	2008				Some
				Single	1 x 1,000-1,300	11,500	
				MIRV	6 x 100	11,500	
Jericho 2B		90	1990	Single	1 x 500kg	>7,800	Some
TOTAL 12(SIPRI) 12(JDW) 11(SIPRI) 11(WIKI) Note [1], [2], [3], [4], [5]		Some					Some
IRBM							
Jericho 2		(50-100)	1990				Some

TABLE 2.9 OPERATIONAL NUCLEAR DELIVERY SYSTEMS, 2012-2013

NAME/DESIGNATION	AKA	NUMBER OF SYSTEMS Active+Spares	YEAR FIRST DEPLOYED	WARHEAD TYPE	NUMBER OF WARHEADS x YIELD (kilotons)	RANGE (km)	TOTAL NUMBER OF WARHEADS Active+Spares
				Single	1 x 750-1,000kg payload	1,500-1,800	
TOTAL 12(SIPRI) 11(SIPRI) 11(WIKI)		(50-100)					Some
NORTH KOREA							
IRBM							
No-Dong-1		Some	1997	Single	1 x 700-1,000kg payload	1,300	Some
Rodong-1		Some		Single		1,300	Some
Rodong-2		Some		Single		2,000	Some
Taepodong-1		Some		Single		2,500	Some
Musudan		Some	(>2011)	Single		3,500-4,000	Some
TOTAL 11(SIPRI) 11(WIKI)		Some					Some
SRBM							
Scud-B		Some	1979-1980	Single	1 x 1,000kg payload	300	Some
Scud-C variant		Some	1989	Single	1 x 700kg payload	500	Some
Scud-D		Some	2006	Single	1 x 500kg payload	700	Some
TOTAL 11(SIPRI)		Some					Some
SLBM							
UNITED STATES							
UGM-133	Trident II D-5	288					
	MK-4		1992	MIRV	4 x 100	12,000	468
	MK-4A		2008	MIRV	x 100	>7,400	300
	MK-5		1990	MIRV	4 x 475	12,000	384
TOTAL 12(SIPRI) 12(BULL) 11(SIPRI)		288					1,152

Table 2.9 Operational Nuclear Delivery Systems, 2012-2013							
NAME/DESIGNATION	AKA	NUMBER OF SYSTEMS Active+Spares	YEAR FIRST DEPLOYED	WARHEAD TYPE	NUMBER OF WARHEADS x YIELD (kilotons)	RANGE (km)	TOTAL NUMBER OF WARHEADS Active+Spares
UNITED KINGDOM							
UGM-135	Trident II D-5	48	1994	MIRV	1-3 x 100	12,000	225
TOTAL 12(SIPRI) 11(BULL) 11(SIPRI)		48					225
RUSSIA							
SS-N-18 M1	Stingray	48	1978	MIRV	3 x 50	6,500	96/144
SS-N-23 M1	Sineva	96	1986 /2007	MIRV	4 x 100	9,000	256/384
SS-N-32	Bulava-30	(32)	(2011)	MIRV	6 x 100?	>8,050	(192)
TOTAL 12(SIPRI) 12(BULL) 11(SIPRI) 11(BULL)		144					352/528
FRANCE							
M-45		32	1996	MIRV	4-6 x 100	6,000	160
M-51.1		16	2010-2011	MIRV	4-6 x 100	8,000-10,000	80
M-51.2		0	(2015)	MIRV	4-6 x TNO	6,000	0
TOTAL 12(SIPRI) 11(SIPRI) 08(BULL)		48					240
CHINA							
CSS-N-3		(12)	1986				(12)
	JL-1			Single	1 x 200-300	>1,770	
	JL-1			Single	1 x 25-50	2,150	
	JL-1A			Single	1 x 25-50	2,500	
CSS-NX-5	JL-2	(36)	(2010)			>8,000	(36)
				Single	1 x 200-300		
				MIRV	3-4 x 90		
TOTAL 12(SIPRI) 11(SIPRI) 11(BULL)		(48)					(48)
INDIA							

TABLE 2.9 OPERATIONAL NUCLEAR DELIVERY SYSTEMS, 2012-2013							
NAME/DESIGNATION	AKA	NUMBER OF SYSTEMS Active+Spares	YEAR FIRST DEPLOYED	WARHEAD TYPE	NUMBER OF WARHEADS x YIELD (kilotons)	RANGE (km)	TOTAL NUMBER OF WARHEADS Active+Spares
	K-4				1 x 1,000kg payload	3,500	0
Sagarika / Arihant	K-15	1	(2010)	Single	1 x 500-600kg payload	700	12
Dhanush		Some	2007	Single	1 x 500kg payload	350	Some
TOTAL 12(SIPRI) 12(BULL) 11(SIPRI)		Some					Some
AIRCRAFT							
UNITED STATES							
STRATEGIC							
B-52H	Stratofortress	91/44	1961	ALCM	5-150	16,000	200
				ACM	5-150		
B-2	Spirit	20/16	1994	Bombs B61-7, 11, B83-1	ACM 5-150	11,000	100
TOTAL 12(SIPRI) 12(BULL) 11(SIPRI)		113/60					300
SUB-STRATEGIC							
F-15E	Strike Eagle	Some	1988	Bomb B61-3, B61-4	1 x 0.3-170, 1 x 0.3-45	2,500	Some
F-16A/B/C/D	Fighting Falcon	Some	1976	Bomb B61-3, B61-4	1 x 0.3-170, 1 x 0.3-45	2,500	Some
F-117A	Nighthawk	Some	1983	Bomb B61-3, B61-4	1 x 0.3-170, 1 x 0.3-45	2,100	Some
TOTAL 11(SIPRI) 09(WIKI) 04(IISS) 08(BULL)		Some					200
RUSSIA							
STRATEGIC							

TABLE 2.9 OPERATIONAL NUCLEAR DELIVERY SYSTEMS, 2012-2013							
NAME/DESIGNATION	AKA	NUMBER OF SYSTEMS Active+Spares	YEAR FIRST DEPLOYED	WARHEAD TYPE	NUMBER OF WARHEADS x YIELD (kilotons)	RANGE (km)	TOTAL NUMBER OF WARHEADS Active+Spares
Tu-95 MS6	Bear H6	28	1981	ALCM	6 x ?	6,500-10,500	28/168
				Bombs	? x ?		
Tu-95 MS16	Bear H16	31	1981	ALCM	16 x ?	6,500-10,500	31/496
				Bombs	? x ?		
Tu-160	Blackjack	13	1987	ALCM	12 x ?	10,500-13,200	13/156
				SRAM	? x ?		
				Bombs	? x ?		
TOTAL 12(SIPRI) 12(BULL) 11(SIPRI) 11(BULL)		72					72/820
SUB-STRATEGIC							
Land-based bombers							
Tu-22M-3	Backfire	150	1974	ASM	3 x ?	4,800-7,000	~450
				Bombs	? x ?		
Su-24	Fencer	264	1974	Bombs	2 x ?	2,100-3,000	Some
Su-34	Fullback	16	2006	Bombs	2 x ?		Some
TOTAL 12(SIPRI) 12(BULL) 11(SIPRI)		~430					~730
Naval bombers, submarines, surface ships							
Tu-22M	Backfire	58	1974	ASM	2 x ?		Some
				Bombs	? x ?		
Su-24	Fencer	58	1974	Bombs	2 x ?		Some
Be-12/Il-38	Mail/May	63	1967/68	Depth bombs	1 x ?		Some
Submarines		Some					Some
Surface ships		Some					Some
TOTAL 12(SIPRI) 12(BULL) 11(SIPRI)		Some					~700
FRANCE							
LAND-BASED							

NAME/DESIGNATION	AKA	NUMBER OF SYSTEMS Active+Spares	YEAR FIRST DEPLOYED	WARHEAD TYPE	NUMBER OF WARHEADS x YIELD (kilotons)	RANGE (km)	TOTAL NUMBER OF WARHEADS Active+Spares
TABLE 2.9 OPERATIONAL NUCLEAR DELIVERY SYSTEMS, 2012-2013							
Mirage 2000N		~20	1988	ASMP	1 x 300	2,750	~20
Rafale F3		~20	2010-2011	ASMP	1 x 300	2,000	~20
TOTAL 12(SIPRI) 11(SIPRI) 08(BULL)		~40					~40
CARRIER-BASED							
Super Etendard		0	1978	ASMP	1 x 300	650	0
Rafale MK3		~10	2010-2011	ASMP	1 x 300	2,000	~10
TOTAL 12(SIPRI) 11(SIPRI) 08(BULL)		~10					~10
CHINA STRATEGIC							
H-6	Tu-16	~20	1965	Bomb	1 x 3,000kg payload	3,100	(~20)
TOTAL 12(SIPRI) 11(SIPRI)		~20					(~20)
SUB-STRATEGIC							
Q-5	Mig-19	~20	1972-?	Bomb	1 x 1,000kg payload	400	(20)
TOTAL 11(SIPRI)		~20					(20)
ISRAEL SUB-STRATEGIC							
F-4E-2000	Kurnass	Some	1989	Bomb	1 x 8,480kg payload	2,200	Some
F-16A Fighting Falcon	Netz/ Hawk	88	1980	Bomb	1 x 5,400kg payload	2,500	Some
F-16B Fighting Falcon	Netz/ Hawk	16		Bomb	1 x 5,400kg payload	2,500	Some

TABLE 2.9 OPERATIONAL NUCLEAR DELIVERY SYSTEMS, 2012-2013							
NAME/DESIGNATION	AKA	NUMBER OF SYSTEMS Active+Spares	YEAR FIRST DEPLOYED	WARHEAD TYPE	NUMBER OF WARHEADS x YIELD (kilotons)	RANGE (km)	TOTAL NUMBER OF WARHEADS Active+Spares
F-16C Fighting Falcon	Barak / Lightning	75		Bomb	1 x 5,400kg payload	2,500	Some
F-16D Fighting falcon	Barak / Thunderbolt	46		Bomb	1 x 5,400kg payload	2,500	Some
F-16I Fighting Falcon	Sufa / Storm	101		Bomb	1 x 5,400kg payload	2,500	Some
F-15I Strike Eagle	Ra'am / Thunder	25	1997	Bomb	1 x 10,400kg payload	2,500	Some
TOTAL 12(SIPRI) 12(JDW) 11(SIPRI)		351					Some
INDIA SUB-STRATEGIC							
Jaguar IS/ IB	Shamsher	76 12(BULL)	1979	Bomb	1 x 4,760kg payload	1,600	Some
MiG-27M	Bahadur	165 07(WIKI)	1982	Bomb	1 x 3,000kg payload	1,000	Some
Mirage 2000H	Vajra	49 12(BULL)	1998	Bomb	1 x 6,300kg payload	1,850	Some
TOTAL 12(SIPRI) 12(BULL) 11(SIPRI)		290 12(BULL) / 07(WIKI)					Some
PAKISTAN SUB-STRATEGIC							
F-16A/B	Fighting Falcon	32	1983	Bomb/ Babur LACM	1 x 4,500kg payload	1,600	Some
Mirage 2000-5		Some	2002	Bomb	1 x 4,000kg payload	2,100	Some
Q-5	MiG-19	Some	1980s	Bomb	1 x 1,000kg payload	1,200	Some
TOTAL 12(SIPRI) 11(SIPRI) 09(BULL)		>32					Some
NORTH KOREA SUB-STRATEGIC							

TABLE 2.9 OPERATIONAL NUCLEAR DELIVERY SYSTEMS, 2012-2013							
NAME/DESIGNATION	AKA	NUMBER OF SYSTEMS Active+Spares	YEAR FIRST DEPLOYED	WARHEAD TYPE	NUMBER OF WARHEADS x YIELD (kilotons)	RANGE (km)	TOTAL NUMBER OF WARHEADS Active+Spares
H-5	Il-28	80	1950	Bomb	1 x 3,000kg payload	2,100	Some
TOTAL 11(SIPRI)		80					Some
SLCM							
UNITED STATES							
Tomahawk	TLAM-N	325	1984	Single	1 x 5-150	2,500	(0)
TOTAL 12(BULL) 11(SIPRI) 10(BULL)		325					(0)
RUSSIA							
SS-N-9	Siren	Some	1972	Single	1 x 200	110	Some
SS-N-12	Sandbox	Some	1959-1960	Single	1 x 350	550	Some
SS-N-19	Shipwreck	Some	1980	Single	1 x 500	550	Some
SS-N-21	Sampson	Some	1984	Single	1 x 200	2,400	Some
SS-N-22	Sunburn	Some	1980	Single	1 x 320kg payload	120	Some
TOTAL 11(SIPRI) 10(BULL)		Some					-280
ISRAEL							
Turbo-Popeye 3		Some	2000	Single	1 x 200kg payload	1,500	Some
TOTAL 04(IISS)		Some					Some
ALCM							
UNITED STATES							
AGM-868		1,140	1982/1991	Single	1 x 900-1,400kg payload	2,500	Some
AGM-129		460	1990	Single	1 x 5-200	3,500	Some
TOTAL 11(SIPRI) 08(BULL)		1,600					Some
RUSSIA							
AS-4	Kh-24 Kitchen	Some	1964	Single	1 x 1,000	310	Some

Table 2.9 Operational Nuclear Delivery Systems, 2012-2013							
NAME/DESIGNATION	AKA	NUMBER OF SYSTEMS Active+Spares	YEAR FIRST DEPLOYED	WARHEAD TYPE	NUMBER OF WARHEADS x YIELD (kilotons)	RANGE (km)	TOTAL NUMBER OF WARHEADS Active+Spares
AS-15A	Kh-55 Kent	Some	1971	Single	1 x 200-250	2,500	Some
AS-15B	Kh-55SM Kent	Some	1986	Single	1 x 200-250	3,000	Some
AS-16	Kh-15 Kickback	Some	1980	Single	1 x 350	150	Some
TOTAL 11(SIPRI) 08(BULL)		Some					Some
FRANCE							
ASMP		Some	1985	Single	1 x 300	250	Some
TOTAL 11(SIPRI) 08(BULL)		Some					Some
CHINA							
	DH-10	150-350	2007	Single	1 x ?	>1,500	Some
TOTAL 12(SIPRI) 11(SIPRI) 08(BULL)		150-350					Some
PAKISTAN							
Babur	Haft-7	Some	2007	Single	1 x 400-500kg payload	600	Some
Ra'ad	Haft-8	Some	(>2011)	Single	?	350	0
TOTAL 12(SIPRI) 11(SIPRI)		Some					Some
MISSILE AND AIR DEFENSE SYSTEMS							
RUSSIA							
STRATEGIC DEFENSIVE SYSTEMS							
53T6	SH-08 Gazelle	68	1986	Single	1 x 1,000 / 10	30	68
S-300 and S-400	SA-10/20 Grumble, and SA-21 Growler	-1,000	1980 and 2007	Single	1 x low yield	5-150	-340

TABLE 2.9 OPERATIONAL NUCLEAR DELIVERY SYSTEMS, 2012-2013							
NAME/DESIGNATION	AKA	NUMBER OF SYSTEMS Active+Spares	YEAR FIRST DEPLOYED	WARHEAD TYPE	NUMBER OF WARHEADS x YIELD (kilotons)	RANGE (km)	TOTAL NUMBER OF WARHEADS Active+Spares
SSC-1B Sepal	Redut	34	1973	Single	1 x 500	500	17
TOTAL 12(SIPRI) 12(BULL) 11(SIPRI) 11(BULL)		1,102					425
UNITED STATES							
STRATEGIC DEFENSIVE SYSTEMS							
GBI missiles		25(26)					0
Aegis BMD cruisers		3					0
Aegis BMD destroyers		57(70)					0
TOTAL 08(SIPRI) 11(WIKI)		85(99)					0
SUB-STRATEGIC DEFENSIVE SYSTEMS							
PAC-3 missiles		546					0
TOTAL 08(SIPRI)		546					0

ACM advanced cruise missile

AKA also known as

ALCM air-launched cruise missile

ASM air-to-surface missile

MIRV multiple independently targetable re-entry vehicles

ICBM intercontinental ballistic missile

IRBM intermediate-range ballistic missile

SRBM short-range ballistic missile

SLBM submarine-launched ballistic missile

SLCM submarine-launched cruise missile

LACM land-attack cruise missile

GBI ground-based interceptors

BMD ballistic missile defense

PAC-3 Patriot advanced capability-3

SOURCES: SIPRI, BULL, WIKI, IISS, JDW

NOTES.

1) According to an official report which was submitted to the American congress in 2004, it may be that with a payload of 1,000 kg the Jericho 3 gives Israel nuclear strike capabilities within the entire Middle East, Africa, Europe, Asia and almost all parts of North America, as well as within large parts of South America and North Oceania.
2) Henry A. Kissinger (16 July 1969), "Israeli Nuclear Program," Memorandum for the President (The White House), Retrieved 2009-07-26
3) Proliferation of Weapons of Mass Destruction: Assessing the Risks, U.S. Congress Office of Technology Assessment, August 1993, OTA-ISC-559, Retrieved 2008-12-09
4) Missile Survey: Ballistic and Cruise Missiles of Foreign Countries, by Andrew Feikert, Congressional Research Service, Updated March 5, 2004
5) Study on a Possible Israeli Strike on Iran's Nuclear Development Facilities, by Abdullah Toukan, Center for Strategic and International Studies, March 14, 2009

TABLE 2.10 OPERATIONAL NUCLEAR WARHEADS, 2012-2013, STRATEGIC						
OBS	COUNTRY	ICBM	IRBM	SLBM	ALCM/ BOMBS	TOTAL
1	Russia	1,087		528	820	-2,430
2	U.S.	500		1,152	300	-1,950
3	France			240	60	300
4	China	40-60	94	62	40	-240
5	U.K.			225		225
6	Israel	Some				Some
7	India					
8	Pakistan					
9	N. Korea					

ALCM air-launched cruise missile
ICBM intercontinental ballistic missile
IRBM intermediate-range ballistic missile
SLBM submarine-launched ballistic missile

SOURCES: SIPRI, BULL, IISS, JDW

TABLE 2.11 OPERATIONAL NUCLEAR WARHEADS, 2012-2013, SUB-STRATEGIC						
OBS	COUNTRY	SRBM	SLCM, NAVY WEAPONS	ABM, AIR/ COASTAL DEFENSE	AIRCAFT	TOTAL
1	Russia	-164	-700	-425	-730	-2,000
2	U.S.		Some		Some	200
3	Israel	-30-40	Some		-30-40	60-80
4	Pakistan	-35-45			-35-45	70-90
5	India	-30-40			-30-40	60-80
6	N. Korea				6-10	6-10
7	China	Some			Some	Some
8	France					0
9	U.K.					0

SLCM sea-launched cruise missile
SRBM short-range ballistic missile

SOURCES: SIPRI, BULL, IISS, JDW

TABLE 2.12 OPERATIONAL NUCLEAR WARHEADS, 2012-2013, TOTAL STRATEGIC AND SUB-STRATEGIC

OBS	COUNTRY	STOCKPILE			DELIVERABLE			
		12(BULL) 11(BULL)	12(SIPRI) 11(SIPRI)	See [1], [2], [3]	12(BULL) 11(BULL)	12(SIPRI) 11(SIPRI)	10(IISS)	10(JDW)
1	Russia	10,000	10,000		~4,430	~4,430		
2	U.S.	~5,000	8,000		2,150	2,150		
3	Israel	60-80 (115-190)	~80	Up to 400	60-80	~80	~200	100-300
4	France		300		300	290		
5	China		240		236-256	200		
6	U.K.	225	225		160	160		
7	Pakistan		90-110		70-90	90-110		
8	India		80-100		60-80	80-100		
9	N. Korea				6-10			

Notes:

1) "Background Information, 2005 Review Conference of the Parties to the Treaty on the Non-Proliferation of Nuclear Weapons," United Nations, Retrieved 2006-07-02.

2) Brower, Kenneth S., "A Propensity for Conflict: Potential Scenarios and Outcomes of War in the Middle East," Jane's Intelligence Review, Special Report no. 14 (February 1997), p. 14-15.

3) "Nuclear Weapons: Who Has What at a Glance," Arms Control Association, Retrieved 2007-05-30.

4) The Bulletin of the Atomic Scientists puts the Israeli nuclear stockpile at 60-80 but notes that it is believed that Israel has produced nuclear material enough for 115-190 warheads.

5) In 1986, Mordechai Vanunu, a former technician at Dimona, revealed to the media some evidence of Israel's nuclear program. Israeli agents abducted him from Italy and transported him to Israel. An Israeli court then tried him in secret on charges of treason and espionage, and sentences him to 18 years imprisonment. At the time of Vanunu's arrest, *The Times* reported that Israel had material for approximately 20 hydrogen bombs and 200 fission bombs. If we take this information at face value, by now Israel should have material for considerably more nuclear bombs and that seems to corroborate the opinion of the sources from Notes [1], [2], [3] that Israel now may have up to 400 nuclear weapons.

6) Vanunu's information in October 1986 said that based on a reactor operating at 150 megawatts Israel produces 40 kg of plutonium per year. Israel possesses a 200 kg

warhead, containing 6 kg of plutonium (Farr, Warner D. The Third Temple's Holy of Holies: Israel's Nuclear Weapons, USAF Counterproliferation Center, September 1999, retrieved 2007-07-03). For 26 years from 1986 until 2012, Israel could have produced 26 x 40 = 1,040 kg of plutonium; divided by 6, this gives us 173 warheads. Add the 220 warheads which, according to Vanunu, Israel already had in 1986, and we get 393 as the possible number of Israel's warheads now.

7) The substantial discrepancy over data about Israel (between the Bulletin of the Atomic Scientists and the Stockholm International Peace Research Institute on one side and the International Institute for Strategic Studies, Jane's Defense Weekly, and sources from the notes [1], [2], [3] on the other side) may be explained by the following:

7.1) "Israel's nuclear weapons are not believed to be fully operational under normal circumstances" (Bulletin of the Atomic Scientists, article "Nuclear Notebook: Worldwide deployment of nuclear weapons, 2009").

7.2) As Zbigniew Brzezinski stated on Book TV in 2009, Israel had acquired a second-strike capability.

7.3) The opinion of Brzezinski is supported by other less prominent sources stating that Israel's nuclear weapons can now be launched from land, sea and air (Douglas Frantz, Israel Adds Fuel to Nuclear Dispute, Officials confirm that the nation can now launch atomic weapons from land, sea and air, Los Angeles Times, Sunday, October 12, 2003). This gives Israel a second strike option even if much of the country is destroyed (David Eberhart, Samson Option: Israel's Plan to Prevent Mass Destruction Attacks, NewsMax.Com, October 16, 2001).

7.4) The second strike strategy may mean that at any given time some of Israel's nuclear weapons are in storage.

TABLE 2.13 – STATES POSSESSING, PURSUING OR CAPABLE OF ACQUIRING WEAPONS OF MASS DESTRUCTION, 2012 — 2013

STATE	NUCLEAR ENERGY	URANIUM ENRICHMENT	PLUTONIUM PRODUCTION	NUCLEAR WEAPONS	CHEMICAL WEAPONS	BIOLOGICAL WEAPONS	MISSILE TECHNOLOGY
Algeria				Pursuing			
Argentina	Possessing		Possessing	Capable			Pursuing
Armenia	Possessing		Possessing				
Australia				Capable	Capable	Capable	Capable
Belarus				Capable			
Belgium	Possessing		Possessing				
Brazil	Possessing	Pursuing	Possessing	Capable			Possessing
Bulgaria	Possessing					Capable	
Burma					Pursuing		
Canada	Possessing		Possessing				
Chile					Capable		
China	Possessing	Possessing	Possessing	Possessing	Possessing	Possessing	Possessing
Cuba						Capable	
Czechia	Possessing		Possessing				
Ethiopia					Pursuing		
Egypt					Possessing	Possessing	Pursuing
Finland	Possessing		Possessing				
France	Possessing	Possessing	Possessing	Possessing	Possessing	Capable	Possessing
Germany	Possessing	Possessing	Possessing	Capable	Capable	Capable	Capable
Hungary	Possessing		Possessing				
India	Possessing	Possessing	Possessing	Possessing	Possessing	Possessing	Possessing
Indonesia					Pursuing		
Iran	Possessing	Possessing			Possessing	Possessing	Possessing
Israel			Possessing	Possessing	Possessing	Possessing	Possessing
Japan	Possessing	Possessing	Possessing	Capable	Capable	Capable	Possessing

Kazakhstan				Capable			
Laos					Pursuing	Pursuing	
Libya					Pursuing	Pursuing	Pursuing
Lithuania	Possessing		Possessing				
Mexico	Possessing		Possessing				
Netherlands	Possessing	Possessing	Possessing				
North Korea	Possessing		Possessing	Possessing	Possessing	Possessing	Possessing
Pakistan	Possessing	Possessing	Possessing	Possessing	Possessing	Possessing	Possessing
Romania	Possessing		Possessing				
Russia	Possessing	Possessing	Possessing	Possessing	Possessing	Possessing	Possessing
Saudi Arabia				Pursuing	Pursuing	Pursuing	Pursuing
Serbia				Pursuing	Capable		
Slovakia	Possessing		Possessing				
Slovenia	Possessing		Possessing				
South Africa	Possessing		Possessing	Capable	Capable	Capable	Capable
South Korea	Possessing		Possessing		Capable	Capable	Possessing
Spain	Possessing		Possessing				
Sudan					Pursuing		
Sweden	Possessing		Possessing				
Switzerland	Possessing		Possessing				
Syria					Pursuing	Pursuing	Pursuing
Taiwan	Possessing		Possessing		Possessing	Possessing	Possessing
Thailand					Pursuing		
Ukraine	Possessing		Possessing	Capable			
Vietnam					Pursuing	Pursuing	
United Kingdom	Possessing	Possessing	Possessing	Possessing	Capable	Capable	Possessing
United States	Possessing	Possessing	Possessing	Possessing	Possessing	Possessing	Possessing

SOURCES: BULL, SIPRI, EST, E, CIA

Developed Market Economies

3.1 GNI Per Capita at Market Exchange Rates of Developed Market Economies

Table 3.1.1 GNI Per Capita at Market Exchange Rates of Developed Market Economies, Year 1970		
Rank	Country	GPC
1	United States whites	5,187
2	United States	5,010
3	Sweden	4,480
4	Canada	3,930
5	Switzerland	3,800
6	Denmark	3,300
7	Australia	3,280
8	Norway	3,100
9	France	3,000
10	Luxembourg	2,880
11	Germany	2,850
12	Belgium	2,770
13	Netherlands	2,740
14	Iceland	2,520
15	Finland	2,420
16	United Kingdom	2,290
17	New Zealand	2,180
18	Austria	2,030
19	Italy	2,020
20	Japan	1,810
21	Israel	1,750
22	Greece	1,470
23	Ireland	1,450
24	Spain	1,160
25	Portugal	940
26	Cyprus	879
27	Malta	760
28	South Korea	270

TABLE 3.1.2 GNI PER CAPITA AT MARKET EXCHANGE RATES OF DEVELOPED MARKET ECONOMIES, YEAR 1980

Rank	Country	GPC
1	Switzerland	20,130
2	Sweden	16,420
3	Norway	15,460
4	Iceland	15,030
5	Denmark	14,990
6	Luxembourg	14,510
7	Netherlands	13,920
8	Belgium	13,730
9	United States whites	13,723
10	United States	12,950
11	France	12,850
12	Germany	12,600
13	Canada	11,320
14	Austria	11,210
15	Finland	11,110
16	Australia	10,850
17	Japan	10,670
18	United Kingdom	8,510
19	Italy	8,090
20	New Zealand	7,520
21.5	Greece	6,190
21.5	Ireland	6,190
23	Spain	6,060
24	Israel	5,350
25	Malta	4,280
26	Cyprus	3,410
27	Portugal	3,290
28	South Korea	1,810

TABLE 3.1.3 GNI PER CAPITA AT MARKET EXCHANGE RATES OF DEVELOPED MARKET ECONOMIES, YEAR 1990

Rank	Country	GPC
1	Switzerland	35,020
2	Luxembourg	29,530
3	Japan	27,580
4	Sweden	26,360
5	Norway	26,010
6	Finland	25,220
7	United States whites	24,679
8	Iceland	24,150
9	Denmark	24,120
10	United States	23,260
11	Germany	20,630
12	Austria	20,180
13	Canada	20,150
14	France	20,090
15	Belgium	18,960
16	Netherlands	18,820
17	Italy	17,840
18	Australia	17,370
19	United Kingdom	16,600
20	New Zealand	13,430
21	Ireland	12,190
22	Spain	11,880
23	Israel	10,860
24	Cyprus	9,510
25	Greece	8,590
26	Malta	7,600
27	Portugal	7,000
28	South Korea	6,000

TABLE 3.1.4 GNI PER CAPITA AT MARKET EXCHANGE RATES OF DEVELOPED MARKET ECONOMIES, YEAR 2000

Rank	Country	GPC
1	Luxembourg	43,650
2	Switzerland	41,160
3	United States whites	36,820
4	Norway	35,860
5	Japan	35,040
6	United States	34,890
7	Denmark	31,830
8	Iceland	30,800
9	Sweden	29,490
10	Netherlands	26,580
11	Austria	26,000
12	United Kingdom	25,910
13	Finland	25,440
14	Belgium	25,430
15	Germany	25,300
16	France	24,270
17	Ireland	23,220
18	Canada	22,130
19	Australia	21,150
20	Italy	21,010
21	Israel	17,830
22	Spain	15,420
23	New Zealand	13,760
24	Cyprus	13,440
25	Greece	12,460
26	Portugal	12,100
27	Malta	10,510
28	South Korea	9,910

Table 3.1.5 GNI Per Capita at Market Exchange Rates of Developed Market Economies, Year 2010		
Rank	Country	GPC
1	Norway	86,390
2	Switzerland	73,350
3	Luxembourg	71,860
4	Denmark	59,590
5	Sweden	50,780
6	United States whites	50,024
7	Netherlands	48,580
8	United States	47,360
9	Finland	47,130
10	Austria	47,070
11	Australia	46,340
12	Belgium	45,990
13	Germany	43,280
14	Canada	43,250
15	Ireland	42,370
16	France	42,190
17	Japan	42,050
18	United Kingdom	38,410
19	Italy	35,550
20	Iceland	33,920
21	Spain	31,450
22	Cyprus	29,450
23	New Zealand	29,140
24	Israel	27,270
25	Greece	26,390
26	Portugal	21,810
27	South Korea	19,720
28	Malta	18,620

Table 3.1.6 GNI Per Capita at Market Exchange Rates of Developed Market Economies, Year 2011		
Rank	Country	GPC
1	Norway	88,870
2	Luxembourg	77,390
3	Switzerland	76,350
4	Denmark	60,160
5	Sweden	53,170
6	United States whites	51,376
7	Australia	49,790
8	Netherlands	49,660
9	United States	48,620
10	Austria	48,170
11	Finland	47,760
12	Belgium	45,930
13	Canada	45,550
14	Japan	44,900
15	Germany	44,230
16	France	42,420
17	Ireland	39,150
18	United Kingdom	37,780
19	Italy	35,320
20	Iceland	34,820
21	Spain	30,930
22	Cyprus	29,450
23	New Zealand	29,140
24	Israel	28,930
25	Greece	24,490
26	Portugal	21,370
27	South Korea	20,870
28	Malta	18,620

TABLE 3.1.7 GROWTH RATES OF GNI PER CAPITA AT MARKET EXCHANGE RATES OF DEVELOPED MARKET ECONOMIES, 1970-2011

Rank	Country	GRPCMER
1	South Korea	11.19
2	Cyprus	8.94
3	Norway	8.53
4	Ireland	8.37
5	Luxembourg	8.36
6	Spain	8.34
7	Japan	8.15
8	Malta	8.11
9	Austria	8.03
10	Portugal	7.92
11	Switzerland	7.59
12	Finland	7.55
13	Denmark	7.34
14	Netherlands	7.32
15	Italy	7.23
16	Greece	7.10
17	Belgium	7.09
18	Israel	7.08
19	United Kingdom	7.08
20	Germany	6.92
21	Australia	6.86
22	France	6.67
23	Iceland	6.61
24	New Zealand	6.53
25	Sweden	6.22
26	Canada	6.16
27	United States whites	5.75
28	United States	5.70

3.2 GDP Per Capita at PPP of Developed Market Economies

Table 3.2.1 GDP Per Capita at PPP of Developed Market Economies, Year 1970

Rank	Country	GPCPPP
1	United States whites	5,106
2	United States	4,922
3	Switzerland	4,840
4	Canada	3,969
5	Sweden	3,855
6	Luxembourg	3,714
7	Denmark	3,523
8	Netherlands	3,500
9	Australia	3,465
10	New Zealand	3,331
11	United Kingdom	3,273
12	Germany	3,227
13	France	3,215
14	Norway	3,113
15	Italy	3,045
16	Belgium	2,989
17	Iceland	2,980
18	Finland	2,902
19	Japan	2,811
20	Austria	2,757
21	Israel	2,667
22	Spain	2,179
23	Ireland	1,852
24	Greece	1,562
25	Portugal	1,454
26	Malta	1,276
27	Cyprus	1,032
28	South Korea	500

Table 3.2.2 GDP Per Capita at PPP of Developed Market Economies, Year 1980		
Rank	Country	GPCPPP
1	Switzerland	14,250
2	Luxembourg	12,968
3	United States whites	12,899
4	United States	12,180
5	Iceland	11,972
6	Canada	11,031
7	Sweden	10,553
8	Austria	10,379
9	Belgium	10,223
10	Denmark	9,946
11	Germany	9,853
12	Netherlands	9,850
13	Norway	9,550
14	France	9,476
15	Italy	9,230
16	Australia	9,186
17	Finland	8,953
18	New Zealand	8,526
19	Japan	8,525
20	United Kingdom	8,367
21	Greece	8,225
22	Israel	7,470
23	Spain	6,828
24	Ireland	6,163
25	Malta	5,509
26	Portugal	5,399
27	Cyprus	5,061
28	South Korea	2,376

Table 3.2.3 GDP Per Capita at PPP of Developed Market Economies, Year 1990		
Rank	Country	GPCPPP
1	Luxembourg	30,351
2	Switzerland	25,285
3	United States whites	24,444
4	United States	23,038
5	Iceland	21,261
6	Canada	19,499
7	Austria	19,293
8	Sweden	19,275
9	Japan	19,191
10	Belgium	18,678
11	Germany	18,504
12	Denmark	18,424
13	Norway	17,852
14	Italy	17,623
15	Netherlands	17,591
16	Finland	17,561
17	Australia	17,262
18	France	17,177
19	United Kingdom	16,289
20	New Zealand	14,648
21	Israel	13,373
22	Spain	13,300
23	Ireland	12,933
24	Greece	12,656
25	Cyprus	12,303
26	Portugal	11,010
27	Malta	10,925
28	South Korea	7,960

TABLE 3.2.4 GDP PER CAPITA AT PPP OF DEVELOPED MARKET ECONOMIES, YEAR 2000

Rank	Country	GPCPPP
1	Luxembourg	53,648
2	United States whites	37,022
3	Norway	36,131
4	United States	35,082
5	Switzerland	32,509
6	Netherlands	29,403
7	Ireland	28,921
8	Austria	28,905
9	Iceland	28,839
10	Denmark	28,818
11	Canada	28,407
12	Sweden	27,952
13	Belgium	27,650
14	Australia	26,272
15	United Kingdom	26,039
16	Japan	25,909
17	Germany	25,757
18	Italy	25,754
19	Finland	25,670
20	France	25,168
21	Israel	23,520
22	Spain	21,312
23	New Zealand	21,130
24	Cyprus	19,439
25	Malta	19,042
26	Greece	18,246
27	Portugal	17,794
28	South Korea	17,197

TABLE 3.2.5 GDP PER CAPITA AT PPP OF DEVELOPED MARKET ECONOMIES, YEAR 2010

Rank	Country	GPCPPP
1	Luxembourg	84,764
2	Norway	56,976
3	United States whites	49,826
4	Switzerland	48,720
5	United States	46,612
6	Netherlands	41,673
7	Ireland	40,883
8	Denmark	40,588
9	Austria	40,401
10	Sweden	39,251
11	Australia	39,125
12	Canada	39,075
13	Belgium	37,834
14	Germany	37,652
15	Finland	36,030
16	Iceland	35,506
17	United Kingdom	35,298
18	France	34,262
19	Japan	33,625
20	Italy	32,110
21	Cyprus	31,780
22	Spain	31,575
23	New Zealand	30,194
24	South Korea	28,613
25	Greece	27,520
26	Israel	27,048
27	Malta	26,672
28	Portugal	25,519

TABLE 3.2.6 GDP PER CAPITA AT PPP OF DEVELOPED MARKET ECONOMIES, YEAR 2011

Rank	Country	GPCPPP
1	Luxembourg	88,797
2	Norway	60,392
3	Switzerland	51,227
4	United States whites	50,839
5	United States	48,112
6	Netherlands	42,779
7	Austria	42,172
8	Australia	41,974
9	Sweden	41,484
10	Denmark	40,933
11	Ireland	40,868
12	Canada	40,420
13	Germany	39,456
14	Belgium	38,723
15	Finland	37,455
16	Iceland	36,483
17	United Kingdom	35,598
18	France	35,247
19	Japan	33,668
20	Italy	32,672
21	Cyprus	32,254
22	Spain	32,087
23	New Zealand	31,082
24	South Korea	29,834
25	Israel	28,809
26	Malta	27,504
27	Greece	25,858
28	Portugal	25,564

Table 3.2.7 Growth Rates of GDP Per Capita at PPP of Developed Market Economies, 1970-2011

Rank	Country	GRPCPPP
1	South Korea	10.49
2	Cyprus	8.76
3	Luxembourg	8.05
4	Ireland	7.84
5	Malta	7.78
6	Norway	7.50
7	Portugal	7.24
8	Greece	7.09
9	Austria	6.88
10	Spain	6.78
11	Belgium	6.45
12	Finland	6.44
13	Iceland	6.30
14	Germany	6.30
15	Netherlands	6.30
16	Australia	6.27
17	Japan	6.24
18	Denmark	6.16
19	France	6.01
20	United Kingdom	5.99
21	Israel	5.98
22	Sweden	5.97
23	Italy	5.96
24	Switzerland	5.92
25	Canada	5.82
26	United States whites	5.77
27	United States	5.72
28	New Zealand	5.60

3.3 Infant Mortality of Developed Market Economies

Table 3.3.1 Infant Mortality of Developed Market Economies, Year 1960		
Rank	Country	INFMRT
1	Sweden	16.2
2	Netherlands	16.4
3	Iceland	17.0
4	Norway	18.6
5	Australia	20.5
6	Denmark	21.4
7	Switzerland	21.8
8	Finland	22.0
9	New Zealand	22.5
10	United Kingdom	23.0
11	United States whites	23.1
12	France	24.0
13	United States	26.0
14	Canada	28.1
15	Cyprus	29.8
16	Belgium	30.0
17	Japan	30.1
18	Ireland	30.5
19	Israel	30.8
20	Luxembourg	31.5
21	Germany	35.0
22	Austria	36.9
23	Malta	37.2
24	Italy	43.8
25	Spain	47.6
26	Greece	47.7
27	Portugal	82.1
28	South Korea	84.3

Table 3.3.2 Infant Mortality of Developed Market Economies, Year 1970		
Rank	Country	INFMRT
1	Sweden	11.3
2	Iceland	12.4
3	Netherlands	12.5
4	Norway	12.9
5	Finland	13.1
6	Japan	13.4
7	Denmark	13.7
8	Switzerland	14.9
9	France	15.0
10	New Zealand	16.8
11	Australia	17.5
12	United States whites	17.8
13	United Kingdom	18.0
14	Luxembourg	18.1
15	Canada	18.4
16	Ireland	19.4
17	United States	19.9
18	Belgium	20.2
19	Germany	22.1
20	Israel	24.1
21	Malta	24.3
22	Austria	25.1
23	Spain	25.3
24	Cyprus	26.0
25	Italy	29.3
26	Greece	34.3
27	South Korea	38.6
28	Portugal	53.5

Rank	Country	INFMRT
1.5	Finland	7.2
1.5	Sweden	7.2
3	Japan	7.4
4	Iceland	7.6
5	Denmark	8.2
6	Norway	8.3
7	Switzerland	8.4
8	Netherlands	8.8
9	France	10.1
10	Canada	10.4
11	Luxembourg	10.8
12.5	Australia	10.9
12.5	United States whites	10.9
14	Ireland	11.9
15	Belgium	12.0
16	United Kingdom	12.1
17	Germany	12.5
18	United States	12.6
19	New Zealand	12.8
20	Austria	13.9
21	Italy	14.3
22	Malta	14.6
23	South Korea	15.3
24	Spain	15.5
25	Israel	15.6
26	Cyprus	20.3
27	Greece	21.2
28	Portugal	23.2

Table 3.3.3 Infant Mortality of Developed Market Economies, Year 1980

Table 3.3.4 Infant Mortality of Developed Market Economies, Year 1990

Rank	Country	INFMRT
1	Japan	4.6
2	Iceland	5.2
3	Finland	5.6
4	Sweden	5.7
5	South Korea	6.4
6	Switzerland	6.6
7.5	Canada	6.8
7.5	Netherlands	6.8
9	Norway	6.9
10.5	Germany	7.0
10.5	Luxembourg	7.0
12	Denmark	7.2
13	France	7.3
14.5	Australia	7.5
14.5	Ireland	7.5
16	United States whites	7.6
17	United Kingdom	7.8
18	Austria	7.9
19	Italy	8.4
20	Belgium	8.5
21	New Zealand	9.1
22	Spain	9.3
23	United States	9.4
24	Cyprus	9.5
25	Israel	9.6
26	Malta	9.7
27	Portugal	11.4
28	Greece	11.5

TABLE 3.3.5 INFANT MORTALITY OF DEVELOPED MARKET ECONOMIES, YEAR 2000

Rank	Country	INFMRT
1	Iceland	3.0
2	Japan	3.3
3	Sweden	3.4
4	Finland	3.5
5	Norway	3.8
6	Luxembourg	3.9
7.5	France	4.4
7.5	Germany	4.4
9.5	Austria	4.6
9.5	Denmark	4.6
11.5	Belgium	4.7
11.5	Switzerland	4.7
13	Italy	4.8
14	South Korea	4.9
15.5	Australia	5.1
15.5	Netherlands	5.1
17	Canada	5.3
18	Cyprus	5.4
19.5	Portugal	5.5
19.5	Spain	5.5
21.5	Israel	5.6
21.5	United Kingdom	5.6
23	United States whites	5.7
24	Ireland	5.8
25	New Zealand	6.0
26	Malta	6.5
27	Greece	6.8
28	United States	7.1

Table 3.3.6 Infant Mortality of Developed Market Economies, Year 2010		
Rank	Country	INFMRT
1	Iceland	1.8
2	Sweden	2.3
4	Finland	2.4
4	Japan	2.4
4	Luxembourg	2.4
6	Norway	2.7
7	Cyprus	2.8
8	Portugal	2.9
9.5	Denmark	3.3
9.5	Italy	3.3
11.5	Germany	3.4
11.5	Ireland	3.4
14	Austria	3.5
14	France	3.5
14	Netherlands	3.5
16	Belgium	3.6
17.5	Israel	3.7
17.5	Spain	3.7
19	Greece	3.9
20	Switzerland	4.0
21.5	Australia	4.2
21.5	South Korea	4.2
23	United Kingdom	4.5
24	New Zealand	4.8
25	Canada	5.0
26	Malta	5.1
27	United States whites	5.4
28	United States	6.5

TABLE 3.3.7 INFANT MORTALITY OF DEVELOPED MARKET ECONOMIES, YEAR 2011

Rank	Country	INFMRT
1	Iceland	1.7
2	Sweden	2.2
3.5	Finland	2.3
3.5	Luxembourg	2.3
5	Japan	2.4
6.5	Cyprus	2.6
6.5	Norway	2.6
8	Portugal	2.7
9	Denmark	3.1
10.5	Ireland	3.2
10.5	Italy	3.2
12	Germany	3.3
13.5	France	3.4
13.5	Netherlands	3.4
16.5	Austria	3.5
16.5	Belgium	3.5
16.5	Israel	3.5
16.5	Spain	3.5
19	Greece	3.7
20	Switzerland	4.0
21.5	Australia	4.1
21.5	South Korea	4.1
23	United Kingdom	4.4
24	New Zealand	4.7
25	Canada	4.9
26	Malta	5.1
27	United States whites	5.3
28	United States	6.4

Table 3.3.8 Decrease in Rates of Infant Mortality of Developed Market Economies, 1960-2011

Rank	Country	DRIM
1	Portugal	6.92
2	South Korea	6.11
3	Luxembourg	5.27
4	Italy	5.26
5	Spain	5.25
6	Greece	5.14
7	Japan	5.08
8	Cyprus	4.90
9	Germany	4.74
10	Austria	4.73
11	Iceland	4.62
12	Finland	4.53
13	Ireland	4.52
14	Israel	4.36
15	Belgium	4.30
16	Sweden	3.99
17	Malta	3.97
18	Norway	3.93
19	France	3.91
20	Denmark	3.86
21	Canada	3.48
22	Switzerland	3.38
23	United Kingdom	3.30
24	Australia	3.21
25	Netherlands	3.13
26	New Zealand	3.12
27	United States whites	2.93
28	United States	2.79

3.4 Life Expectancy of Developed Market Economies

Table 3.4.1 Life Expectancy of Developed Market Economies, Year 1960

Rank	Country	LIFEXP
1	Norway	73.550
2	Iceland	73.427
3	Netherlands	73.393
4	Sweden	73.006
5	Denmark	72.177
6	Israel	71.684
7	Switzerland	71.313
8	New Zealand	71.237
9	Canada	71.133
10	United Kingdom	71.127
11	Australia	70.817
12	United States whites	70.700
13	France	69.868
14	United States	69.771
15	Belgium	69.702
16	Ireland	.69.692
17	Germany	69.620
18	Cyprus	69.591
19	Italy	69.124
20	Spain	69.109
21	Finland	68.820
22	Greece	68.726
23	Austria	68.586
24	Luxembourg	68.322
25	Japan	67.666
26	Malta	67.602
27	Portugal	63.037
28	South Korea	52.999

TABLE 3.4.2 LIFE EXPECTANCY OF DEVELOPED MARKET ECONOMIES, YEAR 1970

Rank	Country	LIFEXP
1	Sweden	74.649
2	Norway	74.088
3	Iceland	73.934
4	Netherlands	73.586
5	Denmark	73.343
6	Switzerland	73.020
7	Canada	72.700
8	Cyprus	72.527
9	Spain	72.027
10	United Kingdom	71.973
11	Japan	71.950
12	United States whites	71.700
13	Greece	71.694
14	France	71.659
15	Italy	71.559
16	New Zealand	71.273
17	Israel	71.213
18	Australia	71.019
19	Ireland	70.996
20	Belgium	70.972
21	United States	70.807
22	Germany	70.641
23	Malta	70.443
24	Finland	70.180
25	Austria	69.891
26	Luxembourg	69.876
27	Portugal	67.073
28	South Korea	61.207

Table 3.4.3 Life Expectancy of Developed Market Economies, Year 1980		
Rank	Country	LIFEXP
1	Iceland	76.847
2	Japan	76.092
3	Netherlands	75.743
4	Sweden	75.741
5	Norway	75.672
6	Switzerland	75.459
7	Spain	75.349
8	Canada	75.078
9	Cyprus	74.748
10	Greece	74.415
11	United States whites	74.400
12	Australia	74.334
13	Denmark	74.102
14	France	74.051
15	Italy	73.943
16	Israel	73.876
17	United Kingdom	73.676
18	United States	73.659
19	Finland	73.440
20	Belgium	73.207
21	Malta	72.932
22	New Zealand	72.829
23	Germany	72.819
24	Ireland	72.549
25	Austria	72.424
26	Luxembourg	71.960
27	Portugal	71.215
28	South Korea	65.802

Table 3.4.4 Life Expectancy of Developed Market Economies, Year 1990		
Rank	Country	LIFEXP
1	Japan	78.837
2	Iceland	78.036
3	Sweden	77.537
4	Canada	77.377
5	Switzerland	77.242
6	Australia	76.995
7	Greece	76.939
8	Netherlands	76.878
9	Italy	76.859
10	Spain	76.838
11	Israel	76.607
12	France	76.600
13	Norway	76.537
14	Cyprus	76.505
15	United States whites	76.100
16	United Kingdom	75.880
17	Austria	75.530
18	New Zealand	75.378
19	Germany	75.316
20	United States	75.215
21	Malta	75.176
22	Belgium	75.052
23	Luxembourg	74.853
24	Finland	74.813
25	Denmark	74.805
26	Ireland	74.741
27	Portugal	73.966
28	South Korea	71.295

Table 3.4.5 Life Expectancy of Developed Market Economies, Year 2000		
Rank	Country	LIFEXP
1	Japan	81.076
2	Switzerland	79.680
3	Iceland	79.654
4	Sweden	79.644
5	Italy	79.427
6	Canada	79.237
7	Australia	79.234
8	Spain	78.966
9	France	78.959
10	Israel	78.954
11	New Zealand	78.637
12	Norway	78.634
13	Malta	78.200
14	Austria	78.027
15	Netherlands	77.988
16	Cyprus	77.957
17	Germany	77.927
18	Greece	77.888
19	Luxembourg	77.873
20	United Kingdom	77.741
21	Belgium	77.722
22	Finland	77.466
23	United States whites	77.300
24	United States	76.637
25	Denmark	76.593
26	Ireland	76.541
27	Portugal	76.315
28	South Korea	75.855

Table 3.4.6 Life Expectancy of Developed Market Economies, Year 2010		
Rank	Country	LIFEXP
1	Japan	82.843
2	Switzerland	82.246
3	Iceland	81.898
4	Italy	81.737
5	Australia	81.695
6	Spain	81.627
7	Israel	81.602
8	Sweden	81.451
9	France	81.368
10	Norway	80.998
11	Malta	80.949
12	Ireland	80.895
13	Canada	80.798
14.5	Netherlands	80.702
14.5	New Zealand	80.702
16	Luxembourg	80.632
17	South Korea	80.566
18	United Kingdom	80.402
19	Greece	80.388
20	Austria	80.383
21	Belgium	80.234
22	Germany	79.988
23	Finland	79.871
24	Cyprus	79.380
25	Denmark	79.100
26	Portugal	79.027
27	United States whites	78.800
28	United States	78.541

Table 3.4.7 Life Expectancy of Developed Market Economies, Year 2011		
Rank	Country	LIFEXP
1	Switzerland	82.695
2	Japan	82.591
3	Iceland	82.359
4	Spain	82.327
5	Italy	82.088
6	Malta	82.005
7	Australia	81.846
8	Sweden	81.802
9	Israel	81.756
10	France	81.668
11	Norway	81.295
12	Netherlands	81.205
13	Austria	81.032
14	Luxembourg	80.988
15	Canada	80.929
16	New Zealand	80.905
17	South Korea	80.866
18	United Kingdom	80.754
19	Greece	80.744
20	Germany	80.741
21	Portugal	80.722
22	Ireland	80.495
23	Belgium	80.485
24	Finland	80.471
25	Denmark	79.800
26	Cyprus	79.563
27	United States whites	78.900
28	United States	78.641

Table 3.4.8 Growth Rates of Life Expectancy of Developed Market Economies, 1960-2011		
Rank	Country	GRLE
1	South Korea	0.83
2	Portugal	0.49
3	Japan	0.39
4	Malta	0.38
5	Spain	0.34
6	Italy	0.34
7	Luxembourg	0.33
8	Austria	0.33
9	Greece	0.32
10	Finland	0.31
11	France	0.31
12	Germany	0.29
13	Switzerland	0.29
14	Australia	0.28
15	Ireland	0.28
16	Belgium	0.28
17	Cyprus	0.26
18	Israel	0.26
19	Canada	0.25
20	New Zealand	0.25
21	United Kingdom	0.25
22	United States	0.23
23	Iceland	0.23
24	Sweden	0.22
25	United States whites	0.22
26	Netherlands	0.20
27	Denmark	0.20
28	Norway	0.20

3.5 Health Expenditures of Developed Market Economies, Year 2011

Table 3.5.1 Total Health Expenditures of Developed Market Economies as Percent of GDP, Year 2011		
Rank	Country	HLTGDP
1	United States	17.85
2	Netherlands	11.96
3	France	11.63
4	Canada	11.18
5	Denmark	11.15
6	Germany	11.06
7	Switzerland	10.86
8	Greece	10.83
9	Austria	10.64
10	Belgium	10.60
11	Portugal	10.36
12	New Zealand	10.08
13	Italy	9.50
14	Spain	9.44
15	Ireland	9.38
16	Sweden	9.36
17	United Kingdom	9.32
18	Japan	9.27
19.5	Iceland	9.07
19.5	Norway	9.07
21	Australia	9.03
22	Finland	8.85
23	Malta	8.74
24	Israel	7.73
25	Luxembourg	7.69
26	Cyprus	7.41
27	South Korea	7.21

TABLE 3.5.2 PUBLIC HEALTH EXPENDITURES OF DEVELOPED MARKET ECONOMIES AS PERCENT OF TOTAL HEALTH EXPENDITURES, YEAR 2011		
Rank	Country	PUBHLT
1	Netherlands	85.66
2	Norway	85.64
3	Denmark	85.16
4	Luxembourg	84.27
5	New Zealand	83.22
6	United Kingdom	82.70
7	Sweden	80.94
8	Iceland	80.38
9	Japan	80.01
10	Italy	77.25
11	France	76.74
12	Belgium	75.95
13	Germany	75.85
14	Austria	75.59
15	Finland	74.79
16	Spain	73.59
17	Ireland	70.42
18	Canada	70.41
19	Australia	68.51
20	Switzerland	65.42
21	Portugal	64.05
22	Malta	63.99
23	Israel	61.51
24	Greece	61.19
25	South Korea	57.33
26	United States	45.94
27	Cyprus	43.27

3.6 Taxes as Share of GDP of Developed Market Economies

Table 3.6.1 Taxes as Share of GDP of Developed Market Economies, Year 1970

Rank	Country	TAXGDP
1	Sweden	43.4
2	Denmark	40.4
3.5	Austria	38.5
3.5	Israel	38.5
5	Belgium	38.3
6	Netherlands	37.7
7	France	37.4
8	Norway	37.3
9	Germany	37.2
10	United Kingdom	35.6
11	Finland	33.0
12	Canada	31.3
13	Ireland	30.7
14	United States	28.9
15	Iceland	28.1
16	Italy	27.9
17	New Zealand	26.6
18	Australia	25.4
19	Luxembourg	23.5
20	Greece	21.6
21.5	Portugal	20.9
21.5	Spain	20.9
23	Malta	20.0
24	Japan	19.7
25	Switzerland	19.3
26	Cyprus	18.5
27	South Korea	17.5

Table 3.6.2 Taxes as Share of GDP of Developed Market Economies, Year 1980		
Rank	Country	TAXGDP
1	Sweden	50.6
2	Denmark	48.1
3	Belgium	47.4
4	Netherlands	45.9
5	Norway	45.8
6	Austria	44.5
7	Germany	43.9
8	France	43.6
9	Israel	39.9
10	Finland	38.4
11	Luxembourg	35.6
12	United Kingdom	35.1
13.5	Ireland	33.1
13.5	New Zealand	33.1
15	Italy	32.4
16	Iceland	31.8
17	Canada	30.3
18	United States	30.0
19	Spain	29.1
20	Portugal	27.9
21	Australia	27.7
22	Japan	25.6
23	Greece	25.1
24	Switzerland	24.7
25	Cyprus	22.4
26	Malta	21.6
27	South Korea	18.7

TABLE 3.6.3 TAXES AS SHARE OF GDP OF DEVELOPED MARKET ECONOMIES, YEAR 1990		
Rank	Country	TAXGDP
1	Sweden	63.4
2	Norway	55.5
3	Denmark	54.6
4	Finland	53.3
5	Netherlands	49.6
6	Austria	49.0
7	New Zealand	48.7
8	France	47.0
9	Belgium	45.5
10	Israel	43.8
11	Canada	43.0
12	Germany	41.7
13	Italy	41.5
14	Ireland	40.0
15	United Kingdom	39.4
16	Spain	38.7
17	Luxembourg	35.7
18	Iceland	35.6
19	Portugal	34.5
20	Australia	33.7
21	Japan	33.6
22	United States	32.9
23	Greece	30.8
24	Malta	28.0
25	Cyprus	27.5
26	Switzerland	25.8
27	South Korea	22.1

Table 3.6.4 Taxes as Share of GDP of Developed Market Economies, Year 2000

Rank	Country	TAXGDP
1	Sweden	58.7
2	Norway	57.7
3	Denmark	55.8
4	Finland	55.4
5.5	Austria	50.1
5.5	France	50.1
7	Belgium	49.0
8	Israel	47.6
9	Germany	46.2
10	Netherlands	46.1
11	Italy	44.9
12.5	Iceland	43.6
12.5	Luxembourg	43.6
14	Canada	43.2
15	Greece	43.0
16	United Kingdom	40.3
17	New Zealand	40.0
18	Cyprus	39.3
19	Portugal	38.3
20	Spain	38.2
21	Ireland	36.0
22	United States	35.4
23	Australia	35.3
24	Switzerland	35.2
25	Malta	33.4
26	Japan	31.1
27	South Korea	27.9

Table 3.6.5 Taxes as Share of GDP of Developed Market Economies, Year 2010

Rank	Country	TAXGDP
1	Norway	56.7
2	Denmark	55.0
3	Finland	53.0
4	Sweden	52.3
5	France	49.5
6	Belgium	48.6
7	Austria	48.0
8.5	Italy	46.1
8.5	Netherlands	46.1
10	Germany	43.6
11	Luxembourg	42.0
12	Iceland	41.5
13	Portugal	41.4
14	Greece	40.6
15	Israel	40.3
16	United Kingdom	40.1
17	New Zealand	39.1
18	Canada	37.6
19	Spain	36.6
20	Ireland	35.2
21	Switzerland	34.0
22	Japan	32.4
23	Australia	31.6
24	South Korea	31.4
25	United States	31.3
26	Malta	27.0
27	Cyprus	25.9

TABLE 3.6.6 TAXES AS SHARE OF GDP OF DEVELOPED MARKET ECONOMIES, YEAR 2011

Rank	Country	TAXGDP
1	Norway	58.2
2	Denmark	55.7
3	Finland	53.9
4	Sweden	51.3
5	France	50.9
6	Belgium	49.4
7	Austria	48.0
8	Italy	46.1
9	Netherlands	45.4
10	Portugal	45.0
11	Germany	44.6
12	Greece	42.3
13	Iceland	41.8
14	Luxembourg	41.6
15	United Kingdom	40.3
16	Israel	40.2
17	New Zealand	39.3
18	Canada	37.5
19	Spain	35.7
20	Ireland	34.8
21	Switzerland	34.3
22	Japan	33.4
23	South Korea	31.7
24	United States	31.4
25	Australia	31.3
26	Malta	27.7
27	Cyprus	26.1

TABLE 3.6.7 GROWTH RATES OF TAXES AS SHARE OF GDP OF DEVELOPED MARKET ECONOMIES, 1970-2011		
Rank	Country	GRTX
1	Portugal	2.80
2	Greece	2.42
3	Finland	2.13
4	Norway	2.10
5	Luxembourg	2.07
6	Italy	1.95
7	South Korea	1.93
8	Switzerland	1.92
9	Spain	1.83
10	Japan	1.76
11	Denmark	1.52
12	Iceland	1.50
13	New Zealand	1.43
14	France	1.35
15	Belgium	1.11
16	Cyprus	1.08
17	Malta	1.05
18	Austria	0.95
19	Netherlands	0.78
20	Sweden	0.78
21	Germany	0.75
22	Australia	0.71
23	Canada	0.67
24	United Kingdom	0.49
25	Ireland	0.46
26	United States	0.29
27	Israel	0.17

Some Unexpected Results

1. Is Private Health Insurance More Efficient Than a "Public Option?"

To answer this question, let us consider two major indicators of health care quality — life expectancy and infant mortality — for developed market economies/democracies. And let us compare these two major indicators of health care with two indicators that characterize the type of health care delivery system: total health care expenditures as a percentage of GDP and public health care expenditures as a percentage of total health care expenditures.

In terms of life expectancy and infant mortality, the U.S. has been consistently last (or next to last) in recent years (see Sections 3.3 and 3.4).

In terms of total health expenditures as a percentage of GDP, the U.S. has been consistently at the top of the list in recent years (see Section 3.5.1).

In terms of public health expenditure as a percentage of total health expenditures, the U.S. has been consistently last (or next to last) in recent years (see Section 3.5.2).

Let us express our observations mathematically, through correlations.

The correlation (weighted by population to minimize the effect of accidental factors in smaller countries) between life expectancy and total health expenditures as a percentage of GDP is -0.8953; that is, life expectancy declines (worsens) with the increase of total health expenditures as a percentage of GDP.

The correlation (weighted by population) between infant mortality and total health expenditures as a percentage of GDP is 0.8908; that is, infant mortality increases (worsens) with the increase of total health expenditures as a percentage of GDP.

At the same time:

The correlation (weighted by population) between life expectancy and public health expenditure as a percentage of total health expenditures is 0.8706; that is, life expectancy goes up (improves) as public health expenditure increases as a percentage of total health expenditures.

The correlation (weighted by population) between infant mortality and public health expenditure as a percentage of total health expenditures is -0.8967; that is, infant mortality decreases (improves) with the increase of public health expenditure as a percentage of total health expenditures.

In other words, there are reasons to believe that public health expenditure (a "public option") in developed market economies/democracies is associated with a more effective, cost-efficient health care system than dumping money into health care in the private (American) model of a health care system.

2. Is Taxation Stifling the Economy?

Let us consider all 27 developed market economies/democracies as a group of roughly similar societies.

In terms of the amount of taxes collected, at all levels of government, compared to GDP, the U.S. has been consistently last (or next to last) over the past four decades (see Section 3.6).

The rates of growth of taxes at all levels of government in the U.S. also have been consistently least (or nearly so) over the last four decades (see Section 3.6.6).

Many would suppose that the United States with its lowest (or near lowest) level of taxation should have had the best economic performance in the group of developed market economies/democracies. But we observe nothing of the sort when we compare long-term growth rates with the level and dynamics of tax-to-GDP ratio.

By the rates of growth of per capita GDP (measured by either of the two principal methods: at market exchange rates or at purchasing power parities), the U.S. has been consistently last (or next to last) over the past four decades (see Sections 3.1.6 and 3.2.6).

Let us measure mathematically what we have observed.

The multiple correlation coefficient (weighted by population to minimize the effect of accidental factors in smaller countries) between the two indicators — economic growth per capita and the growth rate of the share of taxes in GDP — is 0.818526. The probability that the correlation is zero (Wilks' Lambda statistic) is 0.0001.

The strong correlation between the growth rates of taxes relative to GDP and the growth rates of GDP per capita is just a mathematical expression of a fact that is obvious if you glance at the tables with the relevant data.

This suggests that among developed market economies/democracies, there are factors mitigating and reversing the effect of increased taxation. It is not unreasonable to assume that these mitigating factors have to do with how resources collected through taxation are spent. Comparing various developed market economies/democracies, one may conclude that such mitigating factors are the results of government efforts to improve social cohesion, increase equality of the general welfare of the population, invest in human capital (through public expenditures in health and education), invest in infrastructure, and invest in research and development.

Appendix: Methodology and Definitions

Selection of Indicators

These parameters were first assembled to illustrate the comparative position of the countries of the world. The aim was to select indicators that were:

- few in number;
- important;
- available for the maximum number of countries;
- statistically reliable;
- independent of the technological and industrial level of the countries.

Missing data was projected with the help of regressions.

Selection of Sources

For most of the tables, the principles for the selection of sources are simple: the most recent year available takes precedence and the corresponding source is indicated. Only if data is unavailable, a regression is used. When faced with a choice among several alternative sources, a deliberate and a priori defined choice between the sources, based on the quality of the sources, is made as described below.

For GNI at market exchange rates per capita and GDP at purchasing power parities per capita, the hierarchy of sources within the latest year is: WB, E, CIA. If either of these two indicators is missing altogether, a regression is used to obtain the other one of the pair.

For the data about infant mortality and life expectancy, the hierarchy of sources within the latest year is: WB, CIA, E. If an indicator is available but not for the latest year, it is weighted against the U.S. for that year and then this weight is multiplied by the U.S. value of this indicator for the latest year. Only if data is unavailable for any year, a regression is used.

For GNI at market exchange rates per capita, GDP at purchasing power parities per capita, infant mortality, and life expectancy, if an indicator is available but not for the latest year, it is weighted against the U.S. for that year and then this weight is multiplied by the U.S. value of this indicator for the latest year. These four indicators belong to the "expanding universe of indicators," which have a tendency to improve from year to year; to leave them at the values of previous years would mean to underestimate the situations in the corresponding countries for the current year.

For the data about civil and political rights index, the source for the latest year is: FH. Only if data is unavailable for any year, a regression is used.

For the data about Human Development Index, the source within the latest year is: UN. Only if data is unavailable for the year in the title of the table, a regression is used.

For the data about Gini coefficient of income inequality, the hierarchy of sources within the latest year is: WB, CIA, GPI. Only if data is unavailable for any year, a regression is used.

For the data about population, the hierarchy of sources within the latest year is: E, CIA.

For the data about military personnel, the hierarchy of sources within the latest year is: IISS, WB, CIA.

For the data about military expenditures as share of GDP, the hierarchy of sources within the latest year is: WB, IISS, CIA.

For the data about foreign military aid received, the source for the latest year is: USAID.

For the data about the nuclear weapons, the hierarchy of sources within the latest year is in the following order: SIPRI, BULL, IISS, WIKI.

For the data about the weapons of mass destruction, the hierarchy of sources within the latest year is in the following order: BULL, E, CIA, WIKI.

For the Developed Market Economies/Democracies data about GNI and GDP PPP per capita, infant mortality, and life expectancy, the hierarchy of sources for all years for which the data is presented is in the following order: WB, Mitchell, SA.

For the Developed Market Economies/Democracies data about the share of health expenditures in GDP and share of public health expenditures in total health expenditures, the source for the year of the table: WB.

For the Developed Market Economies/Democracies data about the share of taxes in GDP, the hierarchy of sources for all years for which the data is presented is in the following order: SA, OECD, WIKI.

Definition of Principal Component 1

I have used "Principal Component 1" for the definition of several indexes.

Principal component analysis is a multidimensional technique for studying the interrelationship between several quantitative variables. For a given set of data with p numerical variables, p principal components can be computed. Each principal component is a linear combination of the initial variables with coefficients equal to the eigenvector of the correlational or covariational matrix. The eigenvectors are typically selected to have a length of one. The principal components are sorted in descending order of characteristic values, which are equal to the variation of the components. Principal components have a number of useful properties; among them are:

- The first principal component accounts for the greatest variation of any linear combination of observed variables of the unit length.
- In geometrical terms, a j-dimensional linear subspace of the first j principal components provides the best possible arrangement of data points measured

as the sum of squares of the perpendicular distances from each point to the subspace.[1]

Definition of the Economic Quality-of-Life Index

I computed an Economic Quality-of-Life Index as Principal Component 1 of the four economic indicators of the quality of life given in this yearbook:

log(GPC)	logarithm of GNI per capita at market exchange rates
log(GPCPPP)	logarithm of GDP per capita at purchasing power parities
log(INFMRT)	logarithm of infant mortality
log(max(LIFEXP) – LIFEXP)	logarithm of the difference between maximum life expectancy and life expectancy in the country in question (in 2006, the maximum life expectancy was that of women of Andorra at 86.61 years)

Definition of the Human Rights Index

In an attempt to give an estimate of the level of human rights, I computed a human rights index as Principal Component 1 of four indicators of the political quality of life:

SCINTX	the index of societal integration
CPR	the index of civil and political rights
HDX	the human development index
GINI	GINI coefficient of income inequality

Definition of the Economico-Political Quality-of-Life Index

I computed an Economico-Political Quality-of-Life Index as Principal Component 1 using the four economic and the four political (human rights) indicators of the quality of life described above.

Definition of Gross National Income at Market Exchange Rates

The Gross Domestic Product is the most frequently used indicator of national productivity. It represents the total value of products and services produced.

GNI (or gross national product, in the terminology of the 1968 United Nations System of National Accounts) measures the total domestic and foreign value added claimed by residents. GNI comprises GDP plus net receipts of primary income (compensation of employees and property income) from nonresident sources.[2]

The GDP or GNI, which is recorded in terms of the national currency, has to be translated into a single currency to enable international comparison. GNI per capita at market exchange rates provides GNI data translated into U.S. dollars on the basis of the market exchange rate. In addition to the actual ratios among the buying powers of different currencies, the market rate is based on a number of other factors. From the point of view of actual buying power, the market typically overestimates the discrepancies in the income earned in different countries. (See also GDP at purchasing power parities.)

1. Mathematics: SAS Institute, Inc. (1988), Kiyosi (2000), Kotz (1985).

2 Economics: Finfacts.

In instances where there was a choice between sources, priority was given to data from the World Bank, since it uses a more advanced procedure for computing the exchange rate, smoothing fluctuations in the market exchange rate.

In cases where values were missing, the following regression was used:

$$\log(GPC) = REG(\log(GPCPPP))$$

where

log(GPC)	logarithm of GNI per capita at market exchange rates
log(GPCPPP)	logarithm of GDP per capita at purchasing power parities
Number of observations	212
Correlation coefficient	0.97

Definition of Infant Mortality

The indicator of infant mortality is computed from number of deaths during the first year of life per 1000 thousand live births. This is one of the most important indicators used, since it indirectly measures the state of health care, transportation, communications, and level of culture of the given country (this list can be extended indefinitely).

In cases where values were missing, the following regression was used:

$$\log(INFMRT) = REG(\log(GPC))$$

where

log(INFMRT)	Logarithm of infant mortality
log(GPC)	Logarithm of GNI per capita at market exchange rates
Number of observations	230
Correlation coefficient	0.87

Definition of Life Expectancy

Life expectancy is probably the most accurate single indicator of the quality of life in a given country. It sums up in one number all the natural and social stresses that affect an individual.

In cases where the data are taken from the Encyclopedia Britannica, I used the arithmetic mean of the life expectancies of men and women.

In cases where values were missing, the following regression was used:

$$\log(\max(LIFEXP) - LIFEXP) = REG(GPC, \log(INFMRT))$$

where

log(max(LIFEXP) – LIFEXP)	Logarithm of the difference between maximum life expectancy and life expectancy of this country
GPC	GNI per capita at market exchange rates
log(INFMRT)	Logarithm of infant mortality
Number of observations	230
Correlation coefficient	0.93

Definition of Gross Domestic Product at Purchasing Power Parities

Typically the GDP is translated into U.S. dollars. The market foreign currency exchange rate, however, does not necessarily reflect differences in actual purchasing power in different countries. The use of purchasing power parities is designed to eliminate this distortion. Purchasing power parities indicate how many currency units are needed in one country to buy the amount of goods and services that can be purchased for a currency unit in another country.

In cases where values were missing, the following regression was used:

$$\log(GPCPPP) = REG(\log(GPC))$$

where

log(GPCPPP)	Logarithm of GDP per capita at purchasing power parities
log(GPC)	Logarithm of GNI per capita at market exchange rates
Number of observations	220
Correlation coefficient	0.98

Definition of the Societal Integration Index

The index of societal integration is an indicator of the intensity of open political life. It is computed as a coefficient of heterogeneity of a parliament (legislature) of a country, under the condition that party seats in the parliament (legislature) are obtained as a result of competitive elections. This indicator can have values between 0 and 1; zero means that all seats in the parliament (legislature) belong to one party or that there are no competitive elections; it approaches 1 if every person in the parliament (legislature) is his own party.

The concept of integration was introduced by Emile Durkheim in his work *Suicide*[3]. Durkheim interpreted integration as a function of the intensity of social communication. I interpreted this conception on the societal level, defining societal integration as the intensity of non-trivial exchanges of information at the highest level of society. I provide a purely structural definition of exchange of information, defining it as a number between 0 and 1 of equal to the probability of interparty (i. e., political party) dialogue in society. As a measure of interparty exchange of information, I took the probability of interparty communication in parliament (the legislative body):

3 Sociology: Durkheim (1993).

$$SCINTX = \sum_{i=1}^{X} P_i \left(1 - P_i\right)$$

where

P(i)	the proportion of members of party number (i) in parliament (the legislative body)
X	the total number of political parties in parliament (the legislative body).

Data about the distribution of seats among parties is taken from an open CIA publication. This indicator can be considered objective because no ruling party would give seats in the parliament (legislature) to the opposition willingly. The introduction of this indicator into the formula for computing the human rights index is based on the concept that the condition of political institutions (and the degree to which they can be called democratic) is closely related to the human rights.

Definition of the Civil and Political Rights Index

The index of civil and political rights is subjective. As such I used index of freedom of the press. It is taken from the publication of the Freedom House based in New York. For the sake of objectivity it should be noted that the Freedom House in the view of many observers is biased in favor of the United States, especially taking into account the drastic change of the political climate in America since the attacks of September 11, 2001. And in the cases of certain foreign countries, it gives absurdly high or absurdly low ratings. The advantage of this indicator is that it is available for all countries in question and is computed annually.

In cases where values were missing, the following regression was used:

CPRX = REG(log(GPC), SCINTX)

where

CPRX	the index of civil and political rights
log(GPC)	Logarithm of GNI per capita at market exchange rates
SCINTX	the index of societal integration
Number of observations	199
Correlation coefficient	0.68

Definition of the Human Development Index

The human development index is an objective indicator. It is the average of the level of income per capita in purchasing power parities, level of education, and level of health care. It is computed annually by a well-respected UN program. The introduction of this indicator into the formula for computing the human rights index is based on the idea that socio-economic rights are part of human rights. Some right-wing lawyers in the U.S. consider the socio-economic rights a bad concept for a well-developed law-abiding state, because it is allegedly difficult to conduct the judicial process if socio-economic rights are recognized as full-blown rights. Even if we agree that there is some truth in this assertion and that there are difficulties for a strict judicial process that would take socio-economic rights as real rights, nevertheless, outside the U.S. socio-economic rights are commonly recognized as a lawful component of human rights. This can be seen, for example, from the Universal Declaration of Human Rights adopted by the UN in 1948.

In cases where values were missing, the following regression was used:

HDX = REG(GPCPPP, log(GPCPPP), INFMRT, LIFEXP)

where

HDX	The human development index
GPCPPP	GDP per capita at purchasing power parities
Log(GPCPPP)	Logarithm of GDP per capita at purchasing power parities
INFMRT	Infant mortality
LIFEXP	Life expectancy
Number of observations	180
Correlation coefficient	0.99

Definition of Gini Coefficient of Income Inequality

The fourth component of human rights index is Gini coefficient of income inequality. This indicator is computed as an integral of distance between equal distribution and the observed distribution of income in a given country. Its values range between 0 and 100; 0 signifies that observed distribution of income is equal, and 100 signifies that all income of the country belongs to one person. The idea of inclusion of Gini coefficient is based on an observation that formal judicial rights are only a potential that can be realized in a specific social context, and that the bigger the inequality, the more difficult it is for an average person of a given society to insist on his or her formal judicial rights. Thus in countries with developed market economies, the price of good lawyers is dictated by material possibilities of the top of the society. For example, in the social context of the U.S., an average person often simply cannot afford a good lawyer. Because of this it is possible to say that for the realization of formally proclaimed judicial rights, a person should possess a certain material potential. The less inequality there is in a country, the more formal judicial rights are realized.

In cases where values were missing, the following regression was used:

GINI = REG(log(GPC), log(INFMRT))

where

GINI	Gini coefficient of income inequality
log(GPC)	Logarithm of GNI per capita at market exchange rates
log(INFMRT)	Logarithm of infant mortality
Number of observations	163
Correlation coefficient	0.53

Definition of Population

Population of a country includes all residents regardless of legal status or citizenship — except for refugees not permanently settled in the country of asylum, who are generally considered part of the population of their country of origin. The values shown are midyear estimates.[4]

Definition of Armed Forces Personnel

Armed forces personnel are active duty military personnel, including paramilitary forces if the training, organization, equipment, and control suggest they may be used to support or replace regular military forces.[5]

Definition of Military Expenditures

Military expenditures data are primarily based on the World Bank data. They are taken from Stockholm International Peace Research Institute (SIPRI) and are derived from the NATO definition, which includes all current and capital expenditures on the armed forces, including peacekeeping forces; defense ministries and other government agencies engaged in defense projects; paramilitary forces, if these are judged to be trained and equipped for military operations; and military space activities. Such expenditures include military and civil personnel and social services for personnel; operation and maintenance; procurement; military aid (in the military expenditures of the donor country). Excluded are civil defense and current expenditures for previous military activities, such as veterans' benefits, demobilization, conversion, and destruction of weapons.[6]

Definition of Operational Offensive Nuclear Delivery Systems

I follow the definition of the International Institute for Strategic Studies and the Bulletin of the Atomic Scientists.

Definition of Operational Nuclear Warheads

Here, I include strategic and sub-strategic operational warheads aligned to an in-service delivery system, excluding artillery shells and mini-nukes.[7]

Definition of the States Possessing, Pursuing or Capable of Acquiring Weapons of Mass Destruction

The main part of this data is taken from the Bulletin of the Atomic Scientists[8] for 2000. The original data of the Bulletin also includes information about WMD programs in Iraq. This information is now thoroughly discredited and therefore is not included. It is worth noting that anybody who looked at military budgets by countries in the beginning of the 2000s would have noticed that Iraq's military expenditures were less than the military expenditures of most countries in the Middle East. Such a person would have considerable doubt that Iraq was economically capable to sustain WMD programs. Similarly, the same table from Bulletin of the Atomic Scientists lists poor countries, like Ethiopia, Laos and Sudan, as pursuing WMD programs. It is

4 Economics: The World Bank (1).

5 Economics: The World Bank (1).

6 Economics: The World Bank (1).

7 Military: International Institute for Strategic Studies.

8 Military: Bulletin of the Atomic Scientists.

highly doubtful that these impoverished countries have the socio-economic wherewithal to pull off the weaponizing of dangerous biological and chemical substances.

Conversely, I concluded that all countries which have nuclear power plants should be considered to some degree capable of acquiring nuclear weapons. The list of such countries is available from Encyclopedia Britannica[9] for 2002 and the CIA[10] for 2006.

I also decided that such highly developed economic powers as United Kingdom, France, Japan, and Germany, should be capable of acquiring the whole range of WMD. In the case of Japan and Germany, which have nuclear power plants, it is reasonable to believe that they have the capability also for biological, chemical, and missile technology. In the case of United Kingdom and France, which are acknowledged by the Bulletin of the Atomic Scientists as nuclear, chemical and missile powers, I think they are also capable of biological weapons. Based on the information about launches of satellites by Japan and Brazil, I consider these two countries as actually possessing the missile technology.

Definition of Developed Market Economies

In section 3, I used data for the period since 1960/1970 for 23 original member countries of the Organization for Economic Co-Operation and Development (excluding Turkey, which is too poor to be compared to the other OECD countries) plus other countries, which also have high per capita GDP and are democracies and for which there exists relevant historical data for the period since 1960/1970 (Cyprus, Israel, Malta, and South Korea qualify for this criteria).

Definition of the Scope of Data for Developed Market Economies

In the tables presented in section 3, I have attempted to look at certain theories popular in the U.S. (and possibly also in the former centrally planned economies of Central and Eastern Europe). I considered, for example, the recent debates about health care reform in the U.S.

Some of the arguments against health care reform in the U.S. are:

1) The U.S. has fewer social programs than other countries and this gives it an advantage in economic competition.

2) The U.S. has the best system of health care in the world, so why to disrupt it?

3) The U.S. has the most economically effective system of health care and social efforts to improve it may only destroy it, creating an ineffective bureaucracy (a variant of the preceding thesis).

4) The current American economic model with lower taxes and lesser social programs provides for faster economic growth and a better quality of life.

5) Even if health care reform could produce better social/economic results, it presents a risk (in the form of a putative socialist order) to freedoms in the U.S. It would be better to remain the freest country in the world.

For item number 5, I refer the reader to the political quality-of-life indicators presented in section 1. For items 1 through 4, the relevant statistics for the developed market economies are presented in section 3.

9 Economics: Encyclopedia Britannica.

10 Economics: Central Intelligence Agency.

Definition of Total Health Expenditures

Total health expenditure is the sum of public and private health expenditure. It covers the provision of health services (preventive and curative), family planning activities, nutrition activities, and emergency aid designated for health but does not include provision of water and sanitation.[11]

Definition of Public Health Expenditures

Public health expenditure consists of recurrent and capital spending from government (central and local) budgets, external borrowing and grants (including donations from international agencies and nongovernmental organizations), and social (or compulsory) health insurance funds.[12]

Definition of Taxes as Share of GDP

Taxes refer to general government sector, which is a consolidation of accounts for the central, state, and local governments plus social security.[13]

Definition of Growth Rates of Taxes as Share of GDP

Growth rates of taxes as share of GDP are defined as such relative growth rates, which cause the observed changes of taxes as share of GDP. The corresponding formula for computation is

$$GRTX = (((100 / (100 - TAXGDP_1) * (TAXGDP_1 / TAXGDP_0) - (TAXGDP_1 / 100)) ** (1 / N) - 1) * 100$$

where

GRTX	growth rates of taxes as share of GDP
TAXGDP0	taxes as share of GDP at the beginning of the period
TAXGDP1	taxes as share of GDP at the end of the period
N	number of years in the period

11 Economics: The World Bank (1).
12 Economics: The World Bank (1).
13 Economics: U.S. Bureau of Census (1).

References

Reference

Encyclopedia Britannica (1983) *The New Encyclopedia Britannica*, 15th edition, in 30 Volumes, Chicago

Law

Freedom House, *Freedom of the Press: A Global Survey of Media Independence*, Rowman & Littlefield Publishers, Inc., New York, annual

Sociology

Durkheim, Emile (1993) *Suicide: A Study in Sociology* (Translated by John A. Spaulding and George Simpson), Routledge, London

Military

Bulletin of the Atomic Scientists

International Institute for Strategic Studies, *The Military Balance*, Oxford University Press, annual

Stockholm International Peace Research Institute, *SIPRI Yearbook: Armaments, Disarmament and International Security*, Oxford University Press, annual

Union of Concerned Scientists

Economics

Central Intelligence Agency, *The World Factbook*, annual

Encyclopedia Britannica, *Book of the Year*, annual

Eurostat Press Office, *Tax Burden and Structure of Taxes*, annual

Finfacts, http://www.finfacts.com/biz10/globalworldincomepercapita.htm

Israel Finance Ministry, Press Releases

Maddison, Angus (1995) *Monitoring the World Economy, 1820-1992*, OECD, Paris

________ (2001) *The World Economy: A Millennial Perspective*, OECD, Paris

________ (2003) *The World Economy: Historical Statistics*, OECD, Paris

________ (2007) *Contours of the World Economy, 1–2030 AD*, Oxford University Press, New York

Mitchell, B.R. (2003)(1) *International Historical Statistics: Africa, Asia and Oceania, 1750–2000*, Palgrave Macmillan, London

________ (2003)(2) *International Historical Statistics: Europe, 1750–2000*, Palgrave Macmillan, London

________ (2003)(3) *International Historical Statistics: The Americas, 1750–2000*, Palgrave Macmillan, London

OECD, *Revenue Statistics*, Paris, annual

The World Bank (1989-1994) *World Tables*, annual, The John Hopkins University Press

________ (1995) *World Data 1995*. World Bank Indicators on CD-ROM

________ (2008) *World Development Indicators Online*

U.S. Agency for International Development, *U.S. Overseas Loans and Grants [Greenbook]*, http://qesdb.cdie.org/gbk/index.html

U.S. Bureau of the Census (1) *Statistical Abstract of the United States*, annual

________ (1975) *Historical Statistics of the United States, Colonial Times to 1970*, Vols 1 and 2, Washington, D.C.

United Nations Development Programme, *Human Development Report*, annual, Oxford University Press, New York

Mathematics

Itô, Kiyosi, Ed. (2000) *Encyclopedic Dictionary of Mathematics*, by the Mathematical Society of Japan, The MIT Press, Cambridge, Massachusetts

Kotz, Samuel, Norman L. Johnson, Eds. (1985) *Encyclopedia of Statistical Sciences, Vols. 1-9*, John Wiley & Sons, New York

SAS Institute Inc. (1988) *SAS/STAT User's Guide, Release 6.03 Edition*, Cary, North Carolina